It's When You Sell That Counts

To Matthew and Laura and Michael

and

To Members of

The American Association of Individual Investors and of

Better Investing

It's When You Sell That Counts

Third Edition

Donald Cassidy

GLOBAL
professional
publishing

Global Professional Publishing Ltd
Random Acres
Slip Mill Lane
Hawkhurst
Cranbrook
Kent TN18 5AD
Email: publishing@gppbooks.com

ISBN 978-0-85297-686-9

Printed by Berforts, United Kingdom

Table of Contents

Introduction

Several years ago, as an equities analyst for a regional brokerage firm, your author was in conversation with an experienced broker to discuss the recommended sale of a certain stock, of which the broker's client held 500 shares.

"Well," said the analyst, "a sale sounds nice since the stock is up several points here. He ought to be glad to take the profit." To his surprise, the broker replied, "I wish it were that easy. You see, this guy is funny. He really hates to pay taxes, so I have an awful time getting him to sell to take a profit."

The analyst responded that he had heard that tune more than a few times and joked that maybe the broker should point out to the client that he ought to like paying taxes on thousands in profit rather than having a loss to worry about. The analyst then suggested some offsetting losses to close out, to help soften the tax blow and put the client's portfolio in better shape. "Oh, no," said the broker, "he absolutely refuses to take a loss. I cannot even mention that; he has threatened to fire me if I do!"

In disbelief the analyst asked, "Are you saying that you have a client who is invested in the stock market but will not take a profit to avoid capital-gains tax, and who will not take a loss as a matter of pride? I will wager lunch that he would refuse to sell a stock unchanged because it has not done what he expected." At that point, the broker scheduled that lunch because her client, indeed, insisted on continuing to hold stocks if unchanged because he also hated paying commissions.

Whether the foregoing tale amuses or alarms the reader, there is a lesson in it. Here was an intelligent person, professionally successful, who owned a significant-sized portfolio. Not atypically, he had difficulty selling stocks whether they were up, down, or unchanged. Market participants like this always prompt that enduring question: Why is it that he cannot sell? The broker, too, was seemingly powerless to provide help.

There are many reasons investors have trouble selling their stocks. Brokers have their own distinct lists of hesitations about getting clients to sell. In fact, selling out of stocks is a universal problem. The inescapable conclusion is that people need help cashing in whether they are typical Main Street investors or professionals such as brokers or money managers. One of the reasons assistance is needed is that there is very little information on selling provided in the marketplace. Much more attention must be given the art of selling out stocks, whether at a gain or at a loss. And an understanding must be developed that today, many brokers are product marketers rather than investment experts and so cannot be leaned on for the needed help.

Investors need to pay attention to the psychology of selling; to individual stocks and how they behave; to how both large and small participants think and act; and to brokers and the roles they play. Overwhelmingly, most books dealing with the stock market in any form focus on the buying transaction, neglecting the sell side of the equation almost completely. Selling may not be as exciting and certainly is a narrower topic, but it is absolutely necessary and has its own myriad twists and curiosities.

This book is divided into four sections. The first describes the external and internal problems and pitfalls that investors face when confronted with a hold/sell choice. These obstructions tend to be structural in nature. The second section covers several necessary aspects of the mind-set needed to approach the hold/sell decision. These problems are related to a natural avoidance of closure, which can represent with deathlike finality the mortality of an investor's judgment. The third section prescribes important strategies that should be applied to generate smart selling decisions. The fourth section explores multiple specific tactics for executing a liquidation strategy more effectively and profitably.

The final two chapters provide readers with a checklist, to be used with each transaction, and with the ultimate sell-versus-hold test question, both of which function as learning devices.

There is no difference between a long-term investor and a short-term trader when it comes to stock market success: To profit and to remain a participant rather than merely a frozen, fully-invested collector, one must know how, and be ready, to sell when the time is right. Profits are made only when both a purchase and the subsequent sale have been implemented well. The pages ahead shed light on that latter, more challenging process.

Acknowledgments

A book, like any product of the human mind, is an amalgam formed of conscious and unconscious experiences that affect the author over many years. Thus, a writer might well acknowledge almost anyone who has ever touched his or her life. Publishers prefer that such lists be brief, however. This imposes a discipline at once useful and harsh. With due apologies to others whose names fell off the short list, then, I thank, in chronological order:

Richard Randlett, a teacher of junior high school mathematics, who introduced me to investments: He will never know the horizons he opened in my mind.

Robert Scotland, a teacher of U.S. history at Wayland High School in Massachusetts: he demanded the best of good students. He allowed me to study the Great Depression as a history project and required me to deliver a lecture on that topic to classmates; that experience built self-confidence.

The late Roger Spear, who founded an investment advisory firm later sold to Fidelity Management and Research Corporation: He patiently guided and taught an impetuous young man and let him learn on company time.

Charles Kline, a finance instructor at the Wharton School: His favorite expression was simple but profound, "Everything goes in circles and cycles."

Richard Hurwitz, formerly Research Director at Boettcher and Company: He had the confidence and vision to hire as an investment analyst a management consultant with no previous experience, a courageous act for a manager in late 20th century corporate culture. He was a tough and, therefore, valued mentor and remains a fine friend.

Heather White, a colleague at Boettcher and a dear friend: She taught me things about brokers that otherwise would have taken years to crystallize in my mind. She also told me I was good enough to undertake the perilous task of writing a first book. Then she led me through friends to my first publisher, saving much pain and frustration.

Robert Davis of Davis-Hamilton Associates, one of several research directors I served: His profound sense of proportion and cool, logical mind under stress taught me much more than he thinks.

Michael Lipper: He has been an invaluable Wall Street mentor, teacher, and mental coach, especially in the areas of contrarian and value investing.

Belita Calvert, my wife: She has helped in many hardly visible but important ways, from proofreading and graphics tricks to listening and energizing and encouraging. She remains surprisingly patient in allowing me space and time for my work.

Wayne Baxmann, national chapter development officer of AAII: He added me to its national speakers bureau despite the radical topic on which I spoke (selling rather than buying and hoping). The more than 180 talks I have been privileged to give since then have exposed me to countless investors' thinking and made me some dear friends.

Michael Jeffers, then president of Probus Publishing and now of Edgewater Editorial Services in Chicago: He agreed to publish my first book (that door is the most difficult to open) and convinced me that this volume on selling is freshly required in this new century.

PART I:

Understanding the Selling Problem in Depth

CHAPTER I

External Roadblocks

Keys for Successful Selling

- ◆ Understand Today's Broker
- ◆ Wall Street Rarely Uses One Four-Letter Word: Sell
- ◆ Acknowledge the Importance of Changed Fundamentals
- ◆ Understand Buying and Holding as Conditioned Behaviors

Selling is a lot less fun, and a lot less easy, than buying. Our first two chapters examine in detail two major clusters of factors and forces that inhibit or confound good selling. These first several pages will focus on the external environment in which an investor or trader must operate. Chapter 2 will look at the myriad problems that operate to make selling a difficult challenge. We begin with this information because in order to win one must identify and understand the enemies he or she is facing.

Today's Broker

A description of broker skills as they have evolved over the past decade is not the focus of this book. However, an understanding of the full-commission brokerage industry orientation is essential for investors intent on making profits in the stock market. While some of the following observations about brokers may seem critical, they are intended to illustrate the broker point of view and to help the investor facilitate his relationship with a broker if he or she chooses to use a traditional full-service firm.

There are different kinds of brokers; to compound the confusion, each brokerage firm has its own broker terminology: account executive, registered representative or investment counselor are some examples. Although the title does not matter, what does matter to investors is the training, experience and basic professional orientation of their brokers no matter what they are called and no matter what firm employs them. In mid-2007, the National Association of Securities Dealers (NASD) was challenging terminology for brokers such as financial advisor, contending that such words imply a fiduciary role while in reality the broker is a salesperson.

This is not simply to say, get a well-trained broker. It is a recommendation to identify the broker's orientation and to find out how she deals with the investing public. Note that the term stockbroker has not been used in this book; the term broker is favored. The choice of words has been deliberate: Most of today's brokers, especially those younger than average, are not really stockbrokers in the classical, historical sense. And there are many reasons.

Fallout from the Fidelity Phenomenon

With 20/20 hindsight, it is now possible to conclude that probably the largest single early factor in the gradual extinction of the traditional stockbroker was the phenomenal success of Fidelity Management & Research Corporation's money market funds in the mid-1970s. Fidelity's ability to attract billions of dollars, first to its Daily Income Trust and then to its lower-minimum Cash Reserves Fund (see Figure 1-1), triggered a chain of events that has led, over 20-plus years, to the relative scarcity of the traditional stockbroker—a lamentable consequence, but not one that Fidelity's management either foresaw or intended. The success of Cash Reserves—among other similar funds—rippled like a pebble dropped in a pond and widened into a series of tidal waves.

First, Fidelity's Daily Income Trust acted as a parking place for billions of dollars of investor funds during the disintermediation period of the mid-1970s. When interest rates subsided, Fidelity encouraged and educated its money-fund holders to transfer assets to other (equity and bond) mutual funds within the corporate family. The effect was not only to offer Fidelity investors a newly attractive equities climate but also—and much more importantly—to demonstrate profoundly to Fidelity managers and financial services industry competitors alike the success of asset gathering as a corporate strategy.

Whether by brilliant forward planning or not, Fidelity executed a strategy of gathering and maintaining control of billions of dollars in investor assets. The number is now in excess of one trillion. It was highly profitable—indeed, imperative—for Fidelity to maintain and extend its investment pool once the basic move had been made. And at the same time, it became obvious to competitors that they not only should, but indeed must, compete on equal footing by attracting their own client assets to a broad array of funds or products.

Figure 1.1: Fidelity Cash Reserves

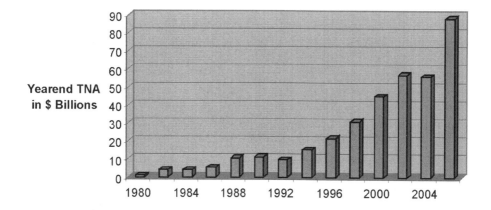

Thus asset capture became a competitive necessity for every firm in the industry. Had Fidelity been able to continue playing the asset-capture game solo, it seemed plausible on a perceived-threat basis for it to have assembled all the public's investable assets—clearly a massive threat to the jobs, egos and incomes of investment executives in all competing firms.

Not only mutual funds were affected; all financial services providers visualized their turfs invaded and captured by the asset-gatherers. Insurance companies feared that billions of dollars would be drained from their coffers, and new-policy sales choked off as investors soaked up the mutual funds offered by Fidelity and its like. Banks envisioned, accurately, both a permanent disintermediation of deposits and a likely diversion of assets from their money-management (trust) departments. Brokerage firms saw both a threat and an opportunity in the lure that mutual funds' professional management represented: It meant a probable drain on the assets held by individual investors in stocks and bonds, which generate periodic transaction revenues. By themselves entering the funds-management business, brokerage firms could stabilize their revenue streams and mute their profit cyclicality by relying on asset-based fee income.

One-stop Shopping

As a result of the asset-capture game, many financial organizations became supermarkets; the department store image fits equally well. Sears, Roebuck & Co., no longer the largest U.S. department store, became a financial supermarket. Starting with a powerful distribution base (the customer list and the walk-in traffic) and with an insurance company (Allstate), Sears added a family of mutual funds and a brokerage firm (Dean Witter), created the Discover credit card, and even got into real estate brokerage and financing. (Starting in the 1990s, it would spin off many of these businesses to enhance shareholder value.) Most financial services providers concluded, at roughly the same time, that the only survival strategy for long-term business success was to become a financial supermarket—the provider of essentially all services under one corporate or holding-company roof. By its nature, asset-gathering became an activity of prime importance because, once assets were captured, they were likely to remain under management or control until the investor needed them for spending. Fees accruing for the management of those assets grew huge as the asset base rose from tens of billions of dollars to a few trillion (the amount in money funds alone, as of May 2007, exceeded $2.4 trillion). One percent of the equity- and bond-fund pie as an approximate annual management fee had become an extremely attractive prize.

So banks and insurance companies bought brokerage firms and started their own mutual funds. Mutual fund firms created insurance and annuity products and started brokerage operations. And most significantly, brokerage firms responded by marketing funds and similar products intensively, in the process reducing their historical emphasis on stocks per se.

The upshot was that individual brokers who had originally been stock and bond brokers now were trained to handle a wide variety of additional investment instruments or products, including annuities, certificates of deposit, unit investment trusts, closed-end funds, guaranteed investment contracts, variable annuities, mutual funds of all descriptions, tax shelters, gold bullion, precious metal coins, exchange-traded funds (ETFs) and options and index futures. Since the new century's arrival, even hedge funds are on the list for brokers to peddle.

Not only were existing brokers now re-educated in some or all of these new offerings, but the standard training programs for new brokers hired by nationwide brokerage firms soon included, and indeed emphasized, such specialized products. Smaller, regional firms, forced to compete on as equal a footing as they could create, followed in lockstep. Thus, an entire new generation of entrants into the brokerage business was conditioned and taught to offer a full array of manufactured financial products rather than to focus on stocks as in the past.

These firms became the personal analog of the financial shopping mall, where ideally customers never leave the premises to satisfy any or all their investment needs. Asset capture became a way of life in the investment and brokerage industry. By the mid-1980s, standard training programs for new sales personnel had relegated stocks and bonds—once the staple of the business—to literally a 10 percent or less share of time and emphasis. A stock or bond became only one of a series of financial concepts or products that the newly trained salesperson learned how to offer to prospects and client-investors. A 1988 Barron's article estimated that 40 percent of the brokers in the business in 1987 had entered since 1980. Similar short incumbency persists today. Their training reflects this era of wholesale de-emphasis on stocks. Not only were individual stocks accorded less emphasis in training programs, but they also became palpably less attractive to the average individual investor.

This major development of the 1970s and 1980s was also, at least in part, a fallout from the Fidelity phenomenon. Huge pools of investable funds came under the control of professional money managers, whether in funds, pension plans or insurance/annuity assets. The live trading marketplace became highly institutionalized as an increasing fraction of each session's trading was initiated by professional portfolio managers rather than implemented directly by individuals.

Individual investors—regardless of their age or Wall Street experience—became painfully aware that they were competing as relative rookies on a playing field dominated by giant players who, right or wrong, moved the market just by playing. This realization, brought home in a series of bear markets from 1973 to 1982 and coming again as no surprise in October 1987, convinced millions of individual investors to reduce their direct participation in stocks. In large numbers they quit altogether, went into hibernation, or turned their money over to the professional money managers, thereby accelerating the institutionalization trend.

These packaged investments or products are sold to investors; they are not actively bought by investors. So the operational dynamic is not that an individual investor goes to a broker who responds by identifying a product or service to sell to that investor. Now, in order to gather assets in the new competitive marketing era, asset managers create packaged investment products to be proactively sold to an investing public by brokers who spend considerable time prospecting for new money rather than studying stocks and the stock market per se.

New Techniques in Sales

The most efficient way to sell a mass-produced product is to train a sales force in a standardized and rehearsed technique. And because, for regulatory compliance reasons, certain representations must be made and certain caveats offered, a sales presentation is delivered essentially from a script. The extreme version is a verbatim or canned script or pitch that the salesperson is supposed to read from top to bottom.

The point? Prepackaged products and rehearsed sales pitches require persuasiveness and persistence, in contrast to the choosing of individual securities that requires informed intelligence and incisive investment expertise. Played out through cold calling of fresh prospects, the sale of products results in successful asset capture. Prepackaged products also generate larger commissions than do stocks and bonds.

Imagine a securities broker with a prospect or existing client whose objective is income and safety of principal. He might place $10,000 in the Consolidated Income Fund, which is professionally managed and offers a 4.5 percent commission or perhaps a 0.5 percent annual trailing commission as long as held. One or two individual income stocks, the alternative to the fund, pay an up-front gross commission of maybe one percent. And at most brokerage firms, the broker's personal percentage of total commissions is higher on packaged products than on stocks and bonds. Which vehicles will the broker sell? The packaged products. Even if commissions were equal, the packaged products come with an easy, prepared script and the assurance of a proven professional management team; individual already-traded stocks do not. There is less post-sale hand holding with the packaged product because, presumably, it is less complicated. And many such products are one-decision (i.e., buy) in nature, further reducing demands on broker time for after-sale client tending.

Consider one more important broker aspect of the asset-gathering revolution: the nature of investment sales personnel. They are paid to distribute investment products created for the benefit of management. This process usually is performed most effectively with conservative, long-term investments. The salesperson of today is trained to help the client make a decision to buy a product. Professional training, mind set and daily work habits all focus exclusively on a relationship in which the broker suggests instruments that should be bought and that the prospect then agrees to buy.

So the modern-era broker is not trained in the process of convincing clients that they should sell investment assets. This is, in effect, a structural buy bias: a focusing of the investment industry on the process of distributing packaged products designed to be bought by the public. Brokers are simply more practiced and more comfortable suggesting that clients buy something rather than that they sell something. This shift evolved because brokers became channels of distribution as a result of asset-gathering, rather than sources of investment advice.

One of the ways to identify a broker's professional point of origin—asset-gathering or investment expertise—is to find out how long he or she has been in the investment business and what prior career he or she had. If the person was previously an entrepreneur or franchisee or—the surest tip-off—a salesman of other products or services, this broker is at heart a hustling sales professional rather than an investment expert. Another useful and revealing strategy is to interrupt the canned or scripted sales pitch with a question. Make the question really challenging or off the wall. Ask the broker an off-beat question like: What happens to (the proposed investment) if the Swiss franc rallies against the Japanese yen while the value of the dollar and gold both rise? Brokers who actually are investment professionals should have some semblance of an informed opinion. Scripted brokers will be baffled.

Because of this pervasive buy bias, investors should expect little or no selling advice unless their brokers happen to be traditional professionals. An investor must, then, realize that selling decisions are going to be virtually a do-it-yourself project. Clearly, going it alone has long become standard for discount brokerage clients.

There is also a psychological bias against selling stocks: All buys are made in optimism, whereas not all sells conclude successful ventures. In buying, an investor focuses on how correct he or she may be; when selling, uncertainty centers on what kind of mistake might be committed. So selling is not a uniformly happy experience for investors. And virtually every sell, unless made at the historic high price, at least sometimes looks like a wrong and irretrievably completed decision. Unhappy memories of such sales, reinforced multiple times, prompt strong avoidance behavior later.

The Four-Letter Word: Sell

One of the reasons selling is a difficult proposition for a broker is the buy bias. It is easy to appreciate the more comfortable and optimistic sense that both investors and brokers have about buying, especially when it is contrasted with selling. As stated before, buying is, by nature, a beginning based on hope and optimism. Selling is an ending that may not conclude in optimism, so it carries a lot more emotional baggage.

There are additional, very important reasons a brokerage firm almost never says sell. All of them are logical if viewed from the firm's viewpoint. Individual investors must, therefore, center on their own profit needs when it comes to making a sell decision, not on the broker's desire for a commission or her sales orientation and not on the profit motive of the brokerage firm. A wise investor must adopt a strong do-it-yourself attitude and discipline about cashing in when the time is right, whether using a full-service firm or not.

The necessity for this go-it-alone investor orientation is that individuals are far from the brokerage firm's only client constituency. Usually, a brokerage firm's most important clients are public companies. This is because the investment-banking side of the firm is in business to raise capital for these companies (or to merge them into other companies), and that is a very lucrative business compared with retail commission revenues.

In fact, when an individual investor buys stocks or bonds in a new issue, the broker usually points out that there is no commission on the purchase. The broker may go so far as to say that the issuing company is paying the commission. This is correct; and except for very small orders, the investment banking, per-share commission is well above what is paid on an aftermarket, stock-exchange, transaction.

The level of commission dollars (politely called underwriting fees) from companies issuing securities is high because the investment banking side of the firm has high fixed costs (salaries, entertainment, technology, legal and accounting consultants) and because nearly all companies (Google was an exception!) cannot raise capital without the brokers. Investment banking departments need to do underwriting for these large corporate clients, or they are not profitable. That means there is an inescapable tension within the brokerage firm between the investment banking side and the research side.

Because investment bankers need to do deals (i.e., bring out securities issues such as initial public offerings), naturally the firm's overall interests are best served if those stocks and bonds prove to be solid investments for the firm's clients. The firm's

9

research analysts must make judgments on the available investment alternatives; they recommend those they think are best to the firm's brokers and clients through published reports and newsletters. A research analyst's job is complete only when he or she fully studies a company and its industry and makes two recommendations: when to buy and when to sell.

Unfortunately, individual investors almost never see a sell recommendation. Why? Selling advice is rarely published because of the negative impact they have on that key relationship between the brokerage firm and its investment-banking clients. Think about these implications. Suppose that in January a brokerage firm brings to market a few million shares of a company called New-Issue Industries. The firm's brokers dutifully place the stock with clients and collect commissions. But suppose something goes awry in the company's affairs shortly after the offering is made: Perhaps in March a competitor introduces a new widget or is acquired by a powerful conglomerate, or sales turn soft, or raw-material costs explode. The research analyst wants to point out the potential problem to brokers and clients, suggesting that the stock be sold.

But sell to whom? Most or nearly all awareness of the company is centered in the firm's own retail clients. How will the clients react if they bought in January and now in March are encouraged to sell because trouble lies ahead? At the least, they will suspect their brokers of churning their portfolios for commissions. At most, they may sue the brokerage firm over alleged misrepresentation or negligence. What happens to the relationship between the investment banking department and the corporate officers at New-Issue Industries if the research department flashes the sell flag and the stock heads south? Future business between the firm and New-Issue Industries becomes highly unlikely. If word gets around the corporate community that the brokerage firm recommends sales of stocks it brought public, other potential issuing companies are very likely to use a different underwriter for their upcoming issues. This is an extremely powerful dynamic.

For these reasons, the sell word is absent from the lexicon of most brokerage firms. It is considered a true four-letter word; although institutional clients might hear it over the phone, it almost never appears in print. The data on lack of selling recommendations are stunning. In the early 1990s a Securities and Exchange Commission (SEC) inquiry into the matter concluded that buy reports by analysts outnumbered sell reports by 46:1. A study by Bloomberg found that sell recommendations constituted a mere 1.9 percent of published broker research. In mid-2007, 5 years after regulatory reform surrounding analyst opinions, sale ratings had crept up to 6.9 percent of analyst advices, again per Bloomberg.

There are several dimensions to the distaste for the word sell, and one of the most important is the reluctance of a broker to activate the sale side of a security transaction. For that reason, consider any broker assistance a gift, and do not count on that help: Brokerage houses almost never say sell, so an investor needs to know the code words brokers use when they really mean sell.

Euphemisms

Other words for sell, however, commonly do appear. Brokerage firms have devised a variety of ways to describe a corporate situation that indicates a sale is the best option. One of them is to write a report covering a corporate finance client, which is labeled a follow-up to the underwriting and carries no opinion or recommendation. Follow-ups need to be read closely. Even if the official policy is to give no recommendation, the tone of the report needs to be evaluated carefully. If it is less than glowing, suspect that the research analyst is not impressed with this stock and, while constrained from saying so, really thinks it should be sold. Another way, short of uttering the S-word, is for the firm to drop analyst coverage of a company altogether. Such silence is not golden.

A diplomatic approach is to give a recommendation other than buy that is kinder and gentler than the S-word itself. The best euphemism for sell, ironically, is its operative opposite: hold. When an analyst does not want to say buy and is not allowed to say sell, the only option remaining is hold. Consider hold almost always as a danger sign. In fact, hold really should generally be interpreted as meaning, do not hold.

Common brokerage euphemisms for sell:

◆ hold
◆ accumulate
◆ long-term buy
◆ market performer
◆ market weight
◆ perform in line
◆ under perform
◆ underweight

Another coded way of saying sell is a carefully worded message such as: The stock is probably a worthwhile long-term holding despite some near-term uncertainties. That is translated by the cynic as: If you hold for quite a while, maybe you will not lose. All such euphemisms should be taken as signals to cash in.

Make it a point to ask a broker about his firm's scale of rating words. For some very few it is buy/hold. Others say buy/accumulate/hold. Others may use words like over perform/in-line/under perform. Some even say strong buy as contrasted with buy or focus list as opposed to a mere buy. Know the range of official analyst word choices. Anything less enthusiastic than the top choice should be interpreted as faint praise or outright damnation. If a broker does not verbally make a compelling case for the stock when the official advice is less than glowing, figure that the profitable decision is to cash out your position promptly.

Politics and Diplomacy

Even when there is no current investment banking relationship between the issuing company and the brokerage firm, there are other important reasons research analysts are unlikely to advise a sale. First, there is the possibility of future business, so they do not want to poison the waters. And more immediately, the analyst needs to have the continuing, cordial, constructive and prompt communication of senior management. Boston Chicken (later Boston Market, before being acquired by McDonald's), as reported by The Wall Street Journal, banned from future meetings an analyst who recommended selling its shares. A sale recommendation, even if it is the correct conclusion, seldom warms up the company's management. They own shares themselves and so are never pleased by a price decline such as usually follows a sale advice. Also, the analyst may have legitimate reason to fear that an adverse recommendation might stifle management's future frankness of disclosures: The worst scenario is to recommend a sale that turns out wrong.

Finally, there is the numbers game. When an analyst writes a research report advising purchase, brokers can use that report to contact every customer whose investment objective makes the purchase of that stock appropriate. That means that a buy advice has a potentially wide audience. For example, suppose that a particular electric utility seems attractive to the analyst. Her recommendation to buy can be presented to every client interested in income.

But a sale recommendation has much smaller business-generating potential. A sale advice applies only to those clients who already own the stock (and to that tiny minority oriented to short selling). Suppose that our utilities analyst now believes interest rates are about to rise or that new lower-cost competitors will become a problem, and she decides to advise the sale of an electric company's shares. Perhaps only one in 10 clients acted on the idea when a buy was advised. These people are the only audience for the sale report. Worse than that, some clients may have bought at higher prices, and their brokers are hesitant to advise taking losses. So the sale report is not likely to be very effective in generating commissions. Research analysts are employed and compensated on the basis of the accuracy of judgment and on the amount of business their reports generate. So analysts have a buy bias too.

Individual brokers face yet another dilemma when making a sale recommendation. The investor tends to blame poor results more on a sale than on a buy. Ask any broker whether clients remember bad buy advice given but not acted on, or do they recall a bad sell advice that was acted on? Overwhelmingly, scoreboard watchers watch the stocks they owned and sold, not those they never bought. That tendency can get brokers into trouble with their clients (and analysts into trouble with a firm's brokers). Another way for a broker to get into even more trouble is to suggest redeploying the funds in another stock that goes down.

In summary, there are five ways a sale advice can backfire on a broker:

1. It can offend the client who is emotionally attached to the stock.

2. Selling can close out a painful transaction (a loss).

3. The sale can be followed by a price rally, which would have provided greater profit or a reduced loss if the stock had been held.

4. Funds liberated by the sale might be reinvested unprofitably, making the sale a double troublemaker.

5. Unless the sale price proves nearly perfect, the broker is resented for generating a commission by suggesting the action.

It is also worth noting here that penny-stock houses never recommend a sell unless it is to generate funds to buy something else. The major reason is that they themselves must buy what investors sell because they, virtually alone, make the market in the stock. And there is a parallel to guard against in non-penny brokerage practice as well. If an investor tells a broker to sell and the response is a pitch not to do so, this is a serious alarm signal. It may mean that the firm is concerned about the price (perhaps it has a long inventory position!) and does not want to put pressure on the stock. Who would turn down an unsolicited sale order? Unless a broker gives solid, specific reasons to hold (buy), insist on selling immediately, at the market.

The most prudent practice is never waiting to hear sell advice. Assume it will not be heard, and plan to make your personal selling-versus-holding decisions with the help of tools and rules that appear later in this book.

The False Security of Low Initial Risk

It periodically becomes fashionable in investment marketing circles to emphasize avoidance of risk, particularly since the October 1987 crash and again the post-bubble bear market of 2000-2002. A balanced emphasis within the industry on risk avoidance—rather than on promising the moon in growth and profits—is healthy. That the investing public is taking this advice to heart is reflected by the noticeable decline in the number of well-known penny-stock brokerage houses, so-called boiler rooms, and other similar operations that prey on investor gullibility, greed and seemingly boundless optimism. (To some extent these have been replaced by glossy-page information mailing houses that tout stocks for a large paid fee and avoid effective regulation under first-amendment cover.)

But even with the rebirth of emphasis on risk avoidance (which has again predictably receded somewhat in the five-year bull market since mid-2002), securities industry marketing efforts focus entirely on buying and virtually ignore the equally important second (selling) side of the transaction. In most public investment seminars, the selling aspect covered most often is the stop-loss order, but speakers rarely cover how and why to use this instrument adequately. Although stop-loss orders can prove useful, their routine use allows investors (and their brokers) to avoid confronting crucial selling decisions. Either a stop-loss order is triggered automatically or it is not activated at all, which neatly truncates the important selling thought-process. For brokers to advise using stop-loss orders routinely is also self-serving: If a client is stopped out of a losing position, the loss is relatively small, and use of these orders shows that the broker exercised diligence in trying to limit losses. And they do generate commissions.

Of course, if stop-loss orders are placed too close to current prices, stops are triggered often; this increases turnover in the account for defensible reasons of caution but protects the client against possible major capital loss in any one stock position.

Many investor seminars promise to highlight specific management techniques for protecting investor money to avoid risk. But managing is an active verb indicating an ongoing process. Managing a factory does not mean hiring workers, sending them through the door and walking away. In the same way, managing invested funds means buying, watching constantly and selling. It consists of much more than an up-front, one-time allocation of assets or just a choice of purchases. Asset allocation—among types of investment instruments, across industries, in world regions and on a time horizon—is not a do-it-once activity. The strategies and tactics taught by a majority of brokerage firms, however, merely list financial instruments rather than teach specific, ongoing money-management techniques.

The lists usually consist of mutual funds, unit investment trusts (UITs), insurance, annuities, bonds and stocks—none of which is a strategy or a tactic. They should be considered only as possible means by which to execute a strategy. Properly timed purchases and sales of these instruments are tactical actions. Of course, three of those six instruments are essentially one-decision (i.e., buy) investments: insurance, annuities and UITs. Notice that not coincidentally these are packaged products manufactured by financial institutions to be sold actively to the public. The broker is compensated at the start to get investors to buy, and there is no back-end action (selling or deliberate cashing in) built into the planned equation.

Generally, these six financial vehicles are properly described and positioned by the brokerage industry within economic cycles. But brokerage and financial planners' seminars focus only on identifying when a cycle has begun and how to take advantage of it by buying at the right time. So in the industry's eyes, managing and avoiding risk in the equities arena becomes a function of buying good stocks and selecting a good time to buy good stocks. What this nearsighted approach ignores is that risk is constantly present in varying degrees over time; managing investments must be an ongoing process that does not end when a purchase is made. Currently, great companies cannot by any means be guaranteed to remain so forever.

Before buying, therefore, assess all the opportunities and associated risks inherent in an investment package, including the illiquidity cost involved in selling. Look at the upside and downside (seen and unseen) carefully. Then, shift focus after the purchase from the broad to the specific. Your question now becomes: Which stock (among many) should be sold? The notion that risk is avoided once a seemingly safe investment has been bought obfuscates the sure reality of changing future events.

Decision time for proactive entry into an investment is not the only juncture when risk is taken on or avoided. By now, the reader's awareness of the one-sidedness of investment marketing should serve to heighten sensitivity to the buy bias. Because greater external attention is always paid to buying, put more of your personal energy and work into selling. Although an investor can sit out an advised buy, once he or she owns an investment there is no way to call a time out. The only way to end game profitably is to sell.

Underestimating the Seriousness of Changed Fundamentals

Today's institutional domination of the market and the increased leverage and fragility of the economy require that investors pay more attention to changed fundamentals than in gentler times past. Success now requires heightened attention to fundamental news about a company—and its industry and broader environment—when an investor owns its shares. If the news is less favorable than expected or if deterioration in the company's prospects is evident or suspected, the best action usually is to sell promptly. The reason is related to momentum: When things go wrong, it takes significant exertion of energy in the opposite direction to make them start going right again. That is true both in the management of the company's day-to-day business and also in the stock market.

In any speculative market, a snowball that starts going downhill tends to keep going. Prices swing emotionally from overvaluation to undervaluation. The extent of overshooting on each side is impossible to predict because it is driven by volatile emotions. So an investor's first job is to become smart enough to realize that the market gyrates and then to get out of the way before the pendulum swings adversely.

While stocks do not always accelerate in decline as an easy telltale signal of having bottomed, it is universally true that an actual reversal to upside price action requires intervention by interested buyers. Such buyers must be big and persistent enough first to stop the price decline and then to stabilize the price against any trickle of further selling that results from boredom. Finally, they must overpower sellers on an ongoing basis to push the stock's price higher. With literally thousands of stocks available to buy, once a company becomes troubled in the collective opinion of the market, it will take considerable time and probably some notable events for improved prices to take hold.

Strategies to Overcome Fundamental Problems

It is well known that running a business successfully takes a great deal of effort and attention. Few companies can be put on automatic pilot: External forces emerge or change; competitors enter the fray or demand-side shifts require product/service changes. Management is paid to anticipate, monitor and overcome difficulties to keep the enterprise moving ahead profitably. The same is true of investing in the stock market: The investor is paid for success in anticipating, monitoring and acting. Those who merely react after trouble is obvious are paid badly or negatively.

Every investor's ego—as well as his or her money—is invested in the market. So he must be on guard to keep his hopes from overruling good judgment. This strongly indicates that an investor should read more than just the annual and quarterly reports; she should read the 10-Ks and the 10-Qs, too. Study management's discussion of challenges and risks foreseen for the quarter or year ahead. Compare what happened against what management's earlier projections were. Compare the content and tone of current outlook statements against those of three or six months ago. Pay particular attention to unfavorable changes.

Remember that because of today's highly litigious climate, executives usually telegraph possible problems early on—to avoid being accused of withholding bad news. Listen to their warnings. If growth in revenue is slowing down or if margins are under pressure or costs are outrunning expansion, find out why. If management does not identify causes, specific remedies cannot be taken, and that is a major fundamental problem. Remember that problems seldom solve themselves.

For this reason, carefully examine what a company's executives say about corporate problems and challenges. Look for discussion of solutions and actions, not whining and excuses. Do not be readily forgiving; executives are paid to manage things. If the president's report bemoans the fact that external forces are causing lost business or higher costs but offers no concrete corporate initiatives to reverse the difficulties, sell your stock. Fire this management team by selling the stock. Hire another team. Do not be patient when your money is on the line and in the hands of managers and directors who may be just drifting while collecting hefty compensation.

It is wiser to lean toward being overly harsh than overly forgiving. Be especially sensitive to the development of negative fundamentals. And paying attention casually just once a quarter, reading the interim report six weeks into the next quarter, is not enough. If the price of liberty is eternal vigilance, the price of investment success is constant observation, evaluation, comparison, decisiveness and a willingness to admit a mistake and move on.

One undeniable reason to be up to date and relatively unforgiving is that institutions moving huge amounts of money into and out of stocks, unfortunately, have a very short-term orientation. Therefore, individual investors must be nimble to nip any potential investment problems in the bud. A smaller investor's inclination may be to give a company the benefit of a little more time to improve. But when a professional investor with a few million shares gets impatient, price will drop even if the patient, small investor later is proven correct about an eventual turnaround. Whether it seems right or wrong in a cosmic sense, developing impatience is actually a virtue for investors in our era of institutional trading domination.

Granted that taking losses quickly on important bad news or disturbing trends means falling into and thereby increasing the pattern of short-term performance orientation. However, an investor must be realistic and do what is required to preserve capital. This willingness to be part of a growing short-term orientation if necessary falls under the broad banner of not fighting the tape. This approach means recognizing that while a market may be wrong in its approach, it is much bigger than an individual.

Buying and Holding: As Conditioned Behaviour

Investors buy stocks for a number of reasons, many of which are ill-advised. From purely an investment perspective, there are only two reasons to buy common stocks. True equities investing consists of identifying those companies with stocks undervalued in terms of future earning power and buying them now because the projected earnings per share (EPS) stream is expected to produce dividends. So the first objective is dividend income. The second objective is capital appreciation. Growth in price tends to occur over time if the fortunes of the underlying company improve, if interest rates do not move sharply higher (squeezing price/ earnings ratios [P/Es]), and if market psychology moves from negative to neutral or positive.

Some investment purists look down their noses and call the desire for capital appreciation speculation. It may or may not be such, but investors buy stocks in order to sell them at a profit in the future, whether it be called intelligent speculation or investment. Whichever it is, to be successful a transaction requires both buying and selling, since both are required before a transaction's final result is established. As stated in the introduction, published books dealing with stock market investing in any form focus overwhelmingly on the buying transaction only and neglect the sell side of the equation almost completely. Selling may not be as exciting, and assuredly it is a narrower topic, but it is absolutely necessary and has its own very interesting twists and curiosities.

Dividend Income

Investors who buy stocks for dividend income should consider the total package of risk and reward more carefully than most of them do. It is tempting to buy common stocks of companies in which the latest year's dividends represent a high percentage of the current stock price. The buyer believes that this high apparent yield will continue. What is often not fully considered is that the collective wisdom and expectations of all knowledgeable market players set current stock prices; therefore, an apparently high yield is usually a sign of high risk. So the buyer of a high-yield stock is accepting two risks: (1) that the dividend income itself may be reduced or stopped and (2) that the stock's price would very likely decline from the buyer's level if such an adverse dividend action occurred.

Table 1.1

Calculation of Annual Total Percentage Return on Investment
(pre-tax; assumes dividend raised 5 percent at year-end meeting)

Year End	Div Rate $	Yield Basis %	Price $	Cap Incr $	Total $ Retn	Total % Retn	Return on Orig Cost	
							Total %	Cash %
0 (Buy)	1.40	7.00	20.00					
1	1.47	7.00	21.00	1.00	2.40	12.0	12.0	7.0
2	1.54	7.00	22.05	1.05	2.52	12.0	12.6	7.3
3	1.62	7.00	23.15	1.10	2.65	12.0	13.2	7.7
4	1.70	7.00	24.31	1.16	2.78	12.0	13.9	8.1
5	1.79	7.00	25.53	1.22	2.92	12.0	14.6	8.5
6	1.88	7.00	26.80	1.28	3.06	12.0	15.3	8.9
7	1.97	7.00	28.14	1.34	3.22	12.0	16.1	9.4
8	2.07	7.00	29.55	1.41	3.38	12.0	16.9	9.8
9	2.17	7.00	31.03	1.48	3.55	12.0	17.7	10.3
10	2.28	7.00	32.58	1.55	3.72	12.0	18.6	10.9
Total:	18.49			12.58	31.07	Average: 15.5		8.8

Table 1.2

Calculation of Annual Total Percentage Return on Investment
(pre-tax; assumes dividend constant at 10 percent of purchase price)

Year End	Div Rate $	Yield Basis %	Price $	Cap Incr $	Total $ Retn	Total % Retn
0 (Buy)	1.40	10.0	14.00			
1	1.40	10.0	14.00	0.00	1.40	10.0
2	1.40	10.0	14.00	0.00	1.40	10.0
3	1.40	10.0	14.00	0.00	1.40	10.0
4	1.40	10.0	14.00	0.00	1.40	10.0
5	1.40	10.0	14.00	0.00	1.40	10.0
6	1.40	10.0	14.00	0.00	1.40	10.0
7	1.40	10.0	14.00	0.00	1.40	10.0
8	1.40	10.0	14.00	0.00	1.40	10.0
9	1.40	10.0	14.00	0.00	1.40	10.0
10	1.40	10.0	14.00	0.00	1.40	10.0
	14.00			0.00	14.00	

Almost continuously since the middle 1950s, common stocks have provided lower current (cash) yields than either long-term bonds or preferred stocks. In this environment, an investor requiring a high current yield should buy senior instruments. They are much less likely than common shares to suffer reduced or omitted income payments, and they usually carry covenants promising to make up the withheld cash returns in the future if those events transpire (barring bankruptcy, of course).

If a buyer has a serious need for current income, he should not take the incremental risk of common stock ownership; instead, he should stick to senior securities. Also, the buyer of common stocks for income should concentrate not on pure current cash income alone but rather on total return (referring to the sum of cash return plus realized or unrealized price appreciation). That appreciation, in turn, is caused by a rising level of dividends over the years. That rate of growth, expressed as a percentage per year, is added to the cash yield (dividend rate divided by stock price) to get total return. (See Tables 1-1 and 1-2.)

Thus, an admittedly uncommon stock currently yielding seven percent with a dividend growth of five percent annually may, on average, be expected to provide a total return of 12 percent per year. Actual results vary as the company's fortunes change and, significantly, as the level of prevailing interest rates shifts. Major capital gains can be achieved with the use of conservative instruments such as utility common stocks and growth-oriented equity real estate investment trusts (REITs) in periods when interest rates are declining. In contrast, even the best in quality among utility and REIT shares decline, in some cases severely, in the face of higher interest rates. Most investors in quality blue chips, and especially in utility shares, consider themselves long-term holders. But because of the major influence that interest-rate cycles exert on stock prices, even blue chip stocks bought primarily for income also should be viewed as subject to sale to capture capital appreciation. (For example, a move from six percent to seven percent in long-term interest rates is a 17 percent change in the valuation equation's divisor, which will swamp one or two years' dividend increases.) So, even for those investors whose stated strategy is a long-term buy and hold, our subject of selling should not be given ostrich treatment. Knowing how to sell is an imperative discipline sooner or later.

Capital Appreciation

As indicated earlier, the other legitimate reason for buying a stock is a prognostication that it will rise in price and thereby reward holders via appreciation in capital value. Some purists argue that any basis for expecting rising value other than higher dividends amounts to the greater-fool theory. Others say that hoping to capture a swing in psychology or interest rates in order to increase a stock's price amounts to speculation because such gains are not driven purely by increased earnings and dividend streams from the company. Suffice to say that very significant rises in price beyond what is driven by dividend streams clearly and frequently do in fact take place. So capturing those increases is a legitimate subject for study and effort.

Other Reasons

Some people buy stocks for other reasons. For example, loyalty induces many investors to buy stock in the company for which they work or shares in a major employer in the community where they live. But such loyalty buys can result in major investment losses because there is a tendency for loyalty to override common sense and, therefore, to prevent timely sales when such action becomes the rational course. Other market participants buy a stock because of a perceived affiliation with the members of management or because they like the products offered by a company. These purchases usually are not entered or timed on a price/value basis; they are not driven by the profit motive.

Other stock purchases are made because of excitement about some concept. In many cases, either the purchaser is ignorant of investment values and just feels warm and fuzzy about owning a company that is involved in the subject business (environmental protection, humane research on new drugs and AIDS cures are forward-looking businesses) or he has purchased this stock to feel trendy. There are also many people who buy stocks primarily for the thrill of participation in the game. They play the market because it is socially acceptable to do so. Or they believe the market can generate the thrills and emotional drama of gambling—but legally and over a longer time period—before their money runs out.

A few psychologists who specialize in patients' money problems even find that some investors participate on Wall Street for deep-seated emotional reasons. Among the darker ones are self-destructive urges and a need to prove oneself to an approval-withholding parent, or even an Oedipal need to compete with father. Such problems and their owners lie well outside our intended range of discussion.

Finally, whether their conditioning is external or self-imposed, some investors should be called collectors. These are people who gradually accumulate a variety of stocks over a period of years. But being a collector of stocks is similar to living as a pack rat: It is most unlikely that a confirmed practitioner of either art can be reformed. Western society emphasizes acquiring things, not disposing of them. This conditioning also subtly supports a buy-and-hold bias.

Financial writers, advisors, mutual-funds advertisements and brokers all constitute powerful external forces focused on buying. This emphasis is perhaps understandable from their perspective, but it needs balance. Equal attention to selling—which is necessary to nail down all profits—is required.

The balance of this book, then, is devoted to assisting investors who buy for financial reasons. No remedy is offered to those who participate mainly for sentimental or psychological reasons. Your author's goal is to provide guidelines for how to cash in profits when appropriate and to limit or prevent losses. A major emphasis is placed on understanding and overcoming the inertia that causes holding rather than selling. Our next chapter looks into various powerful forces that are inside our heads. Sometimes the main enemy actually can be ourselves!

CHAPTER 2

Hidden Reasons We Resist Selling

Keys for Successful Selling

◆ Understand Subtle but Strong Psychological Impediments

◆ Learn and Implement the Difficult 180-Degree Reversal

◆ Battle Perfectionism

◆ Stop Trying to Protect Your Ego; Focus on Your Capital

Chapter 1 cataloged external influences that work against investors' selling their holdings. Those forces will not disappear from our lives just because they have been named, but at least they are readily recognizable when present. We can see and consciously work to neutralize such very visible enemies. Much more challenging are the numerous subtle psychological forces acting within our heads. Each investor is influenced by a different combination of these subconscious drives and motivations, which vary in intensity as well. At the risk of appearing to practice pop psychology, this chapter explores significant things going on inside our heads and our personalities. Only after identifying these forces can we better understand why we feel as we do and why our first instincts in certain situations point us toward actions, or inertia, that can prove counterproductive in our investing (or trading) lives.

Many insightful volumes have been written on human emotion and behavior; it is not the place of this one to attempt a comprehensive psychological examination of investor behavior, not least because your author is not formally trained in that field. Several excellent works providing useful exploration into the psychology of investing are listed in the Appendix. Our purpose here is to expose at a very high level those most central and overriding patterns in our human personalities that adversely influence investment action and inaction. Significantly, many of these affect the selling side of investing considerably more than the buying side. That is why understanding and dealing with these mysteries inside our heads is a very important ingredient in becoming more successful at selling stocks well.

Pain and Pleasure

Considerable agreement exists across various schools of psychological thought that humans are primarily engaged in finding ways to decrease their amount of pain and increase their amount of pleasure; however, those concepts need to be defined in detail. As testimony to how central this is, pain avoidance and pleasure- or comfort-seeking are familiar concepts that certainly dominate marketing and advertising. While numerous other forces are undeniably at work as investors face decisions about selling, comfort-seeking and pain avoidance are extremely powerful. At a most obvious level, it might be observed that making a profit represents pleasure, while suffering a loss equates to feeling pain (at least for all except masochists and neurotics). Our interest here is focused on a deeper layer of forces that dispose us to certain attitudes and behaviors springing from our subconscious pain-avoidance and comfort-seeking tendencies.

Why Holding Feels Right

When we own a particular stock, inaction (holding) keeps us in or certainly closer to a place of comfort than does taking action to change our circumstances (selling). Holding onto a friend keeps us close to our past, to memories and feelings we cherish. Many continue to hold stock in companies whose fortunes peaked years or even decades ago. Logic alone cannot seem to explain why they resist selling despite obviously dim prospects for recovery or gain. Maybe grandfather worked for the company, or we reside in a town where it supported many families or sponsored the softball team. Perhaps ages ago we made a profit, or at least had a good paper profit for a while, in this stock. Or our parents always spoke well of the company or confided they had made a decent sum in its shares at one time. Thus, nostalgic positive feelings surround it and we find it very difficult to end our association.

Without necessarily being rooted in the deep past, our positive associations with a particular stock create a bonded feeling. We have made a good profit on an overall basis and while the annualized return may be unspectacular, a gain is surely better than a loss and the total dollar or point profit feels pleasant. So this stock is our friend. Held for a number of years now, it has been virtually adopted as a family member. Thus, our primary inclination is to not sever such ties by terminating this comfortable relationship. Why end this thing, we think at an unconscious and perhaps also at a conscious level. Living with, rather than without, that stock represents staying in a comfort zone.

Even though the company's fortunes may now have faltered, choosing to sell its stock represents adopting a 180-degree opposite stance. Issuing that order to liquidate means that what we once thought was correct now is no longer so in our minds. This company is no longer under priced, or its prospects or management quality are not what we earlier imagined or expected. Or perhaps we have given up on its price/earnings ratio growing as we had earlier envisioned.

To say sell means that either what we once thought was right is no longer so and/or that maybe we have already been on the wrong side of the market for some time and are now admitting a change in opinion is warranted. Either way, selling represents admitting we now believe what we earlier thought is no longer true. Most of us have great difficulty acknowledging that we were wrong. If you place a very strong value on reputation or esteem in life, the reversal of position inherent in selling is likely to be an especially difficult battle zone for your ego and your comfort. This can be a special problem for professionals such as doctors, attorneys, and others looked up to. Reversing a position is made even more difficult if we have publicly or strongly espoused it. This is a very important reason for keeping our investment holdings secret: reversing ourselves and selling then at least involves no loss of face with others who knew our prior opinion.

We live in a time of high expectations driven in part by ubiquitous computers and the rising speed of communications. Precision in many aspects of life involved in information is possible and increasingly expected; we can all be monitored and our human fallibility documented and used against us. Time is telescoped, and we have become impatient with any delay or error. Seemingly everyone is suing someone else over anything that has gone wrong. We would like to require perfection just as it is expected of us. In our work lives we function in an environment that demands zero defects and expects immediate paybacks. Our children and grandchildren simply must gain entrance to that one best preschool or their lives will be on a path to ruin. Our favorite professional sports team is labeled a failure for not repeating as world champion. Perfectionism is that disease in our minds working to deny us enjoying any good or pleasure because it may not last forever or merely because it is les than an ultimate win.

Perfectionism makes us recoil from the decisions involved in selling our investments. Perfectionism makes avoiding such choices, and therefore holding by default, the least uncomfortable course among available actions. You know, both in terms of actual probabilities and from many experiences, that when you sell you will not receive the top price. That stock's very next tick, its closing price today or tomorrow, a possible piece of good news months hence, or a bull market three years ahead can easily bring a higher price than where you will sell at this moment. Thus, you feel doomed to being wrong sooner or later when you sell. By selling, we predictably and knowingly expose ourselves to yet another instance in which we can be proved less than perfect, in which we again label ourselves as fallible human beings. We feel pressure, either from our external world and/or from ourselves, to avoid such negative feedback, such failure labeling. Therefore, we tend to shun selling, which clearly sets a likely-imperfect result as final (we gained or lost exactly so much, but we may well soon see that a higher price than ours was possible). Selling means deliberately walking outside a zone of potentially improved results, which represents taking a risk, as summed up in a popular phrase about devils we know versus those we do not know.

In a world moving ever faster, in which technology both amazes and scares us and in which we have lost such pillars of security as lifetime employment expectations and permanently nurturing families, we look for and prize any anchors against the storm. Great (often, growth) companies whose stocks have treated us well and whose products and properties we see frequently act as a psychological bedrock to which we can hold firmly. We strongly resist as heretical any suggestion that such stocks ever be sold. No matter that they may have become grossly overvalued in a recent bull craze, or that perhaps their fundamental greatness is actually starting to fade, or that in a new competitive environment the company may survive and continue providing its service or product but at much-reduced profit. We cling to our old favorites no matter their current merit. From the late 1980s into the early 1990s, computer stocks (especially IBM) held such a power over their shareowners, despite a rapid sea change in technology, marketing, pricing and other profit factors. But investors held IBM as a matter of nearly religious conviction due to its past merits (institutions held 50 percent when IBM earnings started declining in 1986 and still held 50 percent in late 1993 when the stock bottomed below $40, down some 75 percent). In developing a mind-set to enable selling stocks successfully, meaning when the time is right, investors must battle against nostalgia and this tendency to cling to old lighthouses.

The common expression, what is wrong with this picture, in the extreme can refer to the psychological concept of cognitive dissonance. Here, a person is experiencing discomfort (and so may behave in strange ways) because new information and perceptions bring conflict with what has long and strongly been known or assumed as true. A spouse betrays our sacred bond of trust; an idol is accused of some crime; a trusted teacher or clergy member is revealed as a pedophile. Our nicely ordered world crumbles in such circumstances, and our first response is to deny it could be possible. We seek to avoid dealing with this terrible new revelation. In investing, we wish that every tree planted in our portfolio would grow forever skyward. Alas, in reality it will not be so. But holding on to existing positions in defiance of newly introduced information enables us to avoid dealing with dissonance: what we happily choose to ignore might go away rather than hurt us. We would rather live with that questionable hope, or turn away altogether, than face the harsh truth that things have changed so much that we need to sell as a result.

Why Selling Feels Uncomfortable

Selling requires of us a significant change in our thinking—indeed a complete reversal! When we bought that stock, its prospects were wonderful, and it represented value and opportunity. Now, whether our investment has since done well or not, to sell requires closing down hope and perhaps admitting defeat. And it is possible that our defeat may have been created by faulty initial thinking, meaning we can place no blame externally since we were actually wrong all along. Not a realization we savor.

Buying involves the opening of possibilities of great things. Buying represents open-endedness; continued holding maintains such hope for gain and pleasure (or, when we have a paper loss, hope for recovery and the righting of a temporary wrong). Selling carries a finality with it because, by definition, it closes the book or ends the game and establishes a final score. We prefer to have our options open rather than foreclosed, to retain chances for improvement and betterment rather than to know that the verdict is sealed and no chance for change exists. We have great difficulty coming to closure since it cuts off further possibilities; it ends hope for any better outcome. Closure includes such experiences as cleaning out great grandmother's attic; graduating and leaving school and friends; acknowledging a failed marriage by concluding a divorce; burying a dear friend or loved one; seeing winter come; leaving an employer and valued colleagues; retiring and therefore wrapping up business. Those are heavy and sad passages, so we are predisposed to resist voluntarily creating any closure experiences that we have power to avoid. Holding does exactly that.

Holding keeps our options open, while selling clearly brings closure and finality. (With surprising myopia, we ignore the fact that once we sell a stock we can just as easily repurchase it. Viewing repurchase as a very real antidote to our revulsion against closure, however, raises visions of again going through that agonizing process of reversing our opinion by 180 degrees, which is painful for all the reasons noted above.) So we hold rather than sell because, at the very least, holding postpones coming to closure. Many a bad stock is held (into an uncertain yet not hopeless future) with palpable likelihood of further financial loss because the (presently avoidable) emotional cost of coming to closure is perceived as so heavy. Investors pay in dollar losses to avoid emotional pain from a closure process; often, as losses get worse, they will later need to pay a higher price in both lost dollars and eventual pain by imposing self-punishment over major mistakes. The closure aspect of selling is a powerful deterrent, one requiring both strong will and courage to overcome.

Behavior Patterns that Protect Fragile Egos

Holding protects our egos in several ways. When we continue to hold a stock that shows a profit, that portfolio position remains conveniently available to stroke us: the good friend smiles at us on the computer screen or from our monthly account statement. We are smart; we are getting rich; we knew enough to hold through that nasty price correction a while back and see a better day. Owning a good stock is having a rich wine cellar, owning a prestigious home, driving the right car, surrounding ourselves with beautiful artworks. A stock that is up makes us feel good. When it goes part way back down, we focus more on the remaining paper gain rather than the lost opportunity. A stock that is up strokes our egos. Holding it makes much more subconscious emotional sense than pushing it away by selling!

Then there are stocks in which we have paper losses. Surprisingly, holding rather than selling these also makes us feel better. This is because of that closure baggage noted earlier. To sell a loser is to admit defeat and our human fallibility and, of our own free will, simultaneously close off any possibility of later vindication or reward. If we sell what is down it cannot recover for us, and we might actually compound our first mistake: It could now rise, meaning that we were wrong twice by having both bought high and sold low! So we preserve hope of eventually being a winner, and thus feeling better, by holding. An objective, updated assessment of this stock's prospects may provide little to encourage optimism (in fact, by going down, the market price is declaring exactly that as indeed the current verdict of most investors). But we can hope for some healing, or perhaps a major miracle, as long as we hold: we can wait to see what comes next, and, if that is not satisfactory we can wait some more to see what comes next after that. Psychologists and behavioral finance students refer to irrational avoidance of selling as myopic loss aversion.

To sell, we must be able to tear down any protective shields we have erected around our ego and stand the consequences of our actions and decisions. One of the aspects of losing in the stock market is that it reflects on our thinking. A loss not only leaves us poorer in dollars but also makes us feel foolish, stupid, or perhaps uncomfortably inadequate to the game. Holding is less painful.

Quite a few books have been written on the subject of fear: fear of losing and, perhaps surprisingly, fear of success (winning). Clearly, keeping the final result with a stock open by holding rather than selling postpones any verdict and thus puts off clearly official, unarguable failure or success to some undefined future time. In a nutshell, it appears that fear of success is related to at least two things: (1) Some Freudians say in the male, great success represents bettering and thus replacing one's father; (2) perhaps at a less complicated or threatening level, a great success sets a standard that we may fear or know we can never again achieve. Thus, selling at a great profit may be a scary thing to do. Holding will allow our gain to run or at least will postpone the scary act of selling and thus officially setting a new lifetime record we may never again equal. Thus, if fear either of failure or of success is a factor, holding works better for us than does selling.

A Look Ahead

This chapter has surfaced some of the often-subconscious or even unconscious psychological reasons why investors seem naturally to prefer holding over selling their investment positions. It is important, as part of the process of becoming a more successful investor (or trader) by selling better, to recognize and understand these hidden drivers of our feelings and behaviors. Chapter 5 exposes some of the symptomatic rationalizations that investors exhibit, in effect acting out and justifying their often irrational predisposition to holding at any cost rather than selling. If you see some aspects of your own behavior there, now you will both know whence that stuff comes and be better equipped to battle against it. Before tackling rationalizations head on, we will first take an important look, for background, at what behavioral finance (Chapter 3) and crowd studying (Chapter 4) say about investing successfully. Investing is indeed a constant battle, in which selling is a clearly more challenging arena than buying. But your newfound knowledge will be providing power to help you prevail!

Understanding and Using Behavioral Finance

Keys for Successful Selling

◆ Know How Anthropology, Sociology and Psychology Affect our Investing

◆ Understand the Nine Mental Mistakes Beyond Fear and Greed

◆ Watch Humor and Advertising as Clues to Market Position

◆ Become Able to Move Deliberately towards Discomfort

Behavioral finance, the intellectual intersection of two formerly far-separated clusters of disciplines, has blossomed during the past quarter century. Until recently investors and finance students were told that the necessary menu of knowledge consisted entirely of economics, corporate finance, accounting and security analysis. Immense richness has now been added by also calling on insights from psychology, sociology and anthropology. These disciplines help us to understand human beings.

That is a crucial increment of wisdom since, after all, investors' actions (which are driven by their perceptions, emotions, wired biases and resulting decisions) are what drive prices of stocks up and down. In the very long run, sure, fundamentals determine values of securities. But between now and that distant future, in the time and place where we as investors live and work, prices are driven by supply and demand. And the balance of those forces is not always rationally based. It is at market-negotiated prices, not values, where we sell (and buy) stocks. And markets reflect people, not fundamentals alone!

Two major implications flowing from behavioral finance can and should be used by investors (and traders) seeking to upgrade their collections of useful tools. The first key finding is that there exist a number of built-in mental errors and unhelpful biases that prompt investors to make mistakes in the markets—unless they learn of and constantly guard against them. In effect, one must know thine enemy! The second implication is narrower, but in my experience it is of huge value in identifying good exit (and entry) points for stocks. This is a simple realization: that crowd behavior frequently drives unsustainable and extreme price behavior at tops and bottoms. It follows from that observation that extra net returns can be earned by those who constantly watch for the crowd and who think of the market not from their own viewpoints alone but rather in terms of what the crowd is thinking. Crowd size can be readily observed in trading volume and, with some lag, in net money flows to/from equity mutual funds. Standing back and discerning where the crowd's often collectively muddled head is will always help you make a better decision.

There is More to Understand than Fear and Greed

Greed and fear are really the byproducts of some unfortunately wired aspects of the human mind. Anthropology teaches us that early humans were risk avoiders (on pain of death); and that they tended to follow the leader rather than be independent thinkers and actors; and that they were prone to superstition. Those tendencies served pretty well in terms of physical survival in cave-dwelling times. But they are unhelpful in the world of modern finance and investing. We now know that you must take risk to have a decent chance at getting rewarded with above-average returns. So any behaviors that stem from ingrained loss-aversion-first are likely to prove sub-optimal for dealing in stocks. Employees who stay in money market funds in their 401(k) and similar plans rather than risk possible interim paper capital losses in stocks (and loss of sleep) will end up with smaller retirement account than those who learn to live with risk and invest in equity funds.

One of the major teachings of sociology is that humans are group animals. We dislike loneliness and prefer the perceived comfort of running with the pack. That is fine in social situations. But it serves us badly in investment markets, because crowd pressure and group opinion are maximized at price extremes, and so guide us exactly backwards in terms of advantageous times and prices at which to buy and sell. I have made an informal study of the positive/negative opinions about stocks expressed in not only financial TV shows, but in cartoons, movies, sitcoms and financial advertising. Those expressions are meant to sell (commercials, books, magazines, newspapers, other products) and the proven way to sell is to give people what they are currently comfortable with. A strong preponderance of either ebullience or despair visible in such media is a useful signal of major market turns.

Nine Mental Mistakes beyond Fear and Greed

From the rich world of human psychology, we can discover—and then profit by guarding against—a number of tendencies and behaviors that come naturally to humans. These nine are listed here first before brief discussions of their details. All of these hurt us generally in investing or trading, and several of them are particularly nasty mental gremlins in the battle to sell well. Some are so big they will get their own later chapters:

◆ overconfidence

◆ ego protection

◆ cognitive dissonance

◆ poor decision-making under high stress

◆ excitement and repetition

◆ closure avoidance

◆ anchoring on past information

◆ misperception from bad framing

◆ backwards dealing with gains and losses

Overconfidence is a problem, in two ways. The more confident a person is in their decisions, the more likely they are to take decisive action! An implication, of course, is that if you are more confident than smart, you will trade a lot and each action is more likely on average to be wrong than brilliant. At a minimum, lots of decisions pile up lots of commissions (in your broker's account, not yours). And commissions subtract from net results. I am definitely not of the long-term buy-and-hope school, nor do I focus primarily on costs and taxes in making investment and trading decisions. But I do agree with the overconfidence critics who say that if you are not as smart as you think, you will not perform very well. A second and less discussed aspect of overconfidence relates to our self perception as an expert, which has implications for holding versus selling. Since we usually think our initial analysis was brilliant, we tend to stick with that original view and therefore are biased not to sell, which would require a reversal of our first decision. We tend to over-count our successes and under report our human frailties—including lack of perfect thinking.

Ego protection is closely related to the prior observation. Face it: We all like to feel good rather than bad. This relates to selling well in two ways. First, when we have an ego-stroking winner our bias is to hold on so it keeps giving us pleasure. Second, however, if pain gets bad enough from a loser, we mentally bury the problem rather than deal with it. Out of sight, out of mind—and thus reduced pain. Each investor and trader must become acutely aware of this strong ego-protecting tendency in order to neutralize its effects.

Cognitive dissonance is a psychological term for the mental equivalent of a head snap. When we hold established belief and are suddenly confronted with jarring contradictory information, our first impulse is to deny that the new version could be true. The neighbor kid takes a gun to school and commits mayhem. The priest we have trusted for years is revealed to be a pedophile. A company management we have grown to admire now is indicted for cooking the books, giving bribes or insider trading. Granted, with what has happened on Wall Street in the past decade, we probably should not be as surprised as we are when something ugly surfaces. But we do recoil in disbelief in such circumstances.

In our daily investing experience, cognitive dissonance makes it difficult to function fully and rationally. Recall the crash day of October 19, 1987, the aftermath of the 911 attacks, or the single-day, 400-point Dow drop in late February 2007. We tend to freeze like deer staring at headlights. Often denial takes over, when probably we should be carefully analyzing our situation and seeing if some industries (airlines after 911) should be sold while other stocks are bargains deserving purchase. But if we totally tune out, we make ourselves passive victims instead of functioning participants.

A somewhat related, although less dramatic problem, is humans' tendency to make sub-optimal decisions under stress. Do you remember how people immersed themselves in the market in 1999-2000, watching financial TV constantly (job permitting) and putting in orders at midnight from their home PCs? When volatility became high –either upside or later on the downside—our pulses quickened and our blood pressure rose. Experimental psychologists have documented that stress hinders our brain chemistry and thus makes it hard to perform at our mental peak. Implications of this are twofold: we should not expose ourselves to more risk than we might need to handle (Bernard Baruch reportedly said he invested only to the sleeping point). And we need to control our daily exposure to stress-inducing market inputs. That means not watching financial TV during market hours! Stress pushes us towards sub-rational or pre-rational actions, and emotional activity is not a profitable way to run a portfolio, on either the buying or selling end of the equation.

Brain research has demonstrated the effects of both excitement (of the neurons) and repetition. Neither one of the results helps us as investors. Sending overloading inputs to the brain tends to push us to take action. In the stock market high volatility therefore will, if left unchecked, prompt us to take action in the direction of the latest motion. After the crazy dotcom IPOs tripled, many could not resist jumping on board. And when the bear's final selling climaxes came in July and October 2002, millions of investors again were excited by the volatility to do the wrong thing at exactly the wrong time. So we need to guard against allowing too much flashy input about the market.

Watching those green and red arrows and charts on our screens, and listening to financial TV and talk radio or reading blogs online (which in many cases are deliberate touts) predictably are means of exciting the brain to do the wrong thing. Similarly, repeated doses of the same input condition our brain to expect more of the same. Lab animals learn to get food by touching the bell. Pavlov's dog salivated on cue. In the stock market, the unfortunate implication of repetition is that we come to expect a continuation of recent direction. That expectation does not occur early in a price rise or fall, but perversely it becomes strongest as the length of a rally (or collapse) builds. For example, net inflows into stock mutual funds become quite strong whenever the market has had about a six-month steady rise. Whether we are traders or investors, the cumulative reinforcement of repeated recent market results will make it difficult for us to sell high (or to buy at bargain prices). We must be constantly aware of this so we un-cloud our thinking. Historically, stocks seldom rise again after three calendar years, four months, five weeks or six days in a row of going up. They have simply gone up too far too fast. But our reinforcement-wired tendency is to become comfortable and expect more at just the statistically wrong time!

Closure avoidance is a special problem pertaining to selling stocks. In our non-financial lives, most closures are unpleasant. The baseball season ends and winter approaches. We finish college and leave our familiar friends and hang-outs. We end a job (voluntarily or otherwise); we leave community to move across country. We attend a colleague's funeral. We clean out the attic in grandma's house now that she is gone. If we had the power to avoid such experiences, most of us would do so. Well, in investing or trading we do indeed have the power to forestall closure: We can simply hold rather than even consider selling. And of course we know on a subconscious level that if we sell that will immediately trigger another stress-inducing decision: what should we buy? So we need to guard against natural inertia that would have us do nothing. This closure problem is a subtle but strong reason why selling is so difficult.

Anchoring on past information is another problem that makes good selling challenging. Experimental psychologists and professors have found that how a question is phrased can strongly influence what answers people give, even if the two different phrasings actually mean the same basic thing. In investing, we hang on some historical stuff that has implanted itself in our brains. Probably the single most problematic example is remembering our cost price for a stock. That is past history, and our trade was like a grain of sand on the beach, pretty meaningless to the whole market. And yet we stubbornly anchor to our entry price. We refuse to take a loss even though objective analysis would say the company's fortunes are now shaky due to new competition, a lost Food and Drug Administration (FDA) approval or other factors. Two other historical prices, which were created in different climates than exist today or going forward, are the stock's all-time high, and its best price since we bought it. Our egos and our skewed views tell us those high quotes were deserved at the time so they could easily be achieved again. The market seems to be telling a different story, so it might be smart for us to step back and listen without the bias of those old-price anchors! Ideally, to become proficient in your market operations you should become able to sell just as easily as you buy. The anchors of past prices tend to hinder that ability, so we need to remember this and fight it.

Misperception from bad framing is closely related, and it can drive both bad selling and sloppy buying. Framing is the researchers' term for the context in which we put an issue. One strong tendency, well documented, is myopic loss aversion. This drives investors and traders to perform backwards by selling the winners and letting the losers run since they mistakenly believe that a paper loss is not real until actually closed out. Again, as with the discussion of anchoring, we need to disconnect from the memory of the past and examine the company and its stock as of today and see if we would buy it if we had cash and it did not violate sound asset-allocation and diversification rules.

Common examples of misperception from bad framing come from the worlds of sports and gambling. A basketball player who has sunk 25 free throws in a row seems on a hot streak, but if he or she has an 80 percent lifetime success rate that is the more relevant statistic. A slot-machine addict mistakenly believes that if he has lost on nine consecutive pulls the odds are now in his favor. Those past hits or misses are part of an overall percentage and streaks will and do occur. The belief that luck is about to turn may drive doubling down, which can raise the risk of losing it all. So in our investing we need to be careful to view situations without personal bias from our experience. A simple example is that you may have always made money when trading XYZ stock. Now, although you may have ignored the fundamental signals because you are fond of the stock/company, fundamentals have soured. You have a long position but refuse to sell because you know that in the end you will be a winner again. Bad framing!

Backwards dealing with gains and losses is an area that defeats many an investor. Professors and lab psychologists have documented that people will allow their current position to influence their decisions more than it should. For example, if you were in a casino and had just won $200 on your latest play, you are much more likely to quit if the win has brought you back to breakeven than if you are now using (net-win) house money. And yet the actual odds of future success are no different—they are random and are equal to one minus the house's win percentage. I do not believe that price movement in stocks is purely random. But I am cautioning you that you need to watch how your recent experience may skew your judgment. Holding on to a loser in the belief that luck should turn in your favor is not rational. Careful analysis may reveal that indeed the stock is now grossly under priced on fundamentals, or that the overall market is deeply oversold. Those findings might justify holding rather than selling, but your personal feeling or a recent run of good or bad luck are irrelevant distractions.

Use Humor and Advertising as Market-State Keys

Two clusters of information can be helpful to the observant investor, giving useful contrarian clues as to the market's psychological position. These are humor and advertising. Clusters of very bullish or bearish observations tell you the market's move is fairly well finished. Humor and advertising function as barometers because they work only if the reader/observer/watcher will definitely get it. So they must reflect broadly held current thinking. For example, cartoons about people jumping out windows, or reminders of 1929 appear only very deep into a painful market decline. They would not make sense in a buoyant setting, and are not seen then. Sitcom plots mentioning how easily a character just made fast money in the market (or movies about Wall Street) appear only when all is very happy in investor land. Watch for such indicators on TV, in your local newspaper, in magazines (The New Yorker is an excellent source) and keep a mental scorecard for recent clusters. There is of course no magic number in a certain time window, but when events rise to the level of feeling recently common that is your signal.

A recent example (as this chapter was written) occurred in June 2007, in a Toyota TV commercial. Mom is sitting at the kitchen table with her two sons; she apparently is working on paying the bills. Mom says words to the effect that: We are saving a lot of money on our great new Toyota lease. What should we do with the money? The apparent 11-year-old son says: I am thinking hedge funds. And the 15-year-old says: No, I lean to emerging markets. This is classic. It appeared just weeks after the S&P 500 Index had finally returned to its old 2000 high of 1,527. The mother did not ask how they should *invest* the money – just what to do with it. Kids would normally suggest buying a Wii or going to Disneyland, but in a high market when everyone knows what is working and making money on Wall Street has again become fun and fairly common, the writers have them suggest investing.

Bottom Line: Learn to Move towards Discomfort

This chapter has dealt with a number of wired tendencies, most of which have to do with making us feel good or bad. Those tendencies repeatedly harm us on Wall Street, so we need to keep them in mind and actively battle them. A major bottom-line action advice to be gleaned from these findings from the non-financial disciplines is that seeking emotional comfort will repeatedly and dependably produce financial discomfort. Moving away from discomfort (as into cash exactly during a market panic) makes you sell low and avoid buying bargains. Needing to be part of the in-crowd (again, seeking comfort or avoiding discomfort) will keep you 100 percent invested in the recently too-hot industry groups. You will be under-diversified and, worse yet, possibly up to your limit on margin. Remember the sad lessons of 2000: You have paid expensive tuition then, so try to learn from the painful coursework you endured!

CHAPTER 4

Always Think about the Crowd!

Keys for Successful Selling

◆ Understand What Technical Analysis Reveals

◆ Note Via Volume the Intensity of Crowd Response to News

◆ Discern When to Join or Buck Strong Crowd Opinion

◆ Honor Major Emotional Turning Points

The two major approaches to investing are fundamental and technical analysis. The former, a staple of what is taught in business schools and the Certified Financial Analyst curriculum, focuses entirely on understanding the company in the context of its industry and competitors, and the overall economy, and then forecasting a stream of future earnings, cash flows and dividends per share. One then applies a suitable discounting rate to that expected stream and compares the computed present value of that stream with the current stock price. As a result, one would conclude that the stock is under-, over- or properly priced and would take action accordingly. Technical analysis looks not at corporate financial reports or the economic outlook but strictly at the price and volume action of a stock (and major market indicators). It assumes that pretty much all of what fundamental analysts know is currently priced into the stock, so it hones in on how the stock is acting—as a hoped-for guide to the important answer, namely what it might do in the future.

Both fundamental and technical analysis can be helpful to us as investors in deciding when it is a good idea to sell. Since the fundamentals generally change fairly slowly— over a period of quarters or years—I find that technical analysis is more helpful in guiding me to profitable action in the nearer term. We know that prices tend to overshoot both too high and then too low in their attempts to reflect proper reality. This tendency towards volatility, which seems to have increased in the age of trading at the speed of the Internet, can either hurt you or help you. How it affects us is driven by how well or badly we understand and handle price volatility.

What drives prices to change? In the long run, yes, definitely the fundamentals or value. But between now and that distant tomorrow, the answer is supply and demand. Suppose that a company reported some news, and that collectively all investors figuratively yawned. Or the board of directors of a quality company declared the regular, expected dividend on its preferred stock. This news, per se, would have no effect on price, and would probably not actually drive anyone to place a buy or sell order. In the extreme, there would be no trading at all, and therefore no change in price.

So we can deduce that it is not the news itself that moves prices, but instead the response of investors and traders to that news. When news fits the existing collective expectation (think of a company hitting its consensus quarterly earnings per share (EPS) target and offering no new guidance about its future outlook), little excitement is created and the supply/demand balance is unchanged, so price is not affected. To the degree that news constitutes a surprise, price will move dramatically. Quarterly earnings misses are frequent examples. If a given company misses or beats its expected quarterly numbers by a penny per share, that added information may have absolutely no change implications for the long-term fundamental cash flow and dividend models. But the deviation from expected numbers drives news stories on financial TV; traders react immediately and sharply. Even some mutual fund managers, if they rely on changing expectations to drive their decisions, may buy or sell a million shares, which surely will create a price change!

The extent of changes in opinion can be measured in trading volume. That tells us the degree of surprise hitting the market and the urgency with which the affected traders and investors feel they need to take action. What studying volume does, in effect, is to reveal what the crowd is thinking and how big that crowd is. If you agree with my belief that the market in the short term is relatively inefficient because of swings in mood and transitory responses to news, it follows that watching, and seeking to gain an understanding of, the crowd is important to being successful as an investor or trader. (Underlying that contention is my assumption that if you are reading this book you are not from the passive buy-and-hope school; that you will not willingly settle for the long-term average of market returns but instead prefer to seek and achieve above-average returns by buying and selling at opportune times.)

Understanding the crowd's collective mind set is crucial to being on the right side of the price action. Contrarians often note that an important indicator of potential change in market direction, which is present sometimes but not constantly, is lack of reaction to good news or to bad news. In the former case, an implication is drawn that the crowd apparently universally expects good news and therefore such news was not market-moving information. Thus in that situation the market may have set itself up for a fall, since all the likely positive expectations are already built in. Conversely, if bad news fails to drive a stock (or the overall market) lower, one can reason that the only likely surprises are less-bad new inputs and therefore prices are more likely to stop going down and begin rallying. Understanding how the crowd is responding to evolving news developments is therefore important to your selling and buying at advantageous times. This is part of the contrarian approach, covered in a later chapter in more detail.

Our focus here is on how the market, which represents a collective crowd, acts. That response is more important in behavioral terms than the actual nature of the news. And occasion exception, of course, is when a specific company or industry/ regulatory news is extremely favorable or damaging. In such cases we need to move in line with the group's reaction. But most news is transitory, not something that would be recalled 10 years from now as a basic turning point for a company. So when there is news, you need to step back and decide how truly important that news is. Your answer will often determine whether taking action is necessary. But, perhaps more interestingly in terms of profit potential, sometimes detecting an overreaction by the crowd will tell you it is actually time to act—in the direction opposite theirs.

There are two aspects of this perceptive challenge. And unfortunately they can seem contradictory at first inspection. The first-level issue is how big the crowd response to a new input is, and whether it is of such proportions as to constitute an unsustainable price driver in the short term. If that is the case, you are looking at a price move (up or down) driven by a volume crescendo or volume spike (covered at more length in Chapter 21). When you really think about it, a crowd that soon dissipates will no longer be there to drive the price in its latest direction. Therefore that price move cannot continue. If the crowd gets excited by good earnings news, or if a crowd is temporarily created by a major brokerage firm's buy recommendation, you can bank on a downside price reversal in short order. Implication? Sell into the strength and buy back later after the temporary price inefficiency has time to be corrected. Remember, too, that momentum traders have a very short-term view. So while they may be buyers today on the price pop, they will almost as surely be sellers in two or three days once the upside momentum stops. So an intelligent market participant who analyzes crowd implications will sell into strength, anticipating what comes next. We must look past the news to the intensity and staying power of the crowd opinion it drives. In the Internet-trading era, intensity is large but predictably brief.

A second aspect has deeper and more lasting implications. On occasion a market move (usually one of a bearish nature) can have truly significant implications for crowd psychology. Such events sometimes are years apart. Stepping way back and looking at history, one could say that the experience of the Great Depression and losing 90 percent of value in stocks at the low in the early 1930s scarred a generation of investors (and some of their home-taught children). A result was that stocks were distrusted. It was not until the middle-1950s that dividend yields on stocks (viewed as risky) finally moved lower than yields on bonds. That is how deeply and enduringly the crash of 1929 and its aftermath affected investor moods and actions!

A somewhat similar event came with the terrorist attacks on September 11, 2001. This changes everything about how we look at the world was a common refrain and response. No doubt the market had been grossly overbought in 2000, but it is hard to imagine that the new atmosphere of caution and background fear that began on 9/11 did not affect the depth and length of the bear market that ensued.

Sometimes market action itself will profoundly affect the mood of the crowd, thus in turn affecting the market. As this was written, we had just felt the reverberations from the one-day 9 percent drop in China's market, which drove a drop of over 400 points in the Dow on February 27, 2007. Remember the Asian contagion of the late 1990s, or the de facto devaluation of Mexico's peso in December 1994? Both of those events deeply affected market trust in overseas stock market investing. Coming as it did after about seven months of steady and confidence-building rising prices in major U.S. market averages, the China event—will it come to be know as the (second) China Syndrome—seems likely to be big enough to begin breaking the back of the upside mentality.

In such instances, your degree of patience with stocks not doing well must be reduced. Your expectations for short-term gains logically should be smaller. Therefore you would follow, rather than counter, the short-term trend and be more prone to selling. The key difference, which is our job to figure out and test, is how important the change in news will prove to be. Our attitude about buying and especially about selling is modified accordingly, or should be! Our conclusion either can be applied in a very short-term sense or can become new basic thinking for a longer period, as appropriate. And the market's ongoing behavior will create further evidence that can support or reshape our initial conclusion, so it is important to continue monitoring how the crowd is acting. You do not want to be caught up in the emotions of the crowd, but you do need to be highly observant of its size, mood and intensity and to honor those if you are sensing a sea change in attitude. This may be a psychological way of expanding the old saying that we should not fight the tape. But watching the crowd and the trading volume it creates will add a new dimension to your market and stock analysis.

CHAPTER 5
Banishing Rationalizations and Admitting Mistakes

Keys for Successful Selling

◆ Overcome Commission and Tax Phobias

◆ Overcome Specialist Phobia (a.k.a. Stop-Order Phobia)

◆ Be Careful of Wishful Thinking

◆ When Trouble Arises, Do Not Think "It Is Different This Time"

◆ Avoid Holding with a Death Grip

◆ Admit and Handle Your Mistakes

◆ Keep Records of Actions; Use a Checklist to Re-assess Stocks

◆ Use a Master Tally Sheet to Detect Your Patterns

Prior chapters have surfaced some of the often-subconscious or even unconscious psychological reasons why people seem naturally to prefer holding over selling their investments. As part of the process of becoming a more successful investor by selling better, it is important to recognize and understand these hidden drivers of our thinking and behaviors. This chapter exposes some of the symptomatic rationalizations that investors exhibit, in effect acting out and justifying their often-irrational predisposition to holding at any cost rather than selling. If you see some of your own behavior here, now you will know whence that stuff comes and thus be better equipped to battle against it. Success in investing is indeed a battle, in which selling is a more challenging arena than buying. But your newfound knowledge is providing power to help you prevail.

Commission Phobia

Most sell-side research analysts hear the lament that investors balk at taking brokers' advice for suspicion their motives are driven by the prospect of earning more commissions. There is no doubt that full-commission brokerages operate to maximize revenue and profit. If you distrust advice-giving brokers, move your account to a no-advice discounter (which of course will rob you of one convenient excuse). Frankly, most commission phobia is a smokescreen that is as dangerous to potential investment profit as it is illogical.

First, look at the logic of commission phobia. Like taxes, commissions are neither a surprise nor a change in rules at mid-game; therefore, paying them cannot logically be a valid objection at the time of sale. There is no way to sell stock without paying commissions except in a handful of very limited exit environments:

- ◆ The company receives a tender offer, so shares are sold for a net cash payment to the soliciting buyer, via its agent (actually, here you will usually pay some fee to the reorganization department).
- ◆ The company conducts a share-buyback tender (a self-tender) in which some or all shares can be sold for a net cash price directly to the company (again, tendering does not occur without a fee).
- ◆ The company can purchase investor shares directly if the position is small (usually an odd lot). Sometimes firms solicit repurchases by mail.
- ◆ Company liquidation occurs, in which common holders receive a net cash payment (often a fee is charged by the brokerage here too).

One individual can sell a stock certificate directly to another individual (perhaps within a family) through a transfer agent by endorsing the back of the certificate (and this also will almost always incur some fee, since banks are not generous charities). This, of course, assumes you actually have a physical certificate—which more and more frequently, investors do not have in their possession.

While the buying decision was the investor's own, commission phobia is most intense when the pain can be blamed on a bad purchase made on a broker's advice.

Effective Commission Strategies

There is one other way to avoid commissions: If the stock becomes worthless in bankruptcy and common holders get nothing, some brokerage firms buy the stock certificates for a nominal price such as $1. This creates a transaction for taxes. In the absence of such a transaction, investors need to amend their tax return for the year in which the stock actually became defunct and worthless. This case is a wonderful example of how an investor can be penny-wise and pound-foolish about paying commissions to cash out: It is much better to pay the exit cost to sell at a partial loss before a stock goes to zero.

Commissions are more visible in stocks and options than in other products or services because securities prices are publicly quoted in newspapers, on quotation machines, on the Internet and on television. Investors pay commissions on these vehicles as a way of compensating the time or expertise of the people actually do the trading for them. When other products are purchased, commissions are paid, but they are built into the purchase price. In fact, in percentage built-in commissions for goods such as cars, shoes or washing machines are immensely higher than are Wall Street stock commissions.

Investors who purchase prepackaged products from brokers, say, front-loaded funds, typically pay from 4.5 percent to 8 percent in commissions. Buy into a load mutual fund by writing a $10,000 check, and only $9,200 to $9,550 is working for you; the rest is commission. Cancel a variable annuity contract, and the exit fee of about 10 percent is a commission under a different name. These percentages are much higher than the typical 1 percent or 2 percent incurred on stocks when one uses a full-service brokerage firm.

Investors most commonly display commission phobia when their stock is down, has done nothing or has gone up so little that its tiny price gain is wiped out by round-trip commissions. When their money is doubled or XYZ Worldwide Conglomerate creates a sudden gain by proposing an attractive merger or spin-off, investors seldom if ever complain about commissions. This difference in response reveals why commission phobia as a smokescreen: It masks investors' pain at admitting and closing out a mistake that caused a loss.

One fairly legitimate complaint about commissions, however, is the wide gap between retail rates and how much big institutional investors pay to play the same game. The retail/institutional commission gap is even more disturbing when individual investors lose money. Actually, in recent years a pleasant irony has come to exist because of the low, flat-rate commissions of deep-discount brokers: While institutions may still pay traditional brokerage of 2 or 3 cents a share, individuals' total commissions may amount to less than a penny on lots of 500 shares or more.

Formula-Based Commissions

A possible remedy for retail investors is commission discounting, with due respect to account executives and their employing firms who need to make a living. For those who continue to use full-service brokerages, one strategy to ease the pain could be to negotiate commissions on a formula basis with your account executive. On the buying side, a full commission is paid when the broker presents an idea the client buys. When the client makes his own selections without service or information provided by the broker, some discount is arguably in order.

At selling time, if the trade results in a gain, the client of a full-service firm should pay the full standard commission without complaint. If there is a loss, a two-tiered discount arrangement can work: the deepest allowable discount should be provided if the broker suggested the purchase; if the buy was the customer's idea, a smaller discount (maybe half the deepest allowable) is granted as a consolation/courtesy and as a psychological inducement to cashing in and moving on. This strategy works best with a small or regional brokerage firm; leading wire-house firms tend to be less flexible, except with their very large customers.

If an investor and her broker mutually agree to such a deal in advance, the commission problem usually can be eliminated. When clients continue to complain about commissions, however, it is then clearly a smokescreen to avoid making the decision (especially to take a loss) and move on.

Discount Firms

Besides failing to trade when it is expedient or to negotiate routine broker discounts, investors also can limit commissions by moving their accounts to a discount firm; clearly millions have done so. But in doing this, they give up access to research and a listening ear. Without taking sides on the sticky question of discount versus full-service brokerage firms' merits, it is clearly accurate that reducing commissions can be an important way of limiting the cost of changing one's mind. Once that problem is addressed, full attention can be devoted to the primary issue: which way the stock is likely to move next. For those disposed to utilizing discount brokers, the American Association of Individual Investors (AAII) provides a valuable reference in the annual January issue of its AAII Journal, which contains a comprehensive listing of discount brokerage firms and their rates. (See the Appendix for the address and telephone number.)

One clear instance when a brokerage client should indeed worry about avoiding commissions is when a broker solicits a sale for the purpose of freeing funds to another purchase. This is not churning per se, but it is an attempt to do two trades where one would do. And despite the language actually used this sale generally is not suggested on fundamental merits (one can always find something wrong with any stock!) It is only a means to enable another transaction and so may be justified on the basis of boredom or possibly greener pastures. A disturbingly enlightening exposé on broker recommendations is found in the book, *License to Steal: The Secret World of Wall Street and the Systematic Plundering of the American Investor*, (Collins, 1999).

Tax Phobia

Most often, however, investors should ignore commissions and sell when the price is right because unwillingness to pay a commission in order to exit a losing position is a self-defeating game. Unless the investor is dealing in a very small block of stock, the sale commission is likely to be a lot less than a point per share. If indeed the stock is going nowhere—or worse yet is going down—a commission saved by cashing in is minuscule compared with the capital loss suffered by holding on. Keep in mind that the capital losses resulting from holding too long include opportunity costs.

Suppose a lazy stock is going nowhere—perhaps a utility with no growth of dividends. Resentfully, the investor refuses to sell because of the exit commission. The proposed replacement may have been a much better utility whose dividend is rising perhaps 4 percent a year and whose stock price appreciates as a result. In this case, refusal to pay a sale commission is very costly. Although such opportunity losses tend to be invisible compared with losses recorded on Schedule D, they are very real and self-inflicted wounds. More investors might be persuaded to pay a small commission to take a loss if they focused on this: That loss is worth the stock's price plus one-third of its paper loss (the combined federal and state tax) if sold, but worth only its current price if retained.

However investors may view the social, economic or budgetary results of eliminating favorable tax treatment of long-term capital gains, the Bush Administration's 2003 capital-gains tax rate cut had at least one positive result: It considerably reduced an artificial excuse for not selling stocks.

Because the tax code makes a strong distinction between long- and short-term gains, many investors use that tax incentive to hold stocks for the long term as a justification for not selling. Unless an extremely large gain was involved and/ or unless the time remaining until the reaching long-term status was very short (thus decreasing the likely risk of losing paper gains), these reasons for not selling are foolhardy. But over-sensitivity to tax treatment remains nearly a religion for many market participants. Here is an interesting context: Have you ever refused to accept a paycheck because that income is taxed at full regular-income rates? Not likely. Favorable long-term treatment of capital gains is a pleasant gift, not a birthright!

The converse of the hold-for-long-term-treatment philosophy on gains, of course, would be a rule that investors should absolutely always sell a losing position before it becomes long term. As an arbitrary discipline, such an operating rule would probably prove quite valuable as a capital preserver for many people. However, this rubric seldom is observed, tending to prove that selective (i.e., one-sided) attention to the long-term-gain rule is more centrally a psychological rationalization for postponing sale decisions than a useful tax-minimizing strategy.

Unfortunately, the existence of federal and state taxation on securities gains remains a major stumbling block; experience suggests that tax phobia is still very real to many investors. Granted no one actively likes to pay taxes; but paying taxes on capital gains and on such taxable investment income as dividends and interest is a reality for all investors. It is not a surprise. Nor is it an unfair mid-game change of rules. Therefore, it is illogical to balk at selling a stock at a gain just because the transaction triggers a tax liability. There are only three logical extensions of refusing to take a gain on a stock to avoid paying income taxes. The investor must have bought the stock in the hope:

1. Of losing money (federal taxes are reduced 28 cents for only a dollar lost);

2. that the stock's price would not change; and

3. that the stock would be held for the remainder of the buyer's life.

The first two alternatives are nonsensical and deserve no further comment. Despite tax reform, the third reason is a clever tax dodge because a legatee's basis is stepped up to the value on the date of the decedent's death. So an investor can enjoy this big loophole only by dying with capital gains unrealized. What a clever way to finally beat Washington! And of course this strategy truly works only of one can dependably never buy a stock that declines.

The objection to paying income taxes due on realizing a gain is just another rationalization for not making a sale decision; it is especially appealing to the habitual rationalizer because it is conveniently external to self. It can be blamed on them, government or on the system. Most other excuses for not selling also rely on illogical or psychological investor weaknesses.

Although taxes are not totally avoidable, they can be postponed—another major pitfall for investors who complain about taxes. The fact that they can be postponed carries another chance at self-satisfaction at the price of financial underachieving. Is beating the system a source of private satisfaction that gets in the way of rational investment action? The reality is that the price/timing of a sale decision would ideally be made based on future price prospects with no regard to tax timing. The best time to sell a stock is at its highest price point; the next best time is as close to that level as possible. The best actual tax situations is to incur huge tax obligations, which accrue only from earning extremely large capital-gains income. Maximum profit should be the goal of every transaction made by every trader or investor, so taxes should be paid cheerfully when due. Remember, also, that the amount of profit desired before or after tax on a given stock position is irrelevant. The amount of profit realistically allowed by the market is a better criterion for timely sale. Similarly, the amount of profit an investor can keep is always defined as after-tax amount, so learn to live with that reality. Ten points is, of its nature, 10 points before taxes, just as a $75,000 annual salary is that amount before taxes!

Income versus Growth Strategies

Income-oriented investors tax-consciously choose among their alternatives: Tax-free municipals and taxable interest or dividend generators are evaluated with advance attention paid to after-tax yields. (The tax-adjusted current yield and yield to maturity are known in advance in the case of fixed-income instruments.) In contrast, in the case of common stocks bought for capital appreciation, the income component has to be imagined because it cannot be quantified with certainty. Therefore, an exact calculation of after-tax return is not made in advance. Because no calculation is performed, the exercise of subtracting projected taxes is, conveniently in a psychological sense, omitted. But that future tax obligation is, nonetheless, real.

The Over-Inflated Ego

Try never to get into the I am-too-big-to-get-out bind because, in effect, any investor who says this looks like he is not ever planning to sell the stock. If he buys so much he is later too wide for the exit door, he will become a collector—he is neither an investor nor a trader.

Stock collectors, people who buy but never sell, inevitably defeat themselves because they usually end up with a long list of stale losers and eventually run out of cash. They are effectively out of the game and stuck with the sour results of past buying decisions. In most cases, as time goes on, the original reasons for buying either do not drive the price to the desired selling point or the reasons fail to work out altogether. Short of legacy at death, there are just two other possible exits for a trader or investor who accumulates a position too big to get out of: the takeover and tender offer (or the subcategory, the Dutch Auction repurchase offer). If an investor is big enough to accumulate a too-large block in advance of a takeover event, either he is dealing in inside information, or he is quite smart and probably already wealthy enough to forgo reading books for investment advice.

Most dispassionate observers would suggest that the my-order-is-too-big syndrome is really just a disguised excuse. Most likely it is the product of an inflated ego and/or an overactive imagination. It tends to reflect the mind-set of a trader never satisfied unless he grabs the last nickel on every move, which of course is an unreal hope. Or it can reflect a market player who is actually involved more with the excitement and action of watching the market and thinking about making decisions than with that all-important goal of taking profits in a systematic way without the burdensome intrusion of emotion, second guessing, or looking back. Finally, of course, taking a too-big position might reflect subtle planning for having a rationalization that will forestall closure. Ways to overcome this obsession are to avoid buying so large a position in the first place or to sell off the holdings in a series of smaller pieces, thus reducing the size of the tax pain each time.

The Persecution Complex

Specialist Phobia (a.k.a. Stop-Order Phobia)

One very popular objection to the use of stop-sell orders is that they tip off the specialist to an investor's intention and so become self-defeating. In this section, we explore that argument and firmly lay it to rest. There certainly is one case in which a stop-order shown advance to the specialist affects the market. But that is only when the stock position to be sold is so large that it represents a significant percentage of an average day's trading volume. The solution is not to withhold any selling order. There are two approaches: First do not accumulate such a large position and second feed a series of small orders at different prices to the floor specialist.

Another mind-set that masks making excuses is also worth noting. Some investors and traders have a persecution complex about the market (and often about much of life). For these people, the market is a very personal struggle of the hapless individual against the world or the establishment. They expect to be less than satisfied every time they take action—and every time they do not act.

They also view market mistakes not as failures of their own logic or as examples of bad luck but rather as traps that were set specifically for them. The specialist system on the exchanges fits their world view of conspiracy. These investors know there is a person on the exchange floor who is uniquely privileged to see many future orders on his official order book. They ask in horror why they should play the game with such a trader by letting him take care of their personal interests when the game seemingly seems so obviously rigged. Those of this mind set should either get over it or leave their money in a bank—or use no-redemption-penalty mutual funds. And besides, the decimalization move away from the old system of quotes in eighths has sharply cut the cost of being slightly wrong in order placement. If indeed the specialist were out to get you, his potential booty is now a penny or two rather than an eighth of a dollar.

Order Strategies

Further, the mechanics of the exchange floor should be examined to understand how likely it is, in reality, that an order will tip the buy-sell balance to work against an individual investor. The alternative tactic, of course, is to stay ever at the ready with quote machine and telephone at hand, and surprise the market with a market order when your designated price is actually hit. That could seriously hamper performance in your day job, possibly costing you a lot more!

When using price rather than market orders, it is not advisable to enter any stop-limit sell order at a round number (e.g., 20,25, 40) or any exact full dollar. This potentially positions you with the crowd; a stampede could develop at any round-dollar level. Such a stop order without a limit might in 20/20 hindsight result in poor execution; a stop-limit could readily result in no execution at all if the investor is the line.

For example, if your target selling price for a stock is $46 per share, place your stop order some small amount lower, in the high $45 price. If your target is a half-dollar level, put the order several cents lower, for example, at $7.44 rather than exactly $7.50. The guiding philosophy is this: If an investor believes that he is sharp enough to pinpoint the high on a stock's move accurately, he ought to be so concerned about getting out for sure that he would sacrifice a small amount per share as insurance against the slight chance that he is a bit off in his calculations or that perhaps some other investors are equally smart. He should be out in this case, instead of still in and sorry for insisting on getting that very last dime.

The only way a sell order above the market can affect the price is if it is so large as to scare away buyers who are so tactically active that they happen to ask about it at right moment. In listed stocks, the specialist on the exchange floor holds the good until canceled stop-sell (and all other) orders in his book and exercises them as market orders when they are touched off. The book is not disclosed to anyone else on floor except in a very limited manner. Upon request, the single best (highest) bid and the best (lowest) asked prices are disclosed to any floor broker, along with the sizes of the total orders at those levels. That is also true on electronic quote machines and on Websites providing quote feeds. In orders placed at the exchange, those currently at a price away from the best spread are never disclosed until the moment they actually become part of the best offer (to sell) or bid (to buy).

And even in this case, remember that the market is a big arena with many participants. Except in very thinly traded issues, it is highly unlikely that one individual trader/investor's order will be the only order on the book at any given time. When he is trying to sell 500 or 1,000 shares at $24.45, there may be another 20,000 shares for sale at that price and probably a similar number to buy at $24.40.

Suppose that an investor buys 500 shares of XYZ at around $19 and targets a sale price of $24.50. Following the earlier suggestion to avoid 50-cent multiples, he places a sell-stop order on 500 shares at perhaps $24.46. If the stock does trade up as high as that level, his order immediately becomes a market order (without limit) to sell. Today, the stock is finally approaching his price. It is up, say, twenty cents at $24.40. The market tone remains firm. The specialist's book shows 1,000 shares bid for at $24.35 and 600 offered for sale at $24.43. That is the quote he provides to floor traders, and that is all. Using common floor abbreviations, the specialist says: at 35 to 43, 10 by 6. He does not mention that there is a bid for 7,500 down at $24.30, or that 1,200 are waiting to be sold at $24.44 or that our investor has 500 for sale at $24.46. None of these orders are relevant yet, so none are disclosed until they become the best orders. So our investor's order does not show until it is just finally the best one away from the most recent trade. Only when that time comes does his order start to show as the next limit sell order above the market.

Incidentally, the investor is in an advantageous position if he exercised the discipline of placing that order some time ago, such as, perhaps, when he bought the stock. Why? Stop-orders and stop-limit-orders are lined up on a first-come, first-served basis. So the longer our order has been in place at that specific price, the earlier it stands in line at that exact level, and the sooner it becomes a market order in the trading sequence. If our trader's 500 shares for sale are part of a total of 3,000 or 4,000 on the book at that same price, his order is filled sooner if it was among the first placed.

Having a GTC order in place is better than putting in a day order at the same price every session until it is executed. Day orders die at the close, and each newly entered day order goes at the back of the line at its price. (Placing multiple orders also requires repeated discipline and frequent decisions.) A strong preference for stop-orders instead of stop-limit orders should be noted. A stop-order says: If the price reaches this level, I want to be considered a seller at market. A stop-limit order is less likely to be executed because it says to the specialist: When the stock hits this price, put me in right away as a seller, but sell me out only if you can do it at this price or better. Do it right away or forget it.

So if the size of your position is generally in keeping with the pattern of average daily trading (i.e., you are not trying to sell big percentage of a whole day's worth), your order will not be big enough to disturb the day's supply/demand balance. Then you should not worry about that order standing as a roadblock for the stock and turning back its advance a fraction short of your level.

One added note about the order book. It is now electronic rather than hand-scribbled as in decades past. Market orders hit the book and are executed electronically, without the specialist having to do anything. This modern computerized approach has reduced the role of the specialist to mainly being the keeper of an orderly market, rather than a juggler of every small order. He will take a position briefly against large market moves to keep prices as smooth as possible. And his entire sequence of actions is monitored by the exchange, so he is very unlikely to risk censure or fines by trying to trap a small investor.

Bottom line about stop and limit orders: Try to be objective and detached enough to recognize that the marketplace is so much bigger than any one participant that it takes no special notice of any individual order. If an investor's ego lets her imagine that her personal 500 or 1,000 shares is going to turn the tide against a stock's advance, she is too heavily involved in competitive success or failure. Huge institutions may move the market or stop a trend, but she will not. Place the order where it should go, and let the market operate.

Paranoia

Anyone who has heard whispers about the ubiquitous they needs to remember that "they" do not exist in the market. This is not to say that attempted—occasional—market manipulation by individuals and/or firms does not exist at all. When they get cited, it is critical to act against the dangerous assumption that as a collective plot they actually exist. Doing this is difficult because it requires leaning against pressure of peers and brokers who give advice that is supposedly based on the urban legend of what they have allegedly decided will happen. Reject the they hypothesis, and act in opposite, contrarian direction—or ignore it altogether.

The underlying assumptions behind the they myth are that everything that happens (especially if it is bad) can be explained readily; that the world, and specifically the world of Wall Street, is ruled by conspirators; that bad guys cannot be reined in because they cannot be tracked down and brought to justice; and that a vast conspiracy is directed at relieving small individual retail investors of their moderate assets. So they become a convenient scapegoat. Basically, anything that supposedly goes on in the plans or hopes of investors who believe in they is other-directed. This conspiratorial orientation absolves they-believers of mistakes in judgment and poor execution strategy, at least in their own minds.

They is a moving target, whose identity cannot be known for sure, including at various times: insiders (corporate officers), floor specialists, corporate raiders, or, lately, program traders and hedge funds. In late 1989, some Japanese buyers of U.S. stocks began to exhibit some qualities often ascribed in the past to they as their national investment preference jumped from one to another of the foreign-stock, open-end mutual and closed-end funds, causing wide price swings without apparent logic or pattern. Foreigners are always favorite targets of conspiracy buffs!

What is heard most about they is that they plan to move the market in a certain direction, at will, to trap small investors. Typically when the market whipsaws traders, word makes the rounds that they were to blame and had laid a trap. As the story goes, they planned to move the market up quickly to suck the naive in at the top, at which point they would unload the stocks in question on the unsuspecting for a profit. Trapped with the stocks, small investors would suffer holding the bad goods for the next price drop once they pulled the plug on the rally. Then investors would get discouraged and sell out en mass at the next bottom, presumably on a drop they would cause by either spreading negative rumors or shorting key stocks to drive quotes lower. At the lows, they would step in and take retail customers' stock away for a bargain price, once again proving that they are in control and that investors are predictably just victims.

In this scenario, every miscalculation is blamed on an outside force, not on personal bad luck or—more to the point—personal lack of expertise, discipline or sophistication. Such thinking also postulates that there is an organized conspiracy to move the market. But such alleged conspirators would need billions of dollars to pull it off; they would need to trust each other totally so that none of them would cheat and step in or out at a better price than the others (or later turn state's evidence).

Strategies for Overcoming This Paranoia

The theory of they, which neatly explains away all problems on the basis of an invincible and overwhelming outside force, is rejected by all rational investors. Of course, if any rational investor really believes the game is rigged, he may question the first loss, but he would quit forever after the second. Firmly convinced that they have all the trump cards, the logical investor would see that folding his hand permanently is the only sensible course for an innocent to follow.

Remember that, the next time someone tries to blame a reverse or a surprise on them. And note who that someone is, to avoid giving them credence again. This someone is naive if they believe it themselves and dishonest if they are using them as a scapegoat for responsibility for the loss. Even if the rationalizer played the same stock and took the same beating, what he is doing is covering his own failing by blaming it on an invisible sinister force. Fault is being conveniently offloaded rather than accepted in an adult manner.

If any doubt remains, consider these questions. If they truly exist and are wealthy and powerful enough to pull off market coups:

1. Why would they bother? They already have more wealth and power than they need; they should buy a country!

2. Why would they take the risk of being caught at it and jailed? (They have more to lose than to gain.)

3. Why would they choose to prey on small investors, who have relatively little wealth to pillage?

4. Why is it never rumored before the fact that they are about to pull off a coup? (After all, even major corporate takeovers are leaked in advance on occasion.)

5. When they are blamed (after the fact, conveniently, after having disappeared), why are those who blame them not able to identify the villains specifically?

If a story is spread that the outside forces plan to run a certain stock up (or down) before it happens, run fast in the opposite direction. Whoever is spreading that story has no better reason to get an investor to buy the stock than they are trying to unload the stock on the unwary. Sell, or sell short, rather than buy. In summary, there are just three simple they rules to remember:

◆ Do not believe people who adduce they as an explanation.

◆ Do not accept they as a reason something will happen or did happen.

◆ Do not rationalize that they were the reason for your failed trade/ investment or even for just bad timing.

As a final note under this topic we must discuss some occasional and brief market moves that do tend to be driven by institutions, but not in a conspiracy. At the end of calendar quarters, some mutual fund managers (but most typically those focused on small-cap, illiquid stocks) have been known to paint the tape just before the close. That phrase means making trades that push up the price of stocks they already own by buying more shares right before the closing bell. Widely-watched performance for the quarter or year can be slightly improved by this tactic. But the reality is that if the price is pushed ahead too much at the close some sellers will drive it down at the next opening, so the next quarter' numbers start out with a small deficit. No one is big enough to rig a free market for long.

Another variant of this, but a more innocent one, involves window dressing by institutions at the end of a quarter. If the market has done very well, they may be buyers on the last couple of days, to get their cash positions down to a low, smart-looking, percentage. They might increase the sizes of positions in stocks that have lately done extremely well, again to look smart. Or they might sell stocks to raise cash after a down quarter, and may tend to eliminate those individual stock names that might be embarrassing to show on their list of holdings. If you are thinking of selling a stock shortly before quarter's end, such patterns might work in your favor if you time your action according to those circumstances.

Holding on with a Death Grip

Traders and investors tend to stretch their investment time horizons for two reasons. The first is that promised or hoped-for hot developments seldom actually take place as quickly as expected. But the second, and more insidious, problem is that human beings hesitate to come to closure, to wrap things up. Selling a stock has a finality akin to acknowledging a death. If one's stock position is kept open, hope for a better result is alive and well. However, this hope can border on rationalization.

An example of this rationalization is a cynical Wall Street cliché☐ that bad traders become investors. Unfortunately for legions of unsuccessful traders, this does not mean they have a religious experience, repent of their wasteful ways and turn their attention to a value-oriented investing approach. It usually means that those owners of unsuccessful stock positions—originally intended to be short-term situations—hold on for a long time out of stubbornness. These traders become long-term holders through the back door; more accurately, they are trapped collectors of bad stocks.

It is important to recognize the trader-turned-investor syndrome as a classic case of switching objectives; this switch usually results from rationalization or lazy thinking. In fact, most traders do not even make a conscious decision to become an investor based on thoughtful consideration. That shift gradually creeps in via inertia. An extreme version of the inertia and psychological baggage that can accompany losses is the investor who says: I expect my stock could go down about 15 percent within the next month or two, but I plan to hold anyway. The logical response, of course, is to question whether, having that expectation and not already owning that stock, the investor would buy the stock today—before the expected 15 percent capital reduction takes place. What he would not buy, he should not hold! In other cases, the investor may not perceive any imminent specific threat to price or to income stream; the investment may have gone bad last month or last year and is presently in a price-dormant phase. Or it may be a recent purchase made for a specific reason—a news scenario that has not matured as expected. Doggedly refusing to accept reality in the situation, this owner holds on; capital remains dormant, depreciates, or, at best, is less successfully employed than other available opportunities would allow.

This critique of the trader-turned-investor syndrome is not in any sense meant to deprecate the conservative, longer-term, value-oriented approach to investing, nor is it an unabashed endorsement of trading for the short term. But it does recognize that money has a time value and that investors mislead themselves dangerously if they allow a mistake or a badly timed purchase to lock up their portfolio contents until some hoped-for but nonspecific future turn of better fortune bails them out.

Think about this aspect of time value and investment logic: The stubborn holder-on not only says he is willing to stand for perhaps a multiple-percent temporary capital reduction, he also says that a return just to current market value at some unknown future date is an acceptable outcome. Holding on for an imaginary non-loss is about as prudent as burying cash in the backyard. There is no return while one is risking loss of that principal and squandering the irreplaceable asset of time.

That is not to say there is not a time to hold. Stocks should be held when market and company prospects are favorable and when the stock would be bought today if not already owned. When the investment strategy is not working out, it is usually a forceful signal to sell out because either the reasoning behind the purchase was faulty or the fundamental nature of the situation (or the psychology of the overall market) has deteriorated since the purchase.

So if an investor would not buy the stock today, it should be sold because others who would potentially buy it ought to be in short supply if the investor is correct. This is a subtle trap for investors who like to hold. Instead of holding when something goes wrong, act like a successful business manager. Assess the situation without delay, and take warranted action. Short of actually selling the stock immediately, set a specific stop-loss limit, an upside goal and a time window. Then, do not deviate. Although this approach will address dramatic and sudden investment problem situations, it is only part of the remedy.

In addition, also review holdings periodically to catch situations that have gone dormant. For sluggish stocks a disciplined, routine approach is needed. Keep a notebook page on which to record stock prices at regular intervals and, for comparison, your major market average of choice. Do this no less than monthly and preferably weekly. When stocks drift, threatening to lull their inattentive investors to sleep, subject them to the tests suggested earlier for emergencies. This practice eliminates the cop-out that you are really a long-term investor. One can be legitimately long-term in intent but should then execute tactics in the nearer term as price and fundamental changes develop. Denver-based Clay Allen, a savvy institutional portfolio consultant, suggests managing one's portfolio like a company in which stocks are workers: Evaluate them frequently and dismiss the underperformers. (His book is titled *The Hidden Order Within Stock Prices*.)

Wishful Thinking

A wise old saying on Wall Street holds that: It is different this time. These are the five most expensive words in the investment business. They are a rationalization trap of the first magnitude. Recall that in the Old Testament the Lord promised Noah that never again would He caused it to rain for 40 days and 40 nights straight. It does not take a meteorologist or an agricultural expert to figure out that rains of even half of 40 days' duration do some pretty devastating damage. Those threatened with waterlog do not blindly focus on the difference between 39 and 40 days; a person threatened with drowning tries to imagine roughly how much rain would be enough to do him in. In the same way, by trying to measure the sameness or differences in investment scenarios with exacting precision, investors will drive themselves to miss the big picture. What is important in comparing a current situation with the past is to recognize common patterns rather than waiting to act until an exact, 100 percent repeating precedent can be detected. In market comparisons, close enough usually is enough.

There are two very different aspects of the this-time-it-will-be-different mantra repeating in investor thinking. One is an outgrowth of the it-can't-really-happen-to-me attitude that many people adopt when considering life's least pleasant realities. This aspect is a logical jump from observation of very real differences to a conclusion that the implied outcome must or will be different. Expecting it to be different involves a blend of reality and unreality that can subtly deceive an investor; it includes both the facts of a situation (fundamentals or trends) and the market's reaction to the facts. While history does tend to repeat itself (or at least rhyme), exact replications hardly ever occur.

So even if it is literally true that at a level of details or specific it will be different this time, investors should not lull themselves into complacency over minor differences. To focus on factual divergences while failing to note significant similarities is to miss the big picture by not seeing important parallels with past events. In doing so, investors can make an erroneous decision to hold based on unfiltered information. A recent powerful example occurred in 1999-2000. Driven by a technology mania (telecomm and the Internet) the world's stock markets blew off speculatively on the upside and then collapsed. The exact high P/E ratio was different, and the exciting new technology was not radio as in the 1920s, but stocks rose again multiple years running before hitting the wall. This time the NASDAQ, rather than the Dow, fell more than 80 percent.

Confronting Reality

While tough business situations are seldom if ever identical, success in business can be studied; patterns of managerial behavior are recorded, categorized and taught as cases in business-school classes. In the same way, there are common contributors discernible in deteriorating investment situations. Following is a list of some of the danger signs:

- ◆ Heavy promotion of stocks by management or agents.
- ◆ Projections of unusually strong/lengthy growth.
- ◆ Use of round numbers for predictions (e.g., 50 percent growth or a $100-billion market).
- ◆ Questioning the motives or expertise of reasonable doubters.
- ◆ Strong claims of being the best, unique or exclusive in a business.

◆ Defining the firm's market narrowly so that, by definition, one is the leader.

◆ Ready excuses that fault outside forces when performance falls short.

◆ Lateness in reporting earnings (against either prior practice or SEC filing deadlines).

◆ Change in outside auditors.

◆ Change in lead banker without improvement in interest rate and/or size of credit facilities.

◆ Substantial insider selling of the stock.

◆ Resignation of key (especially financial) officers or directors.

◆ Sales or margins trends diverging negatively from competitor or industry patterns.

◆ Inconsistent management statements.

◆ Identical (seemingly rehearsed) management statements.

◆ Stonewalling when trouble is obviously present.

Faced with some combination of a few of these signs, an investor reasonably and prudently can conclude that something is wrong and he or she should get out of the stock. To insist that a particular combination of adverse events exactly as seen in another situation must be fully repeated before concluding the stock is in trouble is naive and will probably prove costly. You can salvage a better price for the stock now while suspected further bad news is yet to be disclosed. Once the full ugly truth is finally made public and official, the stock will be down further and may even enter a ghastly free fall.

As already indicated, things do not get better by themselves. When a company's affairs appear to be deteriorating, even if certain negative events have not been reported, a prudent investor is well advised to assume the worst by projecting that the situation is likely to continue deteriorating. The point is, investors should be looking diligently for disturbing general similarities to other problem situations rather than watching for comforting differences. The objective is to detect trouble as early as possible, thereby preventing or limiting loss of one's capital. There is an analysts' cliché that the first earnings disappointment will not be the last. Some call this the cockroach principle. So be suspicious at the first signs of any type of trouble. Unless a neutral or skeptical observer can be convinced that all is well, exit before things have a chance to become worse. Ask dispassionately whether, in light of today's facts, you would think it a good idea to buy right now.

As indicated earlier in this chapter, there is a real but subtle difference between the this-time-it's-different rationalization and the this-cannot-be-happening-to-me thinking. If what is going wrong is like something that went wrong once before, there is quite possibly a reason. Putting it bluntly, many investors tend to make the same mistakes repeatedly. Wishing something would not have happened again, however, is barely across the reality/denial border from this is not happening. This indicates a need to deny that anything is wrong, a blocking of the pain caused by a judgment mistake. And, of course, when a mistake is public knowledge (your broker and, at year's end, your spouse and tax accountant will know as well), the error and pain of a loss is all the more deep and embarrassing.

What usually happens in these situations is that the investor focuses in the wrong direction by turning subjective and inward. But the reality is that whatever is wrong (collapsing earnings, a dividend cut, executive stock sales or resignations of directors) is happening to the company—not the investor—in the objective plane. The problem is only coincidentally connected to this particular investor's current ownership of the stock when it is happening. Bad stuff is happening, period.

The personal internalization that begins with it is happening to me and eventually turns to it cannot be happening to me is a rationalization. Sometimes an investor grasps discernible differences from a disastrous past investment experience and uses these to tell himself shakily that things will be all right, that it is not at all the way it appears. Such thinking (more accurately, freezing of thought) reflects cognitive dissonance. Instead of rationalizing, sell the stock on the first price bounce after trouble at the company and reassess the situation from a cooler distance. Remember that things do not right themselves magically. And realize that after a tarnishing mark some serious buying power from many other investors will be required to get the stock back up to higher levels. A smart investor asks this key question: If I did not own the stock, with today's knowledge would I be a buyer now? When trouble first appears, prepare for the worst rather than hoping for the best. This includes developing a mental scenario of what other shoes might fall, of how long it all will take to play out this situation and jut how adversely market psychology may react to the problem. The less bullish the overall market, the more rapidly other nimble traders will be bailing out. The most important aspect of performing this mental exercise is to examine prior situations in search of their similarities rather than differences; then, from a big-picture standpoint, remember that history does repeat.

Acknowledging Mistakes

How an investor handles mistakes is more important than how many mistakes he or she makes or even how extreme they turn out to be. And one's handling of errors actually affects future frequency and severity as well. Here are three guidelines to remember when contemplating inevitable investing mistakes:

- ◆ Expect to make mistakes and learn to live with them.
- ◆ Mistakes' actual cost will be driven mainly by what you do or fail to do with them.
- ◆ Make the most of mistakes by turning them into learning experiences; keep detailed, real- time records of every transaction from start to finish.

Handling Mistakes

Investors are human beings and therefore fallible. So it follows that, to avoid a downward spiral of self-criticism and emotional depletion, all investors must learn to forgive themselves for the mistakes they inevitably will make. The object of the game is to be right more often than wrong and to be right big and wrong small. The path to success is to keep mistakes under control and in perspective. Put ego aside by remembering that the relevant measuring stick is not the market, the broker or the guy next door—it is the investor's own record.

An investor can be likened to a skier. If he does learn to perform better over time, such improvement occurs because he is learning not to make the same mistakes repeatedly. He also learns to control and channel his intensity, to concentrate on the stock and general-market situation at hand rather than on internal feelings. Another principle that must be learned is not to let market results become enduring baggage; if one can avoid the emotional scars of mistakes, subsequent moves can be made rationally and more skillfully. Another good sports analogy is to a baseball player in a hitting slump, who must concentrate on the next pitch rather than on his past nine hitless at-bats in order to regain success. The beginning of so-called mistake wisdom is acknowledging and taking ownership of investment errors and then letting go of them. As in all of life, we must forgive ourselves or be unable to live with ourselves. In investing, of course, the object over time is to make fewer mistakes in proportion to total transactions and, if possible, to make mistakes less costly and successes more profitable.

People professionally accustomed to winning consistently because of their brilliance and hard work are likely to be frustrated in a very basic way by the stock market; intelligence and diligence are helpful but not sufficient for achieving market profits. Examples are A students, successful lawyers and successful corporate executives. In the same way, people who succeed by precision or by rules are likely to be disappointed that investing cannot be totally controlled, or reduced to a dependable formula. Examples are computer programmers, engineers, research scientists, auditors and civil servants. Similarly, people whose professional lives involve exercising power often find trading stocks psychologically frustrating since they possess no such accustomed control. Examples would be professors, senior managers and military officers or police.

On the other hand, people who have routinely felt life's ups and downs are, by conditioning, psychologically better prepared for the realities of a mix of winning and losing on Wall Street. Salespeople, for example, know the frustration of bad weeks and do not expect perfection; their understanding that winning means just a higher-than-average success rate—not 100 percent perfection—gears them well on an emotional level for the stock market.

Once the psychological art of living with mistakes is mastered, those mistakes must be turned into sources of opportunity if so one can profit from them. In fact, mistakes must be used as building blocks for the next transaction. Think of each buy

57

and sell transaction, both gain and loss, as the tuition required to make progress in the learning process. Like a college student, an investor always pays tuition; the important question is whether she pays attention in class and gets her money's worth by learning something.

Investment success can be built on both right and wrong past moves; those behaviors that result in pain (loss) need most to be understood so they can be changed. One of the most costly causes of error is the tendency to repeat mistakes. And the most costly and troublesome mistakes are those of which the investor is unaware. Many such mistakes are driven, often at a subconscious level, by psychological forces, such as unresolved guilt, narcissism, unvented rage and grandiosity.

Brokers and investment advisors are often unwilling or unable to help investors become aware in this problem area; realistically, they should be viewed only as technical experts in the market and not behavior-modification teachers. They may run money better, but they do not necessarily teach clients how to do it, nor have time to do so. So investors are on their own, with the challenge of learning from past mistakes. They need to overcome rationalization and avoidance behavior in order to focus on this learning opportunity. These are the two most important steps investors can take to analyze their own investing behavior:

1. Face up to errors instead of ignoring or minimizing them.

2. Categorize mistakes and work toward avoiding repetition.

Record Keeping

The most productive way to face and benefit from errors is to record all investment behavior, analyzing what worked and what did not. This way, personal behavior patterns emerge that can be changed. It is helpful to create a computer file (assuming your investment software does not have this feature) and record every transaction, for future analysis. If honest, real-time records are not kept scrupulously—saving confirmation slips until tax time does not count—the result is to lose the learning potential in mistakes. Without recording and analysis, the investor who is unaware of his mistaken behaviors is still flying blind.

Note the suggestion that records be kept in real time. This has four positive effects. First, memory tends to fail when it must process mistakes, so recorded hard facts are a necessary component for accurate analysis. Second, real-time records eliminate cumbersome back-checking, a big task that can be an extremely effective barrier to keeping the analysis up to date. Third, real-time records preclude fudging or minimizing errors, which tends to occur when an investor wants to look back through rose-colored glasses. And finally, if an investor takes time to actually write answers to specific questions and he or she then asks both him or herself (and a broker, if one is used) about tactical mistakes, it is easier to identify mistakes before making another ill-conceived move.

Buy/Review/Sell Evaluation Sheet

Following is a worksheet geared specifically toward catching the most common investor mistakes. These questions are shortened to emphasize key words that identify the most common points in time when mistakes are made. It may be helpful to photocopy this worksheet into a notebook and add blank pages for useful-length answers.

Investor-Mistakes Checklist

Record the following information when each stock is bought:

1.   Whose idea was the purchase (self, broker, advisory letter, friend)?
2.   How long was the stock actively studied before taking action?
3.   Why is the stock expected to perform as projected?
4.   Is the general market in a major uptrend or downtrend?
5.   What was the prior-day closing level of the Dow-Jones Industrial Average? The recent few days' trend?
6.   What was the execution price of the stock purchase (excluding commission)?
7.   What was the prior-day closing price of the stock? Its recent few days' trend?
8.   What was the month-earlier price of the stock? (Was it a case of chasing strength)?
9.   What was the week-earlier price of the stock? (Was it a case of chasing strength)?
10. What is the price objective for the stock, including the implied price/earnings ratio?
11. What is the time of expected workout (date and number of months from now)?
12. What is the implied return in percent per year?
13. Where is the chart's breakdown point (support, trendline)?
14. What is the actual or mental stop-loss price point?

As indicated by these questions, it is very important to establish not only a price objective for each stock holding, but also an associated timeframe. To record this information usefully, mark a calendar or tickler file at the projected workout date. Do that when each stock is purchased. This creates an effective reminder to look at that time at every position and reassess it. This practice helps you to avoid drift.

Stock Reassessment Checklist

At the tickler or projected-workout date, record in real time the following information:

1. What is the closing level of the DJIA?
2. What is its percentage move since the buy date?
3. What is the stock's closing price?
4. What is the percentage move since the buy date (compare with DJIA)?
5. Is the overall market still in a bull or a bear phase?
6. Is the stock in a major uptrend?
7. Has the stock not moved to the established price goal? Why?
8. Why continue holding the stock? Cite specific, realistic reasons, not wishes.
9. What is the new price target (and implied P/E)?
10. What is the new workout date (put in tickler file again)?
11. What concrete factual change, not failure or prior scenario, justifies extending the workout date?

Sale Checklist

When the stock is sold, record the following in real time:

1. What is the DJIA at sale date? (Compute percent moves from buy and review dates.)
2. What was the sale price? (Compute percent moves from buy and review dates.)
3. Did the purchase rationale come true? If not, when did failure become apparent?
4. How long was the time between failure and sale date?
5. Was the stock held for a longer/shorter time than planned? Why?
6. What was the high price of the stock while held? (Compute the percent down from there to sale price.)
7. What was the low price of the stock while held? (Compute the percent down from buy price to that low)
8. Did the stock ever sell at/above the price target while it was held? If yes, why was it not sold then?
9. Was an above-market GTC sale order ever placed? If no, why not?
10. Was a stop-loss order ever placed and then removed or lowered? Did that reduce profit or extend loss?

11. Was the sale execution planned or impulsive?

12. Was the stock sold on strength, weakness, boredom, company news (good or bad), or general market action?

13. Whose idea was the sale?

14. Was the stock sold to provide needed funds for another purchase?

An investor who truthfully answers all the questions in these checklists can expect to be uncomfortable. Good! (Discomfort leads us to modify behavior.) Those questions that cause the greatest discomfort usually identify where the most recurrent mistakes are made or where performance is less than optimal. To learn from prior mistakes, note those portions of the investment sequence, and watch them most carefully the next time a purchase is made. In fact, color-highlight the problem questions on the checklists and refer to them often: before, while, and after subsequent positions are in place.

Tally the mistakes noted, scoring one point for each occurrence, on a master sheet (an example is shown at the end of this chapter)—for example, a tendency to hold longer than planned, to raise the price objective without solid reasons or to develop a pattern of selling from boredom. High scores (repeating points scored) for the most personally troublesome problem areas will emerge. That is where to concentrate improvement efforts in order to become more profitable in the market.

While analyzing mistakes, it is important to disregard the delusion that any investor can ever bat a thousand. (Even professionals have error rates around 40 percent.) But do believe that some worthwhile improvement in performance is possible, indeed likely, if you actually apply systematic effort to noting and correcting mistakes.

Master Tally Sheet

MASTER TALLY SHEET

At Buy Date:

Stocks Scored to Date	1	2	3	4	5	6	7	8	9	10	11	12	13	14	15
Whose idea	☐	☐	☐	☐	☐	☐	☐	☐	☐	☐	☐	☐	☐	☐	☐
Good reason	☐	☐	☐	☐	☐	☐	☐	☐	☐	☐	☐	☐	☐	☐	☐
Study period	☐	☐	☐	☐	☐	☐	☐	☐	☐	☐	☐	☐	☐	☐	☐
Market trend	☐	☐	☐	☐	☐	☐	☐	☐	☐	☐	☐	☐	☐	☐	☐
Chased strength	☐	☐	☐	☐	☐	☐	☐	☐	☐	☐	☐	☐	☐	☐	☐
P/E target	☐	☐	☐	☐	☐	☐	☐	☐	☐	☐	☐	☐	☐	☐	☐

At Tickler Date:

Major trend	☐	☐	☐	☐	☐	☐	☐	☐	☐	☐	☐	☐	☐	☐	☐
Exit-at-goal failure	☐	☐	☐	☐	☐	☐	☐	☐	☐	☐	☐	☐	☐	☐	☐
Stock trend	☐	☐	☐	☐	☐	☐	☐	☐	☐	☐	☐	☐	☐	☐	☐
Conviction re holding	☐	☐	☐	☐	☐	☐	☐	☐	☐	☐	☐	☐	☐	☐	☐

At Sale Date:

Held too long/short?	☐	☐	☐	☐	☐	☐	☐	☐	☐	☐	☐	☐	☐	☐	☐
Relative performance	☐	☐	☐	☐	☐	☐	☐	☐	☐	☐	☐	☐	☐	☐	☐
Scenario right?	☐	☐	☐	☐	☐	☐	☐	☐	☐	☐	☐	☐	☐	☐	☐
Decisive at failure?	☐	☐	☐	☐	☐	☐	☐	☐	☐	☐	☐	☐	☐	☐	☐
Percent given back	☐	☐	☐	☐	☐	☐	☐	☐	☐	☐	☐	☐	☐	☐	☐
Percent overpaid	☐	☐	☐	☐	☐	☐	☐	☐	☐	☐	☐	☐	☐	☐	☐
Exit-at-goal failure	☐	☐	☐	☐	☐	☐	☐	☐	☐	☐	☐	☐	☐	☐	☐
GTC order at target?	☐	☐	☐	☐	☐	☐	☐	☐	☐	☐	☐	☐	☐	☐	☐
Stop tactics	☐	☐	☐	☐	☐	☐	☐	☐	☐	☐	☐	☐	☐	☐	☐
Sale planning	☐	☐	☐	☐	☐	☐	☐	☐	☐	☐	☐	☐	☐	☐	☐
Circumstances/trigger	☐	☐	☐	☐	☐	☐	☐	☐	☐	☐	☐	☐	☐	☐	☐
Whose idea?	☐	☐	☐	☐	☐	☐	☐	☐	☐	☐	☐	☐	☐	☐	☐

PART II

Developing the Proper Mindset

CHAPTER 6

Keep a Clear Head

Keys for Successful Selling

◆ Recognize and Resist Crowd Psychology

◆ Take a Time-Out If Needed

◆ Learn to Deal with Denial and Loss

◆ Benefit from an Actual Case Study

Winning on Wall Street is a challenging pursuit, or at least one that seems easy only late in major bull markets. Following the secondary crash of October 1989, a survey taken for The Wall Street Journal indicated that a majority of the investing public saw the deck as stacked against them: Insider trading was perceived as an essential advantage over individual investors, market manipulation was widely suspected as a result of the recent scandals and celebrity prosecutions, and program trading by huge investing institutions (and brokerage firms for their own accounts) was viewed as an investment barrier for the little guy. Such perceptions predictably returned during and after the 2000-2002 bear market.

Whether an investor is right or wrong about a stock or about market motivation, multi-billion-dollar investors do move the market in whatever direction they think it will go, simply by acting. (See Chapter 10.) Therefore, investing is a challenging endeavor for individuals, even when they play on a relatively even playing field and even if information is fully and equally available to all market participants. Harsh reality is that not every investor functions in the stock market with equal efficiency or earns equal returns. Disparities in performance generally boil down to how well each investor—individual or institutional—can master, or invest against, his emotions. So keeping a clear head becomes the difference between profits and losses in all but the brief upside-runaway periods. Winning means staying clear-headed when everyone else is not, especially during market swings from panicky lows and price despair to manic euphoria—and the reverse.

Statistically, it is known that most market participants in one cycle are again around for a re-enactment of the drama the next time around. Almost incredibly, a majority fall prey to the same mistakes in the subsequent cycle. Most such mistakes have to do not with fundamentals but with investors' emotional reactions to news and price volatility. So it pays to remain emotionally clear-headed.

It is the nature of all speculative markets that they move from one extreme to the other. For example, in a recession, the economy might show a 3 percent drop in real gross domestic product (GDP). Corporate earnings may slide 20 percent or 25 percent. But the major stock averages might fall 30 percent to 40 percent, as if economic life were about to disintegrate.

In this scenario, some individual stocks will fall by 80 percent to 90 percent. And that includes only the survivors; some other companies inevitably go out of business, with their stocks becoming expensive wallpaper. In the recent unwinding of the Internet bubble, most technology stocks fell 90 percent and hundreds of weak companies died.

Crowd Psychology

What takes hold of investors in this kind of extreme market movement is crowd psychology, a total loss of self-control. What ought to be governing is a high awareness of the patterns of one's very recent market experiences, and for a simple but crucial reason. One's degree of recent success or failure has a powerful influence on success during subsequent market moves. Success enables more success, until a point when inhibitions disappear. Failure takes its toll in future failures generated by faulty, irrational or incomplete thinking.

Theoretical Case History

The accompanying figure is a hypothetical stock chart on which are overlaid the buying, holding, and selling decisions—and the emotional reactions—of a mythical investor who can

Figure 6.1: XYZ Common: Emotional Roller Coaster

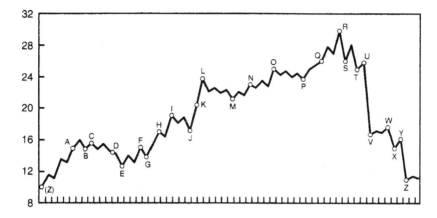

in all respects, be considered real and representative. In fact, this investor is so real in composite as to be the force that moves the stock on the chart in the way it is illustrated. (See Figure 6-1.) On the chart, trace the price movement from one letter to the next, moving from the beginning of the price action to point A for example, and then read the comment corresponding to that letter. Then observe the price movement from there to point B, and look at the relevant comment at B. In that way, you can follow the thoughts and feelings generated by a typical stock's action in a telescoped view.

The feelings, thoughts and actions demonstrated, multiplied by thousands of active buyers and sellers and millions of shares annually, create the type of price gyrations seen in the exhibit. The chart follows a mythical XYZ Corporation; its time scale covers several years from the start of one bull market to the bottom of the following bear market. Given the volatility of individual issues in recent years, the relative rise of 200 percent followed by nearly a 70 percent retrenchment is not at all unrepresentative of reality.

Specific price points on the chart are marked with the letters A to Z, demonstrating the hypothetical composite investor's thoughts, feelings and actions in the comments that follow.

A. Looks like a winner; up 50 percent from the panic lows. Good relative performance. Buy 500 shares at market.

B. Just a little consolidation. The earnings-per-share forecasts are good. Not worried; plan to hold.

C. All right! Finally back above original cost. Now it is really ready to go.

D. Glad I sold here. It both broke down and triggered the stop. That is two strong signals, and I did not miss them.

E. Knew I was right about that dog. Glad I am out.

F. I have seen this price before. That stock is not worth it. Short 300.

G. See, I knew it! Now I have got this one figured out. This baby is headed for nine or even   lower!

H. Aha! A false breakout if I ever saw one. Short another 200.

I. Cannot believe it. This turkey's got a P/E of 22 and it is going up? Another point and I   have to take cover.

J. That is better. Now I am even on my second lot shorted.

K. I've seen this before: another false breakout. I won't be fooled because I know this rally cannot last.

L. I cannot stand it anymore. Cover all 500 at market!

M. Wish I had more guts and stayed short. Look at this downtrend.

N. Hmmmph. Not bad: flat earnings despite recession talk.

O. Look at this uptrend! I have gotta get on board. Tape is saying something's happening that is not apparent. Buy 400.

P. I am scared by this break. Cannot afford a big loss. Sell half.

Q. Guess I was wrong (but that 50 percent sale still felt prudent). Gotta buy back that 200 shares since the market is firmer again.

R. Terrific! $30 and going north. I am not greedy: 32 and I will be gone. That is a reasonable 25 percent profit.

S. Just a correction. Darn market's off 240 points. But there is gotta be a fifth up-wave. I will take 30 when it gets back there.

T. Well, it makes no sense to see the stock way down here. Look how high the yield is. That will support the price. It just cannot go lower.

U. Now that is better. The market's stabilized too. We've seen the worst.

V. Dividend cut 60 percent? Who could have seen that coming? Cannot sell now: too big a loss.

W. Guess the worst is over. I would average down if I had the cash. No, on second thought this one has hurt me enough. Cannot trust it.

X. Margin call? Sell half. I love this stock at these prices but just cannot put more cash into the market.

Y. Glad I did not sell it all. Should have met the margin call and held it for the rally since it was so darn cheap!

Z. Here we go: down again. I cannot stand it anymore. I am done! Get me out; sell at market.

This hypothetical chart reflects a very confused investor, it is true. And the sequence may seem too long to represent any single investor/stock relationship that had gone so badly. But many an individual investor tends to make several, if not all, of these flip-flop mistakes before quitting, and for three reasons:

◆ He has made a profit on the stock before, which generates an affinity for owning it again.

◆ He feels he knows the company or the industry and so believes he understands the stock as well.

◆ He wants to get even, or reach breakeven in dollars, before leaving to engage with another stock.

All of these mind-sets are representative of unclear thinking. Not only do many investors dig in their heels and insist on coming out of the stock relationship whole, but their negative feedback creates more confusion, which makes them dig in their heels even deeper.

Comments associated with this chart include five telling reactions to price behavior that indicate typical investor mistakes when emotions take over:

◆ There are swings back and forth between fundamental and technical explanations and rationales.

◆ There is a tendency to project mentally continuation of the recent trend.

◆ The investor has uncontrolled swings toward extremes of emotional reaction.

◆ The investor believes that the market is out to trap the individual investor.

◆ Prior bad experiences with a stock create damaging confusion.

Taking a Time Out

One useful way to short-circuit such a negative thinking spiral detailed as that above is to quit playing a stock—or industry group—after one or two losses. Whether or not there actually is such a thing as unfavorable chemistry between a stock and an investor, dealing in it again only deepens the perceived destructive pattern and increases risk of additional mistakes. There are thousands of other companies available! In the same way, if there is a pattern of consecutive losses or whipsaws across several stocks, quit all of them for a period of time.

This does not mean selling everything (long-term positions that are working well and would be bought again today need not be disturbed). Just stop trading and clear your mind. Draw up lists of the stocks that are solid and those that are shaky, and describe why. Set price targets. Write down firm resolves not to sell on weakness or buy on strength. This pause in the action will allow one to control his or her actions before a return to the market; thus the tendency to follow crowd hysterics will be diminished.

This pause, however, is best accomplished when some selling has taken place and a cash cushion exists. If an investor stops while fully committed, there is an urgency about getting back to the action because there are still positions causing active worry. A key question to ask is: If action absolutely could not be taken for a month, which stocks would I be most comfortable to own?

It would be a mistake to take a head-clearing pause after every loss. But when there is a run of mistakes, say, three or more, seriously consider calling a halt. That is especially called for if the losses have been stock-specific (not caused by a falling overall market). All errors count, whether in the same stock or across several. Then ask a broker or respected trading friend to take a dispassionate look at current positions and make independent suggestions with which to compare your written evaluations. Ask him to mail a copy of his suggestions on a specified date. If the broker has difficulty helping in this way, the investor has received a telling warning about the broker's usefulness.

Doing solid fundamental research is only one part of the formula for profit. You can lose money in a good stock or mutual fund repeatedly by buying and selling it at emotionally driven times. Only the clearest heads do prevail in the market. A losing streak that the investor does nothing to correct can become self-sustaining as personal confusion gains the upper hand over reason. Psychologists say that losses act to disrupt one's sense of self-unity; losses further cause shame, which also causes disorientation or loss of bearings. So call a halt before your downward mental spiral can set a precedent for future trading failures. Call a halt deliberately before things can get so bad that you shut down completely while holding a collection of performance dogs.

Denial and Loss

The process of deciding to sell a stock is a difficult one at best unless an investor has developed a discipline or methodology and adheres to it faithfully to avoid inevitable internal mental battles. When a loss is involved, the sell decision is even more difficult because the issue of pain avoidance is now present. It is human nature to seek self-preservation, and pain signals to us a danger to our well being. Some investors may be obsessed with safety, while most are reasonably balanced in their tolerance of the risks involved in seeking to earn a profit. But every investor has some threshold at which pain must be avoided, sometimes at horrendous cost.

One of the most convenient but costly ways to avoid the pain of loss—or even of profit squandered—is denial. Dealing with an investment or trading loss involves not only financial pain but also ego pain, a blow to our self-sense of value. At some point, a majority of stockholders will least attempt to avoid both pains by failing to deal with the reality of their losses. They prefer not to think about it, or they minimize it. When specific stock positions go bad, the pain avoider becomes a longer-term holder, or more accurately a collector of stocks. He has no real investment motive or astuteness of value judgment and is, in fact, simply denying the pain of potential (or already apparent) loss.

Unfortunately, most investment brokers are of very little or no help to their clients in dealing with losses; they are unwilling or not equipped to break down client denial or avoidance behavior. Part of brokers' inability to help stems from the bias of their training, which is strongly focused on gathering new assets and then persuading clients to buy, not sell, securities. But the broker problem goes much further.

As a human being the broker too is a pain avoider. He or she needs to remain on cordial and constructive terms with clients. A successful sales person must listen to customers and act on all resulting feedback. So, naturally, when a customer indicates an unwillingness to deal with losses, his or her broker hears that message loud and clear—and heeds it. An unspoken contract develops between investor and broker: I will not complain about my problem if you will please do me the favor of not reminding me of it.

There are several rationalizations that investors use to deny losses, or the importance of their losses. One relies on the rubric of the U.S. tax code. Investors are well aware that, for tax purposes, no loss is recognized as having occurred until a closing transaction actually takes place (and the 31-day wash-sale rule is not violated). Using this tax reality as a psychological crutch, many investors actually talk themselves into believing that they do not have a loss until they actually sell it out. On objective examination, of course, such reasoning is absurd. Few such investors, holding a pleasant 200 percent paper gain, would say they have no profit! And if you die and your heirs look over your account records, they assuredly will see that stock that is down from cost as being a loss.

It is, of course, possible that price might recover and today's paper loss might be reduced or recovered. Best case of all, it might even become a paper (or real) profit in the future. But the truth is that if a stock now trades below what was paid, there is a loss of capital because wealth is measured by the current value of assets less liabilities. Liquidate investments under duress, value an estate or switch investments to obtain maximum current income from available assets, and reality prevails. A stock is currently worth only what it can be sold for now—not what it was bought for, what the owner wishes it would be, or what he thinks it should sell for. If current price is below cost, a loss exists. Period.

If an investor is too smart or too logical to attempt self-deception with the paper-loss-is not-real farce, he may rely instead on a less disprovable assertion: The stock will come back given enough patience. Hope springs eternal, and once in a great while a terrible loser does reverse and rise phoenix-like from the ashes. Then, the investor who has sold out at a loss and later sees the price recover says: See, if only I'd been smarter or more patient and followed my instinct and held on, I would not have had that loss. I will act differently next time.

Closing out a position, especially when at a loss, represents the process of coming to closure. Optimistic by nature, we prefer to see our options remain open rather than have them closed off. Buying a stock involves the grand opening of new possibilities, but selling closes the final chapter. As noted in Chapter 2, many closure processes in our lives carry sadness: graduating from and leaving our alma mater, admitting a failed marriage via divorce, burying a departed friend, cleaning out great-grandmother's attic. These represent some pretty heavy baggage, of a kind we would prefer to avoid lifting if possible. Selling a stock conjures up such feelings, at least at a subconscious level. Holding it allows us potential for greater profit or reclaiming a current loss. If our stock is down, selling labels us with a sign of failure, which we would like to avoid.

Actually placing a sell order and taking the loss on a final basis (the trade confirmations and the Schedule D entry are lasting evidence) goes even further in that it sets up our investor for a possible second source of pain by being wrong again: watching the stock move higher without being on board for its recovery. This possible double horror show can be avoided by refusing to take the loss in the first place, says the person in denial.

What psychologists call denial is, in the investment arena, an umbrella description for a variety of rationalizations and self-deceptions. All are designed to allow possessors of losing investment positions to justify doing nothing about them.

There are several variations on the denial theme. One springs from memory of the purchase price, the highest price ever reached, or the best achieved since our purchase. Old best price levels can each act as a high-water mark that becomes a once-was, a could-be-again, a should-be, then a will-be and all too often a got-to-be. It does not matter how many months or years ago that high-water mark was made. It does not matter that the company's fundamentals or general market psychology have eroded seriously. It does not matter that a rise of several hundred percent from current prices may be necessary for full recovery (example: still-depressed tech stocks long after the end of the 2002 bear market). To avoid accepting and dealing with the loss, the denier waits (and waits and waits some more) for recovery, denying the heavy adverse odds.

The Schuller Corporation Case Study

A specific example, albeit a slightly old one, of how extreme and irrational the predisposition to denial can be will be of some value here. After more than six years under Chapter 11 protection, Denver-based Schuller Corporation (previously Johns Manville and at that time simply Manville Corporation) announced that it would complete its reorganization soon and, in the process, issue a very large number of new common shares to settle the claims of creditors and asbestos-injury victims. Official company documents filed with the SEC indicated that the exiting holders' equity would be diluted 94 percent to 97 percent.

Following local Colorado media coverage of the good news that Chapter 11 status would end, the then-Manville common (old) stock rose from $2.00 to $3.00 on extremely heavy trading volume. Management even took an extremely unusual step by issuing a statement, in response to market action, in which it repeated previous written warnings that its stock involved a high degree of risk.

Part of the reorganization was to be a reverse split on a one-for-eight basis. (Reverse splits are designed to cut the number of shares outstanding and to return a stock's price to a more respectable per-share level.) The long and well documented history of declining value following reverse splits compounded the prospective negative effects of massive dilution from the bankruptcy settlement.

As a local brokerage analyst, your author issued a very strong, urgent recommendation to brokers that they contact all clients who then owned Manville common shares to sell their old stock at market without delay—particularly taking advantage of the recent sharp rally. A dual-trading market existed in the then-Manville shares. The old stock retreated a few days later to $2.00 per share. But the post-split shares were trading at the very same time on a when-issued basis at $8.00 each, which was four and not eight times the pre-split price.

There were technical and mechanical reasons, internal to the market's rules (not relevant here), why such a spread in prices could exist. In fact it did exist. The simple fact was that an investor holding old shares would see a certain loss of 50 percent in capital: 800 shares currently worth $1,600, for example, would in a few weeks become 100 shares worth $800. It was like being able to read a future newspaper and check the quotations in advance. A holder of old stock had an opportunity to sell his or her existing shares, simultaneously replace that position with one-eighth as many when-issued new shares if they so desired, and pocket the difference after commissions in cash.

Neglecting to sell, therefore, represented a fully conscious acceptance of a known imminent penalty to capital: not a tiny marginal loss but a whopping 50 percent slam! To the broker community's (and this analyst's) amazement, some clients could not be convinced to sell their stock even to avoid absolutely certain further losses. Some said: I have held the stock for a long time and see no reason to abandon hope now. Others did not want to create a wash sale, even if it would preserve half the capital involved. One client wanted $2.50 per share and would not sell for less. One client repeatedly swore he did not care about his loss. Dozens of investors in the stock were in total denial of the obvious facts, to the point where they were unwilling to help themselves avoid further damage!

Analyzing Crisis and Loss Situations

Think back for a moment to recall the virtual chaos and near-paralysis on Wall Street after the crash of October 1987. Many brokerage firms were far behind in calculating margin calls to clients; therefore, investors had an unusual but fleeting opportunity to assess their positions and take action before they were absolutely forced to. One of the more insightful client thought processes went something like this:

1. I expect the world to go on.

2. I expect to remain an equities investor.

3. The decline has created some wonderful values right here at today's prices, so I do not want to quit now and return later only to buy back at higher levels.

4. I know I will face a margin call within days or hours. I do not have the courage (or the cash) to put up extra money, so I must do some selling.

5.   It is smartest to keep those stocks whose future prospects seem best from current levels.

6.   Therefore, to raise the needed cash my only logical move is to sell those positions that I would least likely buy again today.

A self-imposed thought process or exercise something like this, developed for an imagined crisis such as a possible future crash, can be helpful by forcing the reluctant investor to focus quickly (these ideas are developed more fully in Chapter 28). Such a process helps him recognize which stocks are not going to be the best choices to hold. Those are the ones to sell. After you go through such a mental exercise several times on a theoretical basis over a period of months or a year, losses generally can be dealt with more easily. The first time through, do it on paper. Then pick up the phone or turn on your computer, and issue an actual sell order. Eventually, this newfound ability to sell without pangs of remorse will improve investment results as tired dollars get repositioned into more promising situations.

Denial Prevention

This Schuller example demonstrates that investors must somehow set up their own ways of dealing with reality, even if that requires what seems like unnatural or artificial devices: stop-loss orders entered at purchase, rigorous periodic reviews of each position, even filling out a questionnaire to justify continued holding.

Another denial-prevention strategy is to sell one stock periodically—perhaps quarterly to avoid too much churning—whether it seems needed or not, just like routine auto maintenance. Pretend that you need to raise some money for tuition bills and a stock sale is your only source. Do such selling dispassionately and regularly, and in the process your most mediocre stock holdings can be sloughed off much more easily. The added practice in making sell decisions will make future ones easier. (Admittedly, this would be an expensive exercise for anyone still using a full-commission brokerage house, and thus the suggestion provides yet another reason for strongly considering opening an online, deep-discount account.)

CHAPTER 7

Cast Off Faulty Mental Anchors

Keys for Successful Selling

- ◆ Learn Fundamental Psycho-Mechanical Realities
- ◆ Require Realism to Support Hope
- ◆ Understand the Aftermath of a Crash
- ◆ Make Sure the Hold Decision Is a Decision
- ◆ Accept the Irrelevance of Your Personal Cost Price
- ◆ Know the Few Cases When Cost Price Might Matter
- ◆ Cease to Misuse Personal Cost Price

It is true that a positive attitude helps produce positive results and, conversely, that believing something to be impossible can be self-fulfilling. However, while wishing may be a necessary component of success in endeavors over which a person has some degree of control, in investing it alone it is not sufficient. In the stock market, where an individual is too small to exert a meaningful influence over price for long if ever, wishing simply will not make it so. For investors with high self-esteem, inability to control the market can act as a subtle source of nagging discomfort; we all must accept what we cannot change and make the best of it.

Thousands of investors—optimistic by natural temperament and encouraged in their buy bias by brokers and the usually upbeat media—spend more energy in hoping than in logical and coolheaded analysis. Their continual wishing is actually counterproductive: In baseless optimism, they deceive themselves and ignore reality by holding a stock that is not working out. Falling into such a trap is quite easy since the stock's price, more than a barometer of wealth, comes to measure an owner's ego; giving up represents admitting defeat, and defeat makes us feel stupid, which evokes shame. So hoping feels better.

Fundamental and Psycho-Mechanical Realities

There are two reasons that hoping against hope fails: One reason is fundamental, the other reason is psycho-mechanical (as distinguished from a technical reason, to use the conventional market vocabulary that contrasts with fundamentals). (See Figure 7-1.)

If a company is not producing expected results, disappointment sets in for shareholders. Fundamental results—an expected product announcement, a technology breakthrough, patent award, sales increase, earnings turnaround or dividend boost—must occur to generate stock-price profits. If this does not happen, the stock loses needed supporters and, eventually, its price takes a deep decline (particularly if positive expectations had been high and/or had persisted for a lengthy period). In strong bull market phases such as those seen in the late 1990s and again from mid-2002 to mid-2007, investors readily become impatient with under performers and dump them for more appealing, faster action elsewhere. This is one more reason hope must be realistic; if it is not, it will be loss-creating.

When fundamentals fail, the implication is very clear: Sell the stock, do not hold it. It can always be bought back later if or when those hoped-for developments do come through. After disillusionment has become the dominant attitude, early signs of fundamental progress will be disbelieved, thus providing ample time to buy back in at a price not too far up from the lows. That is the good news.

The bad news, ironically, is that fundamentals might actually be going according to plan, which naturally encourages optimism. But even though fundamentals may be good, the often-fickle market may cease to be willing to pay up for those fundamentals. All too often, investors are lulled into misguided overconfidence because the company's story works out as anticipated. Therefore, they expect the stock to respond favorably, which sets up a trap: The truth is, it might be up already.

Figure 7.1: Stock-Price Driving Factors

		Fundamentals	
		Good	*Bad*
Psychology	*Positive*	Price up	Price perhaps even
	Negative	Price likely down	Price down sharply

An old market proverb says stocks fall of their own weight, but it takes buying pressure to push them up. At first, it may seem obvious why technicians say that for a stock to remain strong it must rise on increasing volume and that a price advance occurring on declining or low volume is suspect. But there is a second and more profound implication about the difference between fundamental realities surrounding the company and the psycho-mechanical forces that drive its stock price. Do not assume the two will necessarily operate in the same direction in any given time period.

Let us go back to our distinction between technical (which describes a stock's price and volume action) and psycho-mechanical. The latter encompasses all those non-fundamental factors actually operating in the stock market in real time—things that drive investors to take action by placing actual buy or sell orders for a stock. This aspect must be explored to explain why stocks can go down while their fundamentals are positive.

A logical investor sells unless a positive decision can be justified to buy the stock. This approach is supported by the contention that stocks should always be presumed suspect and constantly subject to sale unless there is positive justification for actively deciding to buy. Holding is logical only if others reasonably can be expected to buy.

Why hold a stock at all? There are only two income-based objectives: dividend potential and interest rate volatility. With an income objective, hold the stock if its dividend is secure and is being regularly increased. With interest rate changes, hold only if interest rates will not move adversely enough (i.e., sharply higher) to reduce the market value of the expected dividend stream. Since rates move faster than dividends (a move in long-bond rates from 5 percent to 6 percent is a 20 percent rise in the valuation divisor), this implies being always ready at the sell trigger even with stocks bought for income.

If your objective is capital appreciation and not income, the only justification for holding is a belief that price will begin, or will continue, to rise. Just expecting a stock not to decline is not a good reason to hold it. That is the equivalent of leaving a pile of money in a checking account. Actually it is worse because one's stock-price expectation or overall market-tone assumption might prove overly optimistic, and the stock could decline anyway; the (insured) bank deposit is presumed risk free.

This leads to a key conclusion: Hold a stock only if you expect it to rise (enough to compensate for opportunity cost and risk). The key word is expect, as contrasted with hope. Then logically examine the basis for any bullish expectations by envisioning realistically the stock's positive psycho-mechanical factors. Only a combination of psycho-mechanical factors added to positive fundamental news can drive the price higher; both are required for a price rise. One alone is not enough, except briefly near runaway market tops. At such times, general market euphoria will temporarily reduce selling urgency. But such circumstances must not be assumed to persist for long.

The Aftermath of a Crash

At nearly all other times in the market's march, there is a need for positive upward (buying) pressure (sponsorship) to keep a stock's price from falling. The market for a stock is not like the market for groceries, for example. Stock demand is psychological, not based on necessity. To compound the effect of a lack of compelling stock demand, there tends to be an ongoing supply of shares that, if not matched, pushes prices lower over time. Included are unending sources of selling pressure: settling an estate; retiring and living on one's assets; paying for a college education, vacations or medical expenses; raising capital for a business or to buy other stocks; boredom and disappointment. Those are individuals' reasons for selling. Mutual funds face redemptions and they and other institutions periodically switch to other holdings that seem more attractive. If this supply is not met by equal demand, prices decline.

The central issue then, is the source of buying power or demand for a stock. It is true that at some point a stock can become so compellingly cheap that it finds support. But the problem is that a truly cheap price level may not yet even wildly approximate yesterday's closing price—especially when viewed from bull-market heights. Thus, a logical corollary exists: Do not hold a stock unless it would be a prudent purchase today. If you are not willing to buy it for your portfolio, who else would? If you buy it anyway, this is the practicing greater-fool theory at its worst.

Therefore, look objectively at how purchase decisions favoring a stock are likely to be generated. Think in terms of sponsorship. For sponsorship to exist, it is necessary that corporate management be involved in the process of providing information to the professional investing community and to the public. This does not mean an investor should look for a company that is actively and aggressively promoting its stock; in fact, those situations are suspect and usually best avoided. Sponsorship requires credible executives giving their time and honest answers to research analysts who want to follow the company and who may wish to recommend its stock to their clients or to place or keep it in managed portfolios. Institutional sponsorship is important; its loss can be devastating to share price.

Remember, demand for a stock does not occur in a vacuum. With the exception of a magazine story or news event, themes that catch the public's attention (AIDS or the Internet or global warming), or word-of-mouth recommendations, much retail demand for stocks is generated by stockbrokers who call clients and suggest reasons to buy. Some demand is also created by newsletter advisory services. With so many other prepackaged (and lower maintenance) products available to recommend, most brokers today do not find their own stock stories; they rely on research department recommendations for ideas. Clients of these brokers then buy stocks that have such sponsorship. Other stocks are neglected.

This description of stock sponsorship is likely useful as a screening device for identifying promising stocks to buy. But remember that our primary focus here is on how to make decisions about holding or selling a stock already owned.

Think back to the dark days following the devastation of the 1987 crash. Although the Dow Jones Industrials in late 1988 had rebounded to above 2000, it was a dreary period for common stocks. Many individual investors quit the market altogether and remained too leery to return. Large numbers of those who remained had losses and refused to take any action because they felt locked in. The result was a low level of participation in individual stocks by retail investors. The minimal speculative tendency that did exist was centered on takeovers when the news seemed plausible, or when the reason to buy was based on more than hope or theory.

Starting at that time, many brokerage firms reduced staffing, and many individual brokers left the business because of declining customer activity. Even more important was the reduction in research coverage. This meant the public was far less frequently prodded to buy stocks. Those analysts who remained employed generally concentrated more heavily than ever on large-capitalization issues. The reason is clear: An analyst's time costs the firm money. And that expense must be justified by trading activity that generates commission revenue dollars. Due to their size, mot institutions prefer large-cap stocks.

Since the investing public was in a timid frame of mind following the 1987 and 1989 crashes, people traded for several years in familiar names more than in smaller, fledgling enterprises. As a result, many stocks felt narrower brokerage sponsorship than they had earlier, and some others lost all research coverage. The research department's reasoning goes: If clients will not buy it, why should we bother to recommend it? And if we do not plan to recommend it, why should we even continue to follow it? This general pattern recurs after each bear market. A similar pattern occurred after the 2002 bottom: Merrill Lynch dropped all coverage of closed-end funds; in early 2007 Prudential dropped all research coverage of common stocks.

The resulting implication for stocks in the early years after a bear market is apparent: increased urgency surrounding the hold/sell decision, especially in smaller-capitalization issues and low-priced stocks. It was widely noted (although roundly denied by brokerage firms) during and just after the 1987 crash that the trading market in many unlisted stocks virtually disappeared for a day or more. Market-making firms reduced their exposed capital, causing a lack of depth in the market. Some trading desks reportedly did not answer incoming phone calls. While the problem has become less acute with the passage of time and the broadening of automated electronic trading systems, it remains present.

The penalty suffered by low-priced issues is compounded by margin rules (and to some extent by investors' caution). Most brokerage firms extend credit (margin) of up to 50 percent of the purchase price on stocks priced at $5 per share or higher (some firms have adopted a $3 standard). When a stock declines below the stated level, it becomes worthless for purposes of calculating margin-account equity. Therefore, a price decline through these levels snowballs downhill. Such a decline triggers margin calls, causing further selling. Aware of this, market makers become wary of carrying over-the-counter (OTC) inventory, and tactically savvy investors relinquish their lower priced stocks. Further into a risk-averse climate, most brokers understandably become hesitant to call clients to suggest that they buy low-priced, more speculative stocks. In the fairly buoyant atmosphere of 2006 and mid-2007, such conditions are easily forgotten, but they return with each bear market cycle. Later, Chapter 24 discusses handling low-priced stocks in detail.

This change illustrates psycho-mechanical factors in the market that, together with fundamentals, determine stock prices and trends. Part of the immediate aftermath of each market crash or major decline is a real change in the mechanical inputs that constitute the market for individual stocks. Simply put, many stocks come to have less sponsorship than they previously had. Therefore, for any given disappointment in fundamentals (or general market hesitancy), the resulting decline in share price is likely to be more sudden at first, more substantial in extent and more extended over time than would have been the case before the latest crash or bear market.

Today, with so many millions of individuals having moved heavily into mutual funds and exchange traded funds (ETFs), the number of active, risk-taking individual investors is down. The number of brokers and analysts offering buy advice also is down. As a result, hoping against hope is more dangerous than ever. In addition to assessing whether fundamental news supports an advancing price (remember, just staying even is not good enough), also judge whether current psycho-mechanical forces in the market allow the price to advance. In a negative, cautious post-bear/crash type of environment, lean more heavily than ever toward a guilty until proven innocent attitude. The burden of positive proof must now lie on the stock. Likewise, although it seems intuitively strange, in very strong market phases expect the slightest disappointment to be met with swift and sure price punishment as performance-driven investors abandon an offending stock for perceived greener pastures.

Remember that stocks fall of their own weight, but it takes buying pressure to move them higher. One way to judge a stock's prospects is to look at recent price charts via the Internet: if the price is not in an uptrend and particularly if it has broken down, demand for the shares has weakened. If that is the case, your invested capital will shrink if you hold on in hope. Viewing a stock's price not simply as so many dollars per share but directly as a measure of your wealth will add a degree of urgency to your hold/sell deliberations.

Be coldly objective: Is there going to be buying pressure to move this stock up? Where will it originate? If likely sources of continuing buying cannot be identified (as distinguished from the reasons the stock ought to go up), a decision to hold will lose money. If there is no specific reason for ongoing optimism (on price action as well as regarding underlying fundamentals), an investor is literally hoping against hope.

In these circumstances, not to sell is to make a wager against the odds. And remember, a decision to hold is like a decision to buy again today: It is a reinvestment of your capital for another day in the same stock. Holding is more subtle and does not involve a phone call to a broker, a mouse click or a transaction cost. But that decision to hold should be a decision made consciously and actively, not a default from doing nothing or (worst of all!) of not even thinking about doing something.

The Hold Decision Ought to be a Decision

A hold decision often results from an investor's bias toward a positive outlook on the future, justified by a standard of living that has been generally rising since the Great Depression. This subtle bias can persuade Americans to take enormous personal, career and financial risks in pursuit of reward. It might well be supposed that as demographics work to gray the population, willingness to tolerate risk may decline. As this is written the 78 million Baby Boomers are in their early sixties and becoming risk averse. Such a perspective may seem foreign after a multiyear bull market, but that context will not persist forever uninterrupted.

Investing in the equity market certainly requires a degree of optimism, but that upward bias must be supported by fundamentals in the industry and company, by thoughtful personal judgment, and sometimes also by the judgment of suitable advisors. It is appropriate for an investor to take some risks in search of a stock that doubles or in search of the next Microsoft or Starbucks. But if that risk is too high relative to her personal tolerance, she should put her money into certificates of deposit (CDs) or choose a growth fund with a long-established superior record and accept a lower rate of return that comes with lower volatility.

A word about reliance on fundamentals is necessary at this point. All too often investors make the mistake of transference by projecting attributes of an industry, product or service onto a specific company. Such an error of lazy thinking is especially common when an essential service or product is involved. An example might involve telephone stocks. We cannot conceive of a world without their services' presence. But just because telephone service is necessary does not mean that any particular company providing it is guaranteed to do so profitably enough to keep paying dividends at today's rates, or even to survive. Some companies may endure fierce commodity price competition and come out as winners, but the winner may not necessarily be the one a particular investor has chosen. Work to ensure that lazy thinking about such matters does not creep into your hold/sell equation. A concrete example comes from the grocery field: Floridians still need to be fed, but that did not keep Winn-Dixie from entering Chapter 11.

Unfortunately, brokers make their living by catering to that aforementioned investor optimism, which supports the buy bias described earlier. Investors lose billions of dollars every year because of the optimism and casual thinking they bring to daily living. Money is lost not only on fraudulent too-good-to-be-true, get-rich schemes but also in the buying and too-patient holding phases of legitimate securities transactions. To offset that tendency, proper buy timing and pricing can help reduce the pressure that inevitably surrounds the selling decision. There is a natural tendency to fall victim to excitement and buy a stock when it is already hot. Only the most disciplined of traders and investors consistently refuse to buy stocks on good news, on stories, immediately when they are mentioned on TV, or on excited rallies. Instead they demonstrate self-discipline by staying with buy limits placed below those market prices prevailing at the time a buy decision is first made.

Buying too high on a burst of excitement is the first source of optimism-induced losses for traders and investors. But even greater damage results from holding onto positions because of excessive or unjustified optimism. Ironically, one major difficulty in overcoming this problem is that declining stocks occasionally do rally. An occasional burst of counter-trend strength in a weak stock does its diehard owners more mental harm than financial good.

To illustrate, suppose an investor buys a stock (Figure 7-2) at $100 a share and then watches it decline by exactly twenty cents every single day. In five weeks, the stock eases to $95, and in ten weeks it trails off to $90. The erosion is gradual but relentless. Every day this investor picks up the newspaper or goes online for a quote, and the story is always the same: down again, down twenty cents. Now imagine a second stock (Figure 7-3), also bought for $100 a share. This one also heads south, but in a different pattern, and of course this one accurately reflects true market tendencies. Some days it drops 25 or 50 cents, or even a full point. But on other days it rallies. In fact, sometimes it rebounds consistently for maybe a week or more at a time. Overall, however, its net rate of decline is the same as that of the previous steady 20-cent-daily decliner: Every five weeks it falls by the same net five points.

Figure 7.2: Constant Decliner

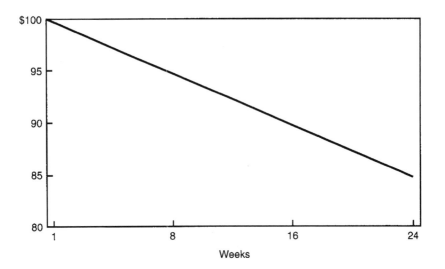

Figure 7.3: Jagged Mover

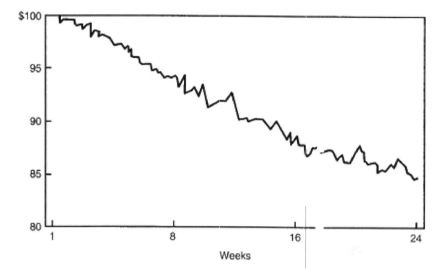

Most investors probably would have a more positive frame of mind toward this second stock-when it reaches 90 or 85 or even 80, than about the first stock, on the same dates and at the same prices. Why? Our second stock, by rallying sometimes, has provided positive feedback more recently and infinitely more often than that constant 20-cent decliner. Each time the stock turns up, a flicker of hope is kindled. The key problem is that even bad (declining) stocks have their good days (or weeks).

Not only does daily price action in the market sometimes renew hope, there can be positive fundamental news as well. A reasonably good quarterly earnings report or an optimistic brokerage recommendation will generate a renewal of optimism in the heart of any holder. Recognize, as the owner of a specific common stock, that you are not an entirely objective human being. Every positive wiggle in the stock price, every time the quote holds steady against a 35-point drop in the Dow, and every good piece of company or industry news is a source of positive psychological feedback. Anything that goes right is a vindication of your personal judgment, a welcome boost to the ego, and a source of renewed feelings of grandiosity. Thus, if the dominant price path of the stock is downward, each and every cause for renewed optimism is actually a false signal. In the cold light of reality, those false signals should be viewed as uninvited distractions from the truth rather than as rays of hope.

When hope begins to spring eternal, the investor must separate the facts of the situation from the fiction. This discrimination process must include not only the hard news background—what is actually true about the company and its industry versus what is rumor and hope—but also the equally important personal psychological environment, in which an investor has linked his or her state of mind with a company and its stock. Guard against being trapped by a personal, renewed sense of optimism when hope springs eternal.

Using Charts

The best way for an investor to calibrate his state of mind against the market is to rely on stock price charts. At the very least, a chart can be useful as an accurate road map of price-movement history. The most accessible and useful charts for the long-term picture are those included on the front side of Standard & Poor's Individual Stock Reports. A mere couple of inches provide a ten-year motion picture of stock movements. (Some analysts argue that a ten-year analysis is questionable because too much fundamental and economic background change occurs, and the data may therefore lose some relevancy.) Fortunately, the Internet age has made it easy to refocus instantly via a mouse click on any desired time window.

Without any expertise in charting techniques, even a typical eight-year-old can spot whether the stock is still in a downtrend or whether its price action has overcome negative momentum for the better. Only rarely will it be true to say: I am not sure; it seems to be right at the point of reversing. If that is true, resolve to look again in a week, and make a yes/no decision then, refusing to take another time extension.

To make this process truly useful, impose a self-discipline by writing down some decision guidelines the first time: something like: The stock seems to be right on the edge of the top of the down-channel at its present price of $39. If it moves up to at least $40, I will be convinced that it has really broken its downtrend, and I will hold. But if it fails on this move by backing down to $37.50, that will be a sign that this latest rally was a false hope. In that case I will sell at market.

Any investor who needs a nudge should mail his or her broker or some trusted friend a copy of this decision rule with a note asking to be called in about 10 days to do the follow-up chart reading jointly. Note that what is written should be confined entirely to the action of the stock and not include anything about fundamentals, feelings, cost, desired price targets or gains or losses. Focus on the factual reality of the stock's action, and give up hopeful desire.

Above all, do not back into a non-decision by default through the insidious process that consultants call analysis-paralysis. The market keeps moving with or without you. So do not wait open-endedly for just a little more news or technical confirmation. There is never going to be a final answer or a point of total closure. So exercise discipline: Make an evaluation and take action accordingly.

Figure 7.4: How Do You Feel?

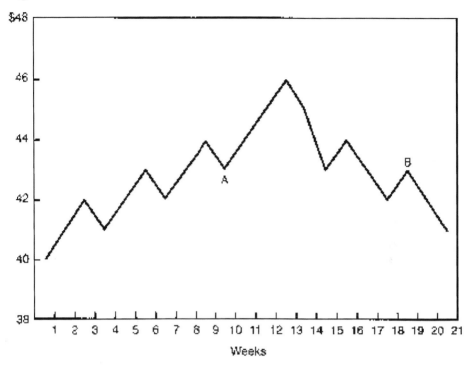

If your stock declines and then rebounds, take note of a change in personal optimism level. (See Figure 7-4.) Keep a daily log in which to record the stock's price and what feelings arise about it; then decide whether a revival of optimism for the stock is truly justified by new facts. Bear in mind that when a declining stock has rallied back to a given price level, it feels better to the owner than when it had earlier fallen that same price. The most recent directional feedback creates hope (and today has more saliency), while the earlier move produced fear. Watch the emotional difference, even at the same price. (See $43 at points A and B in the graph above as an example.)

The price you pay for a stock can get in the way of prudent selling because it influences later willingness to sell in terms of both timing and price. So buying well is important, but it is only half of the transaction. The investor or trader also must exit skillfully. Failure to buy well not only puts all the burden of possible net success on the exit execution, but it also colors the holder's thinking in ways that are damaging.

First, an investor can expect little broker support to sell if he did not buy well (i.e., cheaply). Brokers are paid on their volume of business generated And in the last few years this business plan has been under increasing pressure. In these circumstances, brokers understandably skew their efforts more strongly than ever toward clients and investment suggestions that are likely to generate transactions. As a result, calling an investor to engage in a discussion of a stock that was bought badly is not high on most brokers' to-do lists.

The Broker as Devil's Advocate

Just as a CEO is best served by subordinates who think for themselves and have the courage to speak their minds, investors are best served by a broker who acts as devil's advocate. What the client does not need is a rubber stamp to simply confirm his or her own thinking. Too many of today's brokers are salespersons rather than seasoned investment professionals, so the hunt for a good devil's advocate is difficult because most account executives, if indeed they pay much attention at all to individual stocks, fear being fired for making investors uncomfortable.

A broker's tendency to act in a consensus or status-quo mode is strongest exactly when it is least helpful: at market extremes. When the crowd is unanimous that a big rally has further to go or that the world is about to end, brokers feel the greatest pressure to conform since they are figuratively swimming in the middle of a raging tide every minute. Although it is dangerous to generalize, they often do not dare express with any conviction a heretical contrary view. Therefore, to increase your chance of market success, if indeed you do use and pay a full-service firm, select a broker who operates on a contrarian basis. That way if the impulse to act contrary to the crowd at market extremes fails to arise in you, this rare breed of broker can save the day for having been selected on his or her ability to be a disciplined contrarian. That service can make them worth their cost.

There are two significant aspects to the reluctance of brokers to sell stocks that were not first well bought: time and price. Suppose a broker's research department has advised the purchase of XYZ Widget. It is possible that an investor got on board late: Perhaps his broker paid little attention when the stock was still near its lows, not developing confidence in this analyst recommendation until after a good rally already had taken place—or the client did not become convinced until the broker had pushed it after it was already clearly going up.

The stock has risen from 30 to 40, and the client bought at 38. Now what happens if (1) the research analyst turns bearish, (2) the company's fundamentals deteriorate or (3) the overall market signals it is time to move to the sidelines? Our broker is embarrassed to report the analyst's about-face just after his client got on board, and he well may worry that the investor suspects account churning. The broker also may believe that the market is consolidating before a further rise, as many would in this case. In any event, the broker is subject to an overoptimistic buy bias, so phoning the investor about selling is not attractive to him.

Finally, our broker knows that since she just got in at 38, our investor is less prone to selling quickly at 40 than a luckier or more decisive client who entered at 32 several months earlier. Deep in his gut, the broker hopes that the stock will rally further, allowing the lower-priced (early) buyers out here or higher and getting his late-entry client a few more points' profit and more time from her entry point so that he can phone her later with better news (higher price).

The client should not expect a quick call when the rating drops from buy to hold or (rarely) sell. So one aspect of buying badly is short timing between entry and the new, less bullish recommendation. Of course if the buy was the investor's idea, the barrier is even higher: the broker will expect indignant price resistance (actually driven by a defensive ego) upon daring to call with a suggestion to sell.

The second problem is a price-driven sell, which occurs on a loss. Suppose that the investor gets in at 38 on the way to 40, and our analyst or broker is right in thinking that things have gone sour. The price is now 37 or lower and sinking. Not only does the broker feel squeamish about calling now (an easy 20/20-hindsight criticism is to say he should have called when it was at 40), more bad tendencies result from the client's own mind-set. A typical market player does not sell readily at a one-point loss, especially having first tasted a quick, two-point paper profit. So the investor compounds the broker's weakness: If one of them is inclined to sell, the other probably is not; the phone call may not be made by either party. So both the timing aspect of having entered late (bought recently) and the price aspect of having suffered a loss (bought too high) are dangers to the investor's financial health. A change of mind soon after a buy is an ego embarrassment because it inherently involves an admission of error. Taking a loss is a second blow to self-esteem. It is evident then how both the timing and price of a badly made buy render any selling decision more painful and difficult than it would be on a big gainer.

The truth is that when it is time to sell before the price goes down, it is time to sell, no matter what the timing is or what the cost at entry. But human nature somehow seemingly prevents investors from factoring out in their sell decisions a stock's initial price. And the shorter time an unsuccessful stock has been held, the less an investor is willing to switch mental gears and say sell.

What alone should determine your decision is whether this stock seems likely to go down from here and now; if it does, it should be sold promptly. The central question that should decide the hold/sell dilemma is: Would I buy this stock today? Many investors fail to ask that question at all. Rather, they fall back on hope, their initial reasoning underlying the buy, their unreached initial price target, memories of better past prices or similar factors having no realistic bearing on future potentials.

There is no denying that buying better helps most investors cash in more effectively when the right time comes. Most buying mistakes (aside from acquiring inflated hot new issues and penny stocks) occur not in buying bad stocks but in buying mediocre or even good stocks too late—again, because investors tend to be crowd followers. They wait for confirmation because they lack sufficient courage to act without a feeling of overwhelming optimism. They are most ready to jump in only sometime later, when the overall market, the individual stock, or both have already become overbought.

If a stock is held only because of perceived positive potentials for the whole market, it probably should be sold. Throughout this book, one acid-test questions appears: Would I buy today? A similarly revealing question is whether an investor would consider selling it here if he had bought better. If there is even a hint of an affirmative answer, he must recognize that cashing in is the right thing to do and that a market-irrelevant issue (personal cost price) is clouding his thinking.

Another Word about Brokerage Commissions

Throughout the preceding pages, use of a full-service, full-commission brokerage firm has been assumed. For many readers, this may not be accurate, implying a heightened need to operate in a go-it-alone mode. Investors who are self-starters and do their own research and maintain their own discipline need not pay full (advice-can-be-useful) commission rates. While stock-skilled brokers and their attention to breaking news are sometimes important, many investors prefer to forego these benefits for significantly lower transactions costs.

Those who find themselves frequently considering commission costs as a factor in hold/sell decisions should seriously consider the true, deep-discount brokerage alternative. As of early 2007, more than a dozen firms offered flat-rate commissions regardless of size and type of order if placed online, at $12.95 or less each way. An excellent source listing such choices for self-directed investors is the annual January issue of the AAII Journal (see Appendix for address and telephone). A striking example of the mind-freeing power of low commissions costs is this: If you pay $10 for 500 shares, your round-trip cost, at $20, is four cents per share. In that context, the cost to change your mind, or to buy a little insurance or peace of mind, is so small as to be irrelevant; your only remaining point of mental debate is which way the stock seems likely to move next. And that is exactly as it should be.

Forget Your Cost Price

Traders and investors alike unknowingly attach enormous subjective importance to their own cost price in a stock. When this personal history takes on its a life of its own, it colors future thinking. Awareness of this historical cost-price point is a subtle, powerful, and dangerous influence on a selling decision. Therefore, we will next explore and seek to correct such thinking.

Humbling though it might be, the first reality that must be established regarding history is the total insignificance of any one investor's purchase event. In the markets of the mid-late 2000s decade, on average about 1.6 billion shares are changing hands daily on the New York Stock Exchange alone. Similar or larger trading volumes are seen daily in NASDAQ's listings. A 300- or 1,000-share purchase, which may be a financial event of note and an emotionally charged decision for an individual investor, is completely lost in that avalanche of daily Wall Street activity. Nevertheless, the historic accident of one's buy price predictably becomes psychological baggage of great personal magnitude. Almost always, its effect is detrimental to the eventual execution of a successful sale. (A successful sale does not necessarily mean a profit. It can, under some circumstances, mean a deftly timed exit that prevents a loss or a greater loss from developing or that frees capital for some other more productive use.)

A good sale point is a time/price combination on the stock's historical chart that, when viewed in hindsight, evokes the reaction: Wow, that sure was a good exit point right there! The successful sale point is, therefore, defined only in terms of what occurs after it in time-not at all in terms of the historical fact of any one owner's earlier purchase price.

If a stock is to collapse from 50 to 30 in the next month, a sale at or around 50 now is a good sale for anyone, regardless of whether the stock was bought at 52, 48, 75, 20 or 50.10. This is a key point, so it bears re-emphasis: A good price or time at which to sell a stock is defined by what happens to that stock after your sale occurs and has nothing to do with any prior event (the purchase date or price). A good sale is advantageous in hindsight, regardless of whether it closes out a small or large gain, breaks even, or nets a loss. It is a good sale if it sidesteps a subsequent decline or if it avoids a loss of money's time value (a prolonged sideways market or a period of serious relative underperformance; see Chapter 10 for more detail on this concept.)

All too often, however, the irrelevance of an investor's cost price is not reflected in the way she views her holdings. She has in mind that she owns 200 Home Depot at 36; in fact, she simply owns 200 Home Depot. But her cost price per share, unfortunately, has become a figurative line in the sand and, therefore, an historic hook. When the stock is above there, she feels smart, superior and vindicated (increasingly so, as the margin of paper profit widens). But when a stock trades below cost, our investor feels insulted, cheated, ashamed, stubborn or deprived. Ideas of celebration or bragging have disappeared. The disappointed holder can retreat to thoughts that the market is not as smart as I am but soon will realize its folly and rebound.

When this stock's price is again later at her cost point, that coincidence can trigger any of four conditions:

1.   If the stock has recovered from an interim decline, she feels relief and ego vindication: relief because the pain of having suffered a reversal has been alleviated (ignoring the time value of money, of course); vindication because once again she can look into the mirror and know she was right.

2.   When price rallies back up to her buying level, she experiences excitement: Now the action is really going to get started. If the stock happens to hang

around her personal cost-price level for quite some time, each return to that level is likely to trigger some degree of boredom or frustration. But equally, prolonged trading at her cost level is likely to reinforce in her mind the concept that such a price is totally reasonable, represents demonstrably solid value, and is deserved by the stock (or, more dangerously, by the holder personally). But unfortunately such cathexis, or strength of feelings about a price (in this case, created by frequent reinforcement), is likely to intensify our investor's later difficulty in selling if price moves lower. Conditioned to expecting a given price level and holding out for its re-attainment, an investor can become fixed by her own perception. (For the technical analysts, this is why a broken support level later becomes a resistance level: Get-even sellers are lined up there!)

3. The opposite emotional reaction occurs when a stock once bought has risen but then subsequently falls back to one's cost-price level. The greater the price distance of the now retraced move, the more intense is our investor's emotional reaction. There is a very empty feeling of having given it all back—a sense of sadness and emotional emptiness or loss that anyone who has gambled away a temporary profit will remember all too well. The primary reaction is one of shame or disappointment with one's indecisiveness or lack of discipline. But a stubbornness also takes hold. One recalls previously reached high levels and believes that the company's stock deserved to sell at those quotes and therefore should return to them. Our investor then resolves to hold on for that rally, even though it is one merely fantasized out of hope or desperation.

4. Paradoxically, as an alternative, that decline back to cost price may actually plant the subconscious seeds of resignation to loss. Having done so badly by failing to sell at a profit, our investor begins to feel maybe he is doomed to having a bad experience with this stock anyway. Of course, depending on the size and tenderness of the ego involved, the now-disappointed investor may try to cover up feelings of self-criticism over failure to nail down that earlier paper profit. He can blame it all on bad luck, on a broker or an advisory letter, on the overall market, or even on some outside force.

Therefore, be very wary of the psychological trap that the memory of cost can create. The greatest single problem it creates is a mental line in the sand: the dividing line between gain and loss, between wisdom and foolishness, between celebration and remorse. Remember that an individual trade is an insignificant grain of sand on the market's beach. To quote an old cliché, the stock does not know you own it!

When Might Cost Price be Relevant?

There are only four cases in which price paid actually may have some significance in the market at a later date. But even in these instances, that price's importance is totally coincidental and is not caused by or related to a personal purchase action. What these four circumstances have in common is that they each involve price levels to which large numbers of other investors attach meaning. It is those large numbers, not your participation in the equation, which might make this price have some significance.

The first significant price level at which an investor coincidentally or accidentally may establish a cost occurs when a primary or secondary offering takes place. That level, by definition, involves a large number of shares and a large number of other investors. If a new issue comes to market at $22, that level becomes the mental mark in the sand for thousands of individuals—a win/loss inflection point. Such a point later may be viewed as the level to get out and get even, as a trigger point for a stop-loss order, or as a point where some investors may double up. Whichever kind of reaction a crowd has in relation to this price level, the historical pricing level of a primary or secondary offering can thus have a significant effect on future price action.

An investor may buy into that offering or, just coincidentally, buy at some other time but at the same price. While the price he paid actually does have some significance in the market, in this case it has nothing to do with his few hundred shares. It is the distribution at that price of perhaps several million shares to many investors that matters; they all attach weight to that price and are likely to take buy or sell actions related to its recurrence.

The second event that can make any price important is the so-called price gap. Much has been written by market technicians about the theory and importance of chart gaps in the history of a stock's price action. However, our point here is not to arbitrate repeat or arbitrate that debate.

Briefly summarized, the market lore of price gaps is that all gaps tend to be closed. Actually, it is probably more accurate to say that upside gaps (except in cases of successful takeovers) tend to be retraced and filled. Some downside gaps are caused by such powerful negative fundamental news that they literally may never be filled. So do not be lured into a false sense of optimism about all gaps being filled. The company might not recover, and, in some cases, it may eventually disappear following a devastating chain of events triggered by whatever news caused the downside gap. As this was written in spring-2007, two sub-prime mortgage lenders seemed in possible danger of collapse as loans started going bad. Corporate survival will have overriding impact, not the fact that a downside price-chart gap existed between any two given prices.

The point about gaps is this: Whether or not an investor is a technician or believes that price gaps are important technical phenomena, large numbers of other traders and investors active in the market undeniably do hold that viewpoint. Their collective actions or inactions, based on their beliefs, will have an effect on market-price action. So the gap in price itself becomes important in later market behavior. Say an investor buys right at the moment the gap developed. While the market, in this case, does attach significance to his price, it is for reasons unconnected to him. It is like having a January 1st birthday.

Round numbers also may be significant price points, but for reasons that bear little objective relation to rational investment theory. In the same way that a primary offering or a gap price level creates a memory in the minds of investors, a round number can become a trigger for action. Many recall saying: If Google ever corrects back to 400 (or 350), I am definitely going to buy some. Or: If stock X hits 25, I will take my profit there. In the case of lower-priced issues, it is any full-dollar figure that becomes a target. When large numbers of people act on these targets, such price levels actually do become significant because of bids and asks that cluster at or very near them. Again, however, it is not because of any single investor's 200 shares coincidentally acquired right there.

Finally, any of several technical chart-price patterns may render a particular price level significant. Tops and bottoms of channels, tops of rising triangles, the apex or breakout point of a triangle, a neckline in a head-and-shoulders formation, or that price at which multiple tops or bottoms have occurred can all become significant price points. It is randomly possible that your own purchase price level might coincide, whether it be established before or after those events. Subsequent market action may call renewed attention to this particular price level, fixing it even more firmly in mind as important. But its relevance derives only from that price level's larger technical importance, created by many other participants (some of whom do believe in charts) who attach meaning to that level.

Therefore, avoid building a strategy on an imaginary foundation that your personal price is important to the market just because it feels important to you. In addition to defining the very real (at least pre-commission) dividing line between profit and loss, one's cost price sets up several other private mental constructs that have no operative importance in the marketplace.

Misusing Personal Cost Price

What these constructs all have in common is their being linked to your cost price as a starting point—an accidental moment that then becomes subjectively important history. Personal cost forms the baseline for some calculation that exists only in your head. For example, your goal may be to make five points, 15 percent or 20 percent before commissions, or an ambitious 50 percent gain or even a double. Or you might set either a mental or an actual stop-loss point designed to limit a loss to some predetermined amount in points or percentage. All these formulae share the commonality of a personal entry-price level. But the market is not conscious of any such formula!

Figure 7.5: Locked in a Price Channel

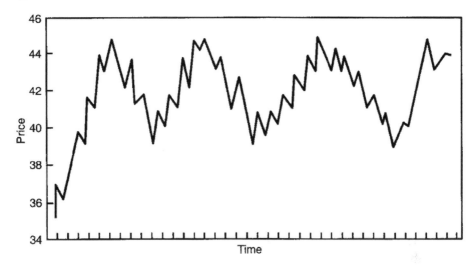

The stock's chart pattern itself defines reasonable resistance and support levels that relate to recent or long-term past history but do not in any way have cause-and-effect ties to any individual's particular entry point. For example, suppose that some investor's stock is locked in a lengthy and well-defined price channel between 39 and 45 (see Figure 7-5). Assume he is lucky or smart enough to have bought at 40. By setting an arbitrary upside goal of 15 percent above cost (before or after commissions), this individual will be frustrated by repeated retreats from the 45 level, just about a point short of his personal target of 46. If, on the other hand, he sets a 10 percent stop-loss error margin, his trigger will be 36, or three full points below a very obvious breakdown level of 39 on a decline.

Setting any formula based on one's entry price could easily be self-defeating in this case. Triggers should be based on the chart's evidence regarding realistic near-term price targets and significant support or breakdown levels, or on reasonable longer-term fundamental valuation measures, not in relation to some accident of personal cost. Here is another reason not to base a stop-loss order on a rigid percentage away from personal cost. Suppose you believe in setting a 10 percent limit on losses. Selling at whatever price that implies would make the concept of bargain hunting at the same price appear wrong. If it is correct (showing patience and discipline) to buy down at a certain price, selling down at that price must be wrong. In Figure 7-5, a protective stop at $39.60 to protect a poorly-timed purchase at $44 would be an example.

A personal entry point and any formulae it generates are not as relevant as the stock's own demonstrated price history and fundamental valuation parameters. Those are totally unrelated to your individual cost. Keeping these psychological and factual perspectives in mind requires deliberate suppression of ego, which may feel humbling when first implemented. But that effort may actually prove easier than what is theoretically more helpful but in practice seems virtually impossible: Literally forgetting what was paid and letting the stock's future action alone indicate when and where to sell.

In summary, the memory-becomes-history syndrome based on personal cost can be highly detrimental to later execution of a good sale. Cost-price history causes a host of psychological reactions to subsequent price action in the stock, most of which battle against a good sale decision and most of which are probably quite unrelated to what the market collectively perceives about that stock.

CHAPTER 8

Understand That You Sell the Stock, Not the Company

Keys for Successful Selling

◆ Mentally Separate the Stock and the Company

◆ Realize That Price Equals the Changing Level of Esteem

◆ Clearly Understand the Different Meanings of Price and Value

To legitimize becoming a long-term holder, an investor must find a comfort zone; there is none better than fundamentals, she will say. When price behavior in an intended shorter-term position becomes unexpectedly negative, the investor rationalizes a flip from the technical to the fundamental orientation: It is a really good company with great R&D so its stock is bound to come back. In fact, the more one knows about a company and the stronger the ties that are felt with it, the more danger there is of switching from a trader/selling mode to an investor/holding mode when a price setback occurs. A switch of investment objectives is a major warning signal; alert, well-disciplined investors must take pains to guard against any such switches. Differentiating the company from its stock is a key skill that will help.

Separating the Stock and the Company

In the same way that weak decision-making causes a trader to become an investor (collector) by default, another confusion can creep in that just as easily prompts holding: the mistaken idea that the stock is the same thing as its company. Although a stock certificate legally does represent some fractional share in the corporation, a company and its stock should never be considered identical.

When a holder's position begins to erode, by default he often silently changes tactical identity from trader to long-term holder. What he has done is mistakenly associate the stock with the virtues and strengths of the underlying company. This is a subtle but critical mistake that investors must strenuously guard against. A further danger arises when our trader then fails to perceive that such confusion of identities has taken place, for this lack of perception only reduces any chance of correcting the situation.

No stock goes up forever, no matter how strong its issuing company. Even during a raging bull market, not every stock price advances. Among those that do score increases over a year or more, none progress in price at a steady rate without interim fluctuations or setbacks. Sometimes even the greatest growth stocks experience meaningful interim declines. While a given company may prosper consistently over time—such as a McDonald's or Coca-Cola with their lengthy near-perfect records of consecutive quarterly earnings advances—its stock often acts independently in the short to medium term. The reasons are usually completely unrelated to company fundamentals; they can include an adverse trend in the general market, temporary factors such as group leadership rotations or simply a short-term correction of an overly exuberant earlier advance.

Therefore, a stock and its issuing company often do not move in harmony: There are times when a firm's business prospers but its shares decline in price; at other times the stock's price can even be advancing, seemingly against all logic, when fundamentals are in a pause or even a brief decline.

Traders most often tend to equate the stock with the company when its share price has fallen since purchase. The trader then becomes an investor through the back door by falling back on fundamentals or generalized faith in the company. Seeking justification for the decision to hold rather than sell, our investor now waxes enthusiastic about the company's virtues (or even its industry's great prospects) rather than focusing on prospects for what is most important to making a profit: likely ongoing stock-price performance.

Usually the symptoms of this misguided switch in investment status are rear-view-mirror in nature. Examples are: They have reported 37 consecutive quarters of rising sales and earnings. Or: You know, they've moved up to number so-and-so in the Fortune 500 now. But, in actuality, something clearly has gone wrong because earnings, reputation and Fortune ranking have not helped the stock to keep rising since purchase.

An even more dangerous influence is a relationship between the stockholder and the corporation. Emotional ties (such as current or pre-retirement employment, enjoyment of company products or warm feelings about its community involvement) are difficult to keep in perspective. Exactly when the time is most critical, such loyalty ties tend to pop up and stand in the way of an objectively prudent tactical sale of the stock. When a stock is up, we praise its technical strength and/or our wisdom in buying and holding it; after a decline, we seek fundamental anchors in support of holding on.

The difficulty of keeping stock and company conceptually separated is compounded when the shareholder's ownership position has been publicized to others. If people around you know that you own stock in your or a relative's employer, you feel in a an even stronger bind when it is time to sell the stock. This psychological complication is avoidable, but only with deliberate effort. It is also a strong reason for never divulging personal investment positions.

Price Equals the Changing Level of Esteem

Another subtle but critical factor in an investor's decision to sell or hold -- or, in this context, to separate the company and its stock—is awareness of some common terminology used when buying. A broker or investor might casually say: I think we ought to own a piece of Microsoft. Or: Our General Electric really has treated us well. Buying with this personalizing attitude, namely, of owning some of the company and its essence, subconsciously encourages the investor to identify with that company as an emotional partner/owner. In an increasingly depersonalized and fast-changing world, we all tend to seek affiliations. Downsizing has taught employees to reject old-time concepts of loyalty to companies; shareholders need pay no greater duty of allegiance, especially when international competition and emerging technologies now change even major companies' prospects faster than ever before. Bygone favorites such as Polaroid, Xerox, Ford and the old AT&T are prime examples of the pain of change.

If an investor cannot sharply distinguish his separate personal identity from his position as shareholder and thus somehow partner, that holding is essentially pre-ordained to become a long-term collector's item since it is effectively already adopted as part of one's family. It is critical, then, always to focus on the concept that a stock is purchased in anticipation of taking advantage of the expected rising esteem level at which other investors hold the company; you are merely a passive rider on the stock's price coattails and do not truly purchase a share of active, participatory ownership in the sense of buying into a contract programming or architectural partnership or some other active business venture.

In reality, a company may reach new heights of prosperity while you as individual stockholder own a bit of it, but you still can lose money. Why? You and other temporary owners have bought merely rights to cash in on whatever changing level of perception other people (taken as a whole, the market) may hold about that company. They may like it less tomorrow because of buying in too late (too high), because interest rates are rising (making all equities less attractive relative to bonds or Treasury bills); because of adverse public opinion about its products or industry; because of press publicity over high executive salaries; because general corporate reputation might deteriorate; because investment tastes shift in favor of other industries; or because of a rising fear of recession. Or the overall stock market may be declining from a too-high prior level. Other investors collectively may be right or wrong about the company over the short to medium term. And you as an individual may prove correct, while the majority are incorrect, about fundamentals.

As Benjamin Graham noted in *The Intelligent Investor*, markets act as voting machines in the short term but in the long run function as weighing machines. Thus, actions and opinions of the crowd determine share price in the short to medium term, which is the most important factor because that share price determines whether you have a gain or a loss, and when. So buy and sell not just on personal judgment of a company behind a stock but on your studied assessment of what other investors think of the company and how that thinking seems likely to change. A great company can be a bad stock (for trading or investing) if bought at just any price without regard to reasonable value.

In the same way, making investment decisions involves mentally and emotionally separating the facts—or the facts as they are perceived or expected to be from what the market (i.e., the collective opinion of investors) believes and will come to believe. The company may, indeed, continue to be profitable and to grow. But when or if it falls out of investor favor, no matter how valid or invalid the reasons for that change in collective esteem, its stock price will suffer. In the 2002-2007 period, this halved the P/E ratio for Wal-Mart while earnings per share (EPS) suffered. The more a company is loved, the sharper will be its stock-price fall when that infatuation ends.

To determine whether now is the time to hold or to sell, focus on changes in perception rather than on long-term fundamentals. An investor can be dead-on right about fundamentals. But if the market collectively decides that it no longer is willing to pay as much for this company's reputation or earnings, its share price heads south. Eventually, an individual's logic may be vindicated again as value reasserts itself and other investors resume their willingness to pay for it. But in that interim, the individual is going to suffer a loss for fighting the tape.

Prices on the tape reflect people's reactions and perceptions and beliefs translated into buying and selling decisions; they do not reflect the truth about a company's fundamentals. So keep in mind that the company and its stock are distinct. You ought to buy a stock out of willingness to bet that others will pay a higher price because of whatever good reasons you perceive in advance. Purchase is a bet based on your judgments of market perception, company reputation and collective psychology; it should not be perceived as acquisition of a piece of the company. Stocks are best used when bought and sold for profit, not when held as nostalgic or affiliation talismans. As in Figure 8-1, holding a stock near interim high point A bets on your fortitude at D and wastes time until B when future value will catch up with today's overoptimistic price; the latter also assumes untarnished future business success. And if you are not adept enough to liquidate near A, how likely Is it that you will have become mentally sharper at point C?

Being able to keep a company and its stock strictly separate in your mind has become ever more critical in recent years. Excellent companies such as Lowe's, GE, or PepsiCo may suffer single-quarter earnings shortfalls against analyst estimates or might even experience actual interim declines in earnings. As will be discussed in Chapter 9, such minor stumbles usually call down immediate and massive institutional selling. While such selling may be vastly disproportionate to any long-term true fundamental meaning of the triggering event, it does signal a coming period of more cautious appraisal by major investors. If you maintain the mental agility to view a stock as merely an opinion barometer because you have separated it from the company's fundamentals, you will be able to sell without costly hesitation. Fail to differentiate a company and its stock in your mind and you will have great difficulty over separation and

Figure 8.1: Market Timing Versus Holding Long Term

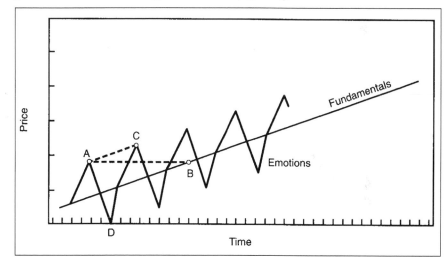

loyalty issues and will be less successful in your investment moves. Figure 8-1 could have substituted the word esteem for the usual price scale on its Y axis. Unless you plan on holding forever, which will produce merely average or even sub-par returns, you need to buy and sell. Swings in market psychology drive prices to fluctuate around true long-term value (if only the latter could ever be known accurately today!). Another way of viewing these price swings is to think of them as changes in the consensus of esteem given to a company by all investors taken together. When esteem runs up above reasonable valuation of fundamentals, price will eventually correct downward to redress that temporary mistake. Above-average profits accrue to those who capture such positive differentials of esteem minus reality. (Similarly, on the buying side of the equation, handsome profit opportunities can be captured when reality minus esteem is a positive number, meaning that the stock in more common terms is temporarily undervalued by the market of opinion.)

When you sell a company's stock, no one else except your broker (who, these days, might very well be a computer!) needs to know, unless you are an insider or 5 percent holder required to file a Form 13-D with the SEC. The company is an inanimate object; it will not be hurt since it will not feel any sense of desertion or disloyalty on your part. By keeping a company and all it represents to the outside world clearly differentiated in your mind from your personal ownership of its stock, you will free yourself to sell without looking back when price rises to your objective or when fundamentals change and render your prior price objective now invalid. Yes, you certainly should want to buy stock in good/strong companies rather than feeble/failing ones since that difference will raise your odds of cashing in on profitable price moves. You should view the world's collective esteem for a company as something to take advantage of rather than to fall in love with and be enveloped by.

CHAPTER 9

Adopt Survival Tactics for the Institutional Jungle

Keys for Successful Selling

◆ Survey Today's Investment Scene: It Is a Jungle Out There!

◆ Learn How to Survive in the Institutional Jungle

◆ Take Smart Tactical Actions to Avoid Being Trampled

In times past many market analysts, advisors and investors considered large holdings by institutional investors a positive factor in evaluating a stock. If those big players like it, such logic said, it must be good. Perhaps that thinking has some value in terms of longer-term fundamentals. However, this chapter makes a case for viewing high institutional ownership as a distinct threat to near-term price stability. And price means wealth to any stock's owners, so sharp, sudden price risk should be taken very seriously. When a stampede gets going, the smallest creatures are at risk of being trampled—unless they are able to move very fast.

Surveying Today's Investment Scene: It is a Jungle Out There!

The past several decades, and particularly those years since 1987, have seen increasing dominance of securities markets by institutions. Today mutual funds get much of the attention, but insurance companies and pension plans also remain major factors. And beginning in the 1990s hedge funds—with $1.3 trillion of assets in 2007—have become major market movers due to their size and fast turnover. As illustrated in the accompanying data (Table 9-1), derived from information compiled by Lipper Inc. and the New York Stock Exchange (NYSE), assets controlled by mutual funds investing in stocks have grown nearly 170-fold, from $37 billion In December 1975 to $6.37 trillion as of December 2006. In the same 31 years, the value of stocks listed on the New York Stock Exchange (to be sure, no longer the uniquely dominant trading market it once was) grew less than sevenfold to just over $15 trillion. With more baby boomers coming into their primary asset-accumulation years and also realizing that they must invest to avoid financial disaster in retirement, market participation will rise. Millions of these boomers are not especially interested in the market and/or are afraid to handle serious money on their own. Thus, institutional control over assets and trading in the stock market will likely continue to grow.

Table 9.1: Rising Importance of Institutions

Year	Value of All NYSE-Listed Stocks ($ Billions)	Value of All Stocks Held by Equity Mutual	Ratio
1975	885	37	1:25
1980	1,200	49	1:24
1985	1,950	124	1:16
1990	2,700	263	1:10
1995	5,700	1,260	1:4.5
2000	11,500	3,940	1:2.9
2006	15,400	6,370	1:2.4

The NYSE estimates that institutional activity accounts for about 70 percent of the value traded on an average day. Such dominance on the trading floor presents both a problem and an opportunity for individual investors. In a nutshell, the problem is that institutional buying and selling de-stabilizes the market, especially since many large investors are increasingly short-term in orientation, often chasing price or earnings momentum rather than focusing on long-term value. Lately, the slightest deviation from analysts' consensus estimates triggers major and rapid price movement. Usually such price adjustments are more extreme on the downside than on the upside, primarily because fear is a stronger motivator than greed.

Yet another and relatively new factor that tends to increase block trading and thus raise price volatility is the huge post-2000 growth of equity exchange traded funds (ETFs). These held $461 billion of equity assets as of May 2007. The recent creation of bear-side and leveraged ETFs can only increase volatility and thereby trigger more-frequent extreme episodes of both fear and greed. Likewise the rules allowing shorting of most ETFs without an uptick!

This environment presents individuals with three choices. First, as millions have already done, they can abandon individual stocks and place their money in mutual funds and/or ETFs. This route, of course, merely makes institutional dominance even greater. Program trading, widely publicized as an alleged cause or at least an aggravator of the sudden October 1987 meltdown, was an excuse for many to take exactly this approach. The rapid May-June 2006 correction had similar results. Such investors add to the problem, but who can blame them individually if they are basically passive and fearful in their investment lives?

A second choice is to ignore the whole problem and let the market do as it will in the short as well as longer term. Here, an investor admits that he can not predict where institutional lightning will strike next but still feels or concludes that ownership of some great (highly institutionally held) growth stock is nevertheless a necessity. Choosing to attempt no protective action is the equivalent of deciding to grin and bear it. Intellectually this means agreeing to ride out fierce storms as they actually occur, which may prove quite difficult emotionally.

A third choice attempts to break the cycle of victimization for individual investors. It involves knowledge, preparation and a proactive approach rather than passive acceptance of short-term price damage compounded by, even worse, personal reactive panic selling. This approach requires independence of mind, decisiveness and, at times, a degree of healthy suspicion about how Wall Street works. Here, an investor includes in his or her assessment of every stock its exposure to being ravaged at the whim of institutional jungle beasts.

Increasing, even accelerating, dominance of daily trading by huge players makes choosing action rather than passive victim-hood a growing and urgent necessity for individuals holding stocks directly. Those unwilling to do the preparation and work, and then actually take necessary action (by placing sell orders!), would arguably be much better served by abandoning individual stockholding for mutual funds than by remaining involved directly in stocks. Why? Funds move much less erratically than do individual stocks and therefore are less likely to generate in their individual owners emotional reactions such as selling in panic when institutional dumping causes sharp and sudden price damage. Index funds clearly are among the main beneficiaries of individual investors' decisions to be passive.

How to Survive in the Institutional Jungle

Knowledge, evaluation, and action are the three essentials for surviving and prospering in today's institutionally dominated markets. Critically important facts to know are as follows:

◆ The proportion of your company's stock held by institutional investors;

◆ the normal level of trading volume (especially in comparison with institutional positions);

◆ expected timing of the next earnings announcement; and

◆ strength of the stock's recent performance, and the implied level of expectations.

Knowing institutional ownership is one item absolutely integral to a buy decision because it helps define price risk. Three readily accessible information sources here are Standard & Poor's *Security Owner's Stock Guide*, individual company reports by S&P (commonly known as tear sheets), and *The Value Line Investment Survey*. Knowing precisely updated levels of ownership by the elephants of Wall Street is not necessary; 60 percent and higher should act as a sign that strong attention must be paid. As percentages rise into the 80 percent to 90 percent range, risk of price volatility becomes extremely great. Table 9.2 is a listing of early-2007 institutional holdings in selected well-known stocks.

Average trading volume is also important since it must be related to institutional ownership. Keeping those annual stock and mutual funds table sections published in early January by The Wall Street Journal and by many major-city newspapers will provide a handy source of trading-volume information. With markets open 252 trading days annually, calculating average daily volume is easy since multiplying an annual total by 0.004 (four-tenths of 1 percent) can be done readily. Again, an S&P monthly stock guide provides a fair approximation because it tracks monthly trading volume (divide by 20 as a fair daily approximation, but realize that this source is based on a statistically less robust one-month sample). Even more prone to error is a quick reference to a weekend newspaper, which provides an even smaller, although very recent, data sample. Those using computerized databases can readily find volume information for longer periods as desired. One excellent example is BigCharts.com, which displays 50- and 200-day average volumes under its printer-friendly chart option.

Table 9.2: Institutional Holdings, 2007

Stock	Percent
Avon Products	86
BankAmerica	60
ConocoPhillips	74
duPont	64
Exxon Mobil	50
Federal Express	72
General Electric	53

Stock	Percent
Humana	83
Intel	57
Johnson & Johnson	63
Kimberly Clark	76
Lowe's	80
Medtronic	75
Nabors Industries	74
Office Depot	88
Procter & Gamble	58
Questar	69
Reynolds American	65
Sears Holdings	90
Travelers	84
Union Pacific	79
Valero Energy	68
Whole Foods Market	79
Xerox	80
Yum Brands	81
Zimmer Holdings	76

Institutional positions must now be related to average trading volume. Suppose an adverse news development, including a company missing the quarterly earnings estimates that analysts have convinced themselves are accurate, should occur. Suppose that perhaps just 5 percent of the institutional shares should be sold in response to bad news. How much stock would that throw into the market, and how many times an average day's volume would that represent? The higher the number of average days' volume, the more likely a stock is to drop severely and sharply for several days. You should not own a stock unless you have done this calculation and envisioned this scenario. It is not theoretical; on the contrary, it is all too common! Institutional money managers are short-term oriented and are personally and competitively driven to perform. Unless professed and practicing contrarians, they sell stocks at the slightest hint of trouble they believe may render those stocks continued under-performers in the few months ahead—and a few months is long term in too many of their views!

Not only must our proactive investor know that important ratio of institutional holdings versus average volume, he or she must also know exactly when quarterly earnings are due for publication. Twenty to 45 calendar days after quarter's end is the common range, but that is hardly accurate enough. Value Line, S&P and other similar sources publish due dates. Except for annual numbers (which require an audit and thus take longer), each quarter's results are usually published about 90 days apart. An electronic news database will reveal the prior quarter's date. To be most precise, phone the company's investor relations office (usually a free 800 number) and simply ask.

The final crucial puzzle piece is how well your stock has performed lately. Quite simply, the greater its recent price strength, the larger the price risk if bad news occurs. Strong short-term price action means positive anticipation is high, so anything short of excellent and expected news will not do. In bull markets (such as in 1998-1999 and 2003-2007), investors impatiently and greedily require continued and preferably rapid gains. Disappointment will not be tolerated; any stock failing to maintain momentum is thrown overboard for the newer, hotter group or concept. As an example of how institutions produce a herd mentality, one major Midwestern-based mutual fund requires its portfolio managers to sell 100 percent of any stock immediately if its quarterly earnings undershoot the in-house analyst's estimate by even $0.01/share. This is an equivalent of shooting first and asking questions later. Their selling will, of course, prompt liquidations by aggressive fund managers whose computer models detect a reversal in price momentum. This, sadly but truly, is the jungle in which individual stock investors must operate at the risk of being trampled.

The listing of crucial factors given earlier does not include what the consensus quarterly earnings estimate is. The reason is that this detail matters little if at all in an absolute sense. Falling short is a crime punishable by massive selling, no matter what the target was. Those interested can find estimated earnings per share (EPS) in Value Line, on S&P tear sheets or in many electronic databases and several chart services. Extremely strong expected percentage gains probably raise both the odds of failure and its consequences. But any level of earnings estimate, if not achieved, will be met with swift and sharp price declines.

An individual investor need not know what the estimate was; market price reaction will immediately reveal whether reported earnings made the grade (or whether management issued some caution for the future). But of course when market reaction is visible, it is already too late to avoid major wealth damage. Thus, knowledge of the estimate is less relevant than preparation for the possible consequences of failure. By analogy, it does not matter exactly what kind of high winds are approaching your property: a hurricane, cyclone or tornado. You can expect damage if in you are their path, and you must prepare your defenses, including having an evacuation plan and proper insurance in place.

Taking Action to Avoid Being Trampled

As any consultant will say, all the information available is worthless unless analyzed and acted upon. How critically true this is in investing. Knowing how heavily exposed a stock is to possible ravages from institutional herd selling will only generate bad headaches unless you take remedial action. The worst action to take when an EPS disappointment makes the big players run for cover usually is to join them. Their selling creates concentrated maximum downward pressure on price and, therefore, peak emotional strain on holders. Unless you monitor your stocks full time during every trading session, you will be late when you do see the EPS and price-change news. If you place market orders after the bad news, you are likely to be making an emotionally driven tactical mistake by joining the crowd led by institutional sellers. The best course is to take anticipatory action based on your previously described analysis. (Chapter 26 covers in more detail how to assess the seriousness and impact of bad news and what holding/selling strategies are implied.)

Four courses of action are available. In a bull market, wherein expectations are already high, mild positive earnings surprises in major, highly institutionally held stocks tend to generate little upside price action. Everyone was already on board, both mentally and financially. In that context, the most prudent course arguably could be to sell such stocks at market on any rally shortly before quarterly-earnings due dates. This means stepping aside to see what happens. For those using deep-discount brokers, this tactic is very inexpensive and provides peace of mind as well as capital insurance. It amounts to clearing out of the jungle just before a predictable stampede season. On the whole, and especially with low commissions, it represents a lot more loss to be saved than gain possibly missed.

A second course of action is to place a stop-loss order fairly close to the current price shortly before the week when the company is scheduled to report its earnings. Stop placement is discussed in Chapter 23, so it will not be covered in detail here. Basically, the purpose of placing this stop is to guard against the greatest possible amount of potential damage in case those wild animals become unhappy. Here you should be less concerned about the virtues of staying in a good long-term position (a looser stop) than about preventing loss (a tighter placement). A temporary but closely placed stop can easily be removed after the EPS news, assuming no damage was inflicted. Good placement would be at the height of the recent uptrend line, at the price support zone, or down just a point or so.

A stop-loss order placed too far away provides little protection against loss and may actually sell you out very near the short-term bottom, entirely defeating your purpose. Two rules to follow in placing such EPS-time stops: (1) Do not use a stop-limit order because, in a fast decline, you will be passed by and thus your order will have been useless and (2) do not play too cozy a game in timing your order entry. If the company reports after the close or before the open, it may already be too late to enter an order since a bad report will result in a deep downside gap opening, and the damage will already be done. Therefore, have your order in several days ahead of that expected announcement date.

But here a major caveat is in order, relating to an unavoidable downside of using stops. Stops are great if they get you out early in a downdraft during a session, when prices are fairly continuous. But a stop can backfire if bad news comes during a trading halt or overnight. In that case, your stop may well be hit, but your execution price may be nowhere near your stop level. So again, being completely out of the stock before the news occurs is safest.

A third approach, and one advocated in Chapters 23 on order placement, is always to have a sell order in place above market. This has the virtue of selling you out on strength rather than on weakness. Thus, it would be wise to have a sell order placed at a price above current levels. Where? Just below the upper line of a rising channel or just below the level where selling resistance has previously been found. Do not be greedy for that infamous last dime: A half point or so is very little to leave on the table if you are being sold out well on a good upward price move. While above-market sells are generally preferable to stop-loss orders, in the case of quarterly EPS-risk time, the latter also must be in place. If your brokerage firm will not allow both orders on the books simultaneously, place an against-the-box, short-selling order above and a stop-loss below, both at technically important levels as just described.

A fourth way to handle this quarterly problem with heavily institutionally owned stocks involves using options. Several good books are available describing options strategies, so no such detail will be attempted here. You need to be prepared; open an options account and sign all necessary forms in advance. It never hurts to have such facilities in place even if they are never used (the same can be said of a margin account). When a price emergency is already occurring, it is far too late to begin options paperwork! The two choices are buying a put option with a strike price below current market (to reduce your premium outlay) and selling a call option with a modestly in-the-money strike, which will get you some premium earned but not risk much loss in case moderately unexpected good news follows. Once the outcome is known for a few days, closing out the put option is generally advisable since time will erode its remaining premium. In addition, bad news will put maximum temporary selling pressure on the stock, raising a put's value and increasing the chance that the next move will be a mild price recovery.

Summary: Beware of the Stampede

This chapter has warned of the occasional acute price pressure likely in institutionally dominated stocks and has provided lists of necessary information to gather and analyze in advance. It has also described order-placement strategies for protecting capital. As you first force and then allow yourself to sell more frequently, the process will, over time, come to feel easier and more natural. Buying back is nothing to cause shame. Often a round-trip commission (particularly with a deep-discount broker) is inexpensive insurance against the injuries to be suffered from being trampled by the jungle's herd. The dangers the herd brings are not only avoidable capital losses but also the chance that you will succumb to emotional strain and sell just as the big players' herd-like selling causes a bottom.

CHAPTER 10

Honor Highly the Time Value of Money

Keys for Successful Selling

◆ Remember the Rule of 72

◆ Note the 9.2 Percent Long-Term Rate

◆ Understand Why Avoiding Losses Is So Critical

◆ Examine the Anatomy of a Loss

Throughout this book our bias favors pushing the reader toward selling out positions instead of holding. The inertia behind holding is powerful and, combined with other psychological factors, often prevents investors from feeling comfortable about selling. Perversely, that inertia favoring holding grows as a bull market gets higher, and it is a very dangerous mode when the market enters a range-bound stage, such as it probably did in early 2000. There is a deliberate effort here to make a strong case for selling, in as many ways as are relevant to individual investing. One of the best arguments, and perhaps most relevant, is the unstoppable march of time.

Although time works against an investor in some senses, it can be a very powerful ally when money is put to work in ways that generate high, compounded returns over a long period. Precisely because of the magic of compound interest, the value of time is great, so the cost of lost time can be staggering. Understanding the somewhat natural inertia that disguises itself as patience should help investors learn to become impatient with under-performing investments.

Probably the most widely cited study of long-term market performance was conducted by Roger Ibbotson and Rex Sinquefield;[1] it examined returns on

FN [1] Roger Ibbotson and Rex Sinquefield, Stocks, Bonds, Bills, and Inflation: the Past (1926-1976) and the Future (1977-2000). Charlottesville, VA: Financial Analyst Research Foundation (now an affiliate of the CFA Institute), 1977.

financial instruments covering a half century ending 1976. As brokers who know about equities are fond of pointing out to hesitant clients, the conclusion of this monumental study was that over a very long period of time common stocks provide higher average returns than the other vehicles studied. They generated, on average, 9.2 percent per annum, including both capital appreciation and dividends. (Because of the extraordinary 16 percent+ compounded returns in the 1982-1999 bull market, more recent versions of the Ibbotson numbers have reached above the 10 percent level; we shall use the longer-window 9.2 percent number here for argument.) Taking a longer-term perspective, it seems more realistic to expect that recent equity return rates will prove extraordinarily strong when seen in hindsight from the year 2025, for example.

Therefore, for our purposes the longer-based assumption of a 9.2 percent return rate remains a useful starting point for evaluating reasonable long-term returns. Investors and traders who take greater risks should aim for higher returns, in the 15 percent range or more per year, as compensation for the intellectual work and emotional energy expended in owning and managing stocks. By rejecting crowd timing and tactics, such a rate can be attained, although mutual fund managers producing it on a sustained average basis with large capital pools become nearly cult figures. In many ways, individuals have certain advantages over money managers handling multiple billions.

The Rule of 72

Many investors are familiar with the Rule of 72, which is an easy way to determine how long it takes to double a sum of money at annual compounded rates (see Table 10-1). It is not 100 percent precise, but it is operationally realistic. For example, 7.2 percent for 10 years, compounded annually, produces $2,004.22 from an original $1,000 investment. There are three formulations of the Rule of 72:

◆ Years times rate equals 72;

◆ 72 divided by rate equals number of years required for doubling a sum; and

◆ 72 divided by available years equals required rate of return to double a sum.

The table is truncated at 14 years because the returns implied by the rule at that point decline to below typical certificate of deposit (CD) or medium-term Treasury bond rates, a level that should be considered very unacceptable for investors assuming the risks of equity ownership.

Table 10.1: The Rule of 72

Years	Rule-Implied Rate in % Starting Sum to Double (%)	Multiple of Actual Rate	Actual Rate to Double (%)
3	24	1.907	26
4	18	1.939	18.9
5	14.4	1.959	14.9
6	12	1.974	12.25
7	10.3	1.986	10.4
8	9	1.993	9.05
9	8	1.999	8
10	7.2	2.006	7.2
11	6.5	1.999	6.5
12	6	2.012	5.95
13	5.5	2.006	5.5
14	5.1	2.006	5.

The 9.2 Percent Long-Term Rate

The Ibbotson and Sinquefield study defined 9.2 percent as the long-term annual rate for equities. And 9.2 percent is close enough to the 9 percent/8 years convention of the Rule of 72, so that eight years can be used as a reasonable investment horizon for doubling money in stocks, low though that may have sounded after investors' giddy experience in the 1990s; bull market and the more recent recovery from 2000 to 2007. In fact, the 9.2 percent rate compounded annually for eight years produces $2,021.99 for each $1,000 invested up front, implying accuracy about doubling within 1.1 percent over eight years.

Suppose an investor has conservative expectations and is willing to settle for the long-term norm of 9.2 percent per annum. Look at Table 10-1 and see what happens when a stock that has been held goes nowhere. If it is held for one year with no gain, the average annual compounded return now required to catch up to the schedule of doubling (in the remaining seven years) becomes 10.4 percent (moving up the first column by one year to a shorter time period to determine the newly required return in the fourth column).

This is not too dramatic. But if this stock goes nowhere for two years, then our required catch-up return rate for the remaining six years jumps to 12.25 percent, which is 35 percent more than the 9 percent required originally to double our investor's money and 33 percent more than the long-term mean rate discovered by Ibbotson and Sinquefield—a significant over-performance that must be achieved over the next six years. This is an indication of the performance required of a stock that is going nowhere when it is patiently—and erroneously—held by a stubborn, fearful, unrealistic or psychologically paralyzed investor.

Table 10.2 Loss and Recovery of Capital

Percent Lost	Years Until Loss Taken	Required Compound Return in
10	1	12.1%/year for 7 years
	2	14.2 for 6
	3	17.3 for 5
	4	22.1 for 4
20	1	14.0%/yr for 7 years
	2	16.5 for 6
	3	20.1 for 5
	4	25.7 for 4
25	1	15.0%/yr for 7 years
	2	17.8 for 6
	3	21.7 for 5
	4	27.8 for 4
33.33	1	17.0%/yr for 7 years
	2	20.1 for 6
	3	24.6 for 5
	4	31.7 for 4
50	1	21.9%/yr for 7 years
	2	26.0 for 6
	3	32.0 for 5
	4	41.4 for 4

To put that 25 percent in context, the legendary Fidelity Magellan Fund achieved a return of 22.4 percent per annum from bear-market bottom in summer 1982 through the end of calendar 1995. That enviable performance over an extended period was achieved by a team of well-paid professional investors (led by individual stars) and only with the help of a rising market slope that has not proved realistic over the long term.

Two other statistics are germane to this example. Suppose that at age 25 an investor invests $1,000 for retirement at age 65, and the long-term average 9.2 percent rate is achieved. If the money lies dormant for only the first year instead of being invested to achieve the 9.2 percent return rate, the retirement kitty is depleted by $2,847. Worse yet, if our young capitalist takes just a $200 loss (20 percent) in the first year and then gets the fund onto a 9.2 percent return track, the final retirement fund is short by $6,759, which is nearly 34 times the early $200 initial loss.

When you as an investor engage in the equities arena seriously for the greater potential it offers, remember that when returns are not helping they are definitely hurting you—even when stocks do no worse than stand still. So, unless one is actually allowing profits to run, patience in investing is no virtue. Keep this urgency context in mind whenever hold/sell inertia sets in.

Why Avoiding Losses is So Crucial

Now consider the major damage that occurs when a stock's performance falls below breakeven. Watch (in Table 10-2) what happens when there is an initial loss of capital and when an investor dawdles before accepting that loss and moving on to better vehicles for recovery. Assuming for illustrative purposes a 9.2 percent long-term rate on equities to double capital over eight years, the required catch-up rates become greatly higher, obviously, as a function of both the severity of the starting loss and the amount of time already consumed.

As this table shows, taking any but a small and brief loss in the beginning requires that heroic returns be achieved to catch up to a doubling schedule in eight years. If a higher expectation such as a positive 15 percent average return is imposed, the required catch-up paces become breathtaking very quickly, even for fairly moderate losses. For example, the 15 percent rate triples money (3.059 times) in eight years. Once the investor starts out with a lazy 20 percent loss in the first 24 months, in order to recover to 15 percent per year over the full eight years, he needs to attain a little more than 25 percent compounded for the final six.

A corollary of money's time value, and a sadly neglected topic, is the importance of avoiding losses. The central objective of equity market participation is to keep making profits over time on balance, much like the effect of compound interest on a sum deposited in the bank. Expect ups and downs, but aim for the main trend to be upward. Your goal in stocks (or equity mutual funds) should be to increase capital more rapidly than is possible in risk-free investments such as an insured bank account or T-bills. The key to making big money in the stock market lies not in making the big gain. Rather the secret is not losing money. To use a baseball analogy, four singles are better than a home run, two strike-outs, and a double play.

The overriding importance of not losing money is illustrated in the old saw about the two rules for successful investing:

Rule #1: Never lose money.

Rule #2: Always follow Rule #1.

The closer and more constant attention an investor pays to not losing money, the more disciplined must be his or her approach to selling, by very necessity. To make good returns in the stock market (or in other investment media, for that matter), investors must both buy right and sell right. Once a stock is owned, the entire focus of attention and effort must shift to the only remaining relevant challenge: executing a close-out of the position with a successful sale.

A successful sale is not defined by the resulting gain or loss reported for tax purposes; more important are the subsequent trends of the stock sold and the actions of other available investments. If the sold stock goes down or sideways in price, or even if it goes up less than the general market (adjusted for beta) or less than your return bogey, its sale is a well-executed decision.

Figure 10.1: Sample Catch-Up Pace

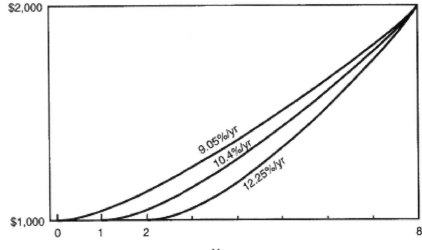

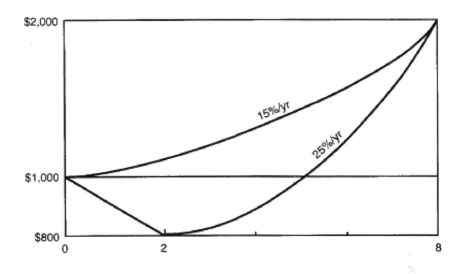

To succeed at not losing money, an investor must focus on and deal with objective realities and must sort out and discard to whatever extent possible the emotional, the irrelevant, and other distracting influences and factors covered in several earlier chapters. If a stock is in a declining trend, rallies in price or good fundamental news items that do not reverse that trend serve only to create false hope. These developments encourage an owner to hold on because they renew his or her belief and hope that prosperity is just around the corner.

As indicated earlier (Chapter 5), an optimistic mind-set rejuvenated by short-term, contra-trend positive feedback can be a serious impediment to achieving capital gains. The reason: False hope tends to forestall a decision to sell just at those times when cool logic alone would dictate an opportunistically timed (i.e., well-priced) sell order. Your hope is rekindled at just the time when smart short sellers are using the rally to increase their short positions. Simple and obvious as it may seem, the way to make maximum profits is to buy near bottoms of declines and to sell near tops of rallies. The losses to be avoided consist not only those of actual sales below cost; missed opportunities to capture better prices often available on rallies in the interim count just as much!

There are several dimensions to the famous first rule. First, in an ideal and perfect world, which does not exist, one would buy stocks that do not go down. Failing the ability to bat a thousand in that fantasy/perfectionist game, an investor must operate effectively at the next-best alternatives. Her capital at all times consists of the value of assets minus liabilities. In the stock market, some days capital goes up and other days it goes down. Each day—in fact, even from moment to moment— she experiences gains and losses as the prices of stocks rise and fall.

Anatomy of a Loss

If an investor buys a stock at 20, watches it go to 30, and then holds on while it falls back to 22, he has suffered just as great a dollar loss as if he had bought it at 20 and watched in horror as it shriveled to 12. That paper loss of eight points is every bit as real in the 20/30/22 case as in the 20/12 disaster scenario. Our hypothetical investor probably does not feel quite as bad about that retreat to 22 because he still has a profit, but he ought to. Even though it is impossible to catch exact tops and bottoms and although we cannot expect a profit on every position, that loss from 30 to 22 is a very real one in terms of opportunity. Our struggling trader missed out on an opportunity to cash in at 30 and do whatever he wanted with all the cash he would receive at that price. Now he has only 22 left.

So in addition to actual losses that get recorded on Form 1040's Schedule D, we need to avoid these opportunity losses. There is another, even more subtle, kind of opportunity loss related to the time value of money. The investor is stung when a stock goes from 20 to 12. He feels unlucky when it goes 20/30/22 but feels that is not quite as bad. Chances are that he does not feel bad at all when the stock fluctuates around 20 for a prolonged period of time. Unless he is collecting a good current income in the form of solid dividend payments or is successfully writing out-of-the-money options against his flat-priced stock, he is losing money in the form of lost time opportunity.

Again, this is not a loss one can deduct for taxes. And it is unlikely to get perceived as a painful loss. It might become acute if the general market is zooming north and all his friends are gloating about their big winners as they were in 1998 to early 2000. Among the three kinds of losses described here, a dead-money one, predictably, is the least painful and therefore the most insidious.

A stock going nowhere, although not as damaging as a stock shrinking in price, is still a source of opportunity loss and therefore is producing a real loss. First, the money could be in the bank, T -bills, or short-term municipals, earning some interest and not at risk in the market.

Second, with the cost of living generally on the rise, a dollar tomorrow is worth less than a dollar today in purchasing power. Third, our unfortunate inertia-saddled holder is losing the one nonrenewable resource he owns in life: time. While this stock meanders back and forth around that long-familiar 20 level, this investor is missing any chance to make money (with these lazy dollars) in other stocks.

And finally, our investor is suffering a psychological loss: He is becoming frustrated with the market and/or is losing confidence in his own market-playing abilities. This negative feedback is doing damage, even if only subtly, to his ability to make future (and other current) trading or investment decisions coolly and smartly.

So in review, setting aside the psychic cost, three kinds of money losses are caused by underperformance in the market: actual Schedule D losses, those losses in the form of profits not taken and then given back on paper and finally the serious implications of lost time value when a stock sits at the same price.

In the real world, stock prices continue to fluctuate. The investor's job is to take advantage of the ebb and flow of prices. One sees a stock that is undervalued and buys. But in order to cash in and realize our rewards for buying cheap, we must also sell dear to capture the difference. You can always buy that same stock back later. Buying and selling does not make us a trader, a short termer, or in any way a bad person. Once we buy, we must sell or become a passive collector with a full cupboard. Such investors will be frozen out of the best of future action until they find more money—or until they change stripes and start learning to sell. It is interesting that stock and funds investors are advised to buy and hold, whereas retailers try to maximize inventory turnover and real estate investors seek to flip properties regularly.

Suppose that for some combination of reasons an investor is relatively comfortable with the fundamental prospects of a company whose stock has an overall flat price over the long term. If she has good foresight and a little lucky too, she could divine the annual tops and bottoms in the stock and buy in and sell out somewhere roughly near those levels a number of times over the years.

In that way, she would make much more money than by holding because, in the long term, the price seems to do no better than come back to its old level. In fact, this approach is the only way she will make money in such a stock (beyond dividends or option premiums). Buying it at 20 and never selling it, or many years later finally selling it in frustration at 20, involves a tremendous opportunity loss compared with taking advantage of periodic fluctuations as they occur. (This concept of capturing periodic rises and falls around fair value, rather than holding on faithfully forever, is critically explored in great detail in Chapter 12.)

Investors should never be frustrated if they cannot capture all of a particular price swing. Take what seems reasonable, what is in agreement with past patterns. If some stock that is stuck around 40 periodically swings between 35 and 45, an investor certainly is doing a creditable job by buying around 37 and passing it along to someone else at 43 or so. Such trades will each book a gain of about 16 percent which is good in itself but excellent from a vehicle that is actually just standing still longer term. Therefore, do not be afraid to pay a broker a little for the opportunity to nail down profits; moving out will prevent expensive opportunity losses, which are just as real as any other kind of loss. Think in your Wall Street dealings as you do in your professional business life: Time is all you have!

One very useful way of visualizing money's time value in the stock market is provided by Better Investing, originally the National Association of Investors Corporation (NAIC), an educational umbrella group for investment clubs (see the Appendix for its address and telephone). B-I created its Stock Selection Guide for investors' use primarily in setting disciplined policy for buying. The Guide can and should also be used for timing sales well; a price plotted well above the future expected-value line indicates likelihood of below-acceptable returns over the balance of the forecast period. (The B-I guidelines suggest that investors members purchase stocks they honestly believe can double in three to five years, implying returns of 14 percent or more under the Rule of 72.) A similarly useful quick assessment of a stock's position and therefore its odds of further gain can be found by checking current price against the plotted line of estimated value in *The Value Line Investment Survey.*

PART III

Mastering the Contrarian Approach

CHAPTER 11

Be a Contrarian

Keys for Successful Selling

♦ Define the Contrarian Approach
♦ Master and Practice Contrarian Principles

Many people who invest look to the perceived professionals or experts for advice. The hope, of course, is that the alleged secret of professional successes can be learned. But it is not evident that investing success can be learned by just anyone who aspires to it; some people have reasonable investing potential and some do not because investing is an art and not entirely a science. As in sports and the creative arts, a certain amount of innate aptitude is required.

For those who have some aptitude, there is no better guru than the person who was at one time reported to be the richest man in the world. Three-time-billionaire J. Paul Getty once said: "Buy when everyone else is selling and hold until everyone else is buying. This is not merely a catchy slogan. It is the very essence of successful investment."

Because this is a book on selling investments, Getty's advice can be slightly reworded: hold until means sell when... The essence of that message is the gospel of contrary opinion. Like any other prescription for investment success, the contrarian approach is never quite as simple to apply as its truth is obvious. This is because there are no exact yardsticks that unfailingly indicate exactly when a trend is overdone. But this is no reason to abandon any attempts to apply contrary thinking to the investment process. To ignore its wisdom because of a personal inability to catch absolute tops and bottoms by using it is like refusing to eat healthy foods because death is inevitable anyway.

This chapter explains why it is necessary to maintain a contrarian mind-set in (both buying and) selling stocks. Statistically, it is known that the majority of investors lose money. Only a minority get richer. It is also well documented that a large majority of professional investors—on the order of 70 percent of mutual funds, for example—fail to match their index benchmarks in an average year. Professional money managers are known for crowd-like behavior; they prefer to own popular stocks and possibly still lose money comfortably rather than come up short by some less conventional means.

But it is also well known that an investor can be successful despite losing more often than winning, provided that his or her losses are cut short while profits are allowed to run. To become more successful at investing, then, it is necessary to act less like the majority and more like the minority, more of the time. Stating it another way, to be successful one must learn to play the game better and/or more nimbly than the other participants: Do not follow the crowd.

Defining the Contrarian Approach

Although the zero-sum-game hypothesis in economics is now mostly discredited, secondary investment markets taken in isolation and as a closed system are a finite-sum game. Assume that a company is going to sell a certain number of widgets this year, achieve certain margins, pay a given tax rate and deliver some specific earnings per share regardless of its stock price. The fundamentals help determine price action, as does industry-related and general market psychology.

Given that a stock will move from one price to another, will retrace some or all of that change, and will arrive at yet a third price or just back at the starting one, and that only a certain amount of trading volume will occur in the process, then some people make money; others lose or forego equal amounts of gain (all before commissions, of course). The entire net price move, in dollars per share, multiplied by the number of shares outstanding equals the increased or decreased combined wealth that all shareholders experience collectively (before commission).

Those who buy at the top lose; those who sell to them win. Those who scalp three points on the way up take potential profits from those who sold to them. Those who hold on and ride the entire price merry-go-round end up back where they started. They have lost the time value of their money by accept profits while prices were up. (They also have failed to learn the failing to contrarian's skill of selling high and have probably done themselves some self-image damage in the process.)

Others who did cash in at higher prices have taken profits and can now buy in again at lower quotes. Those to whom they sold are now holding higher-cost securities. So it is basically a zero-sum game, where one person's gain is equal to the losses or missed gains of his or her counter party in buying and selling transactions. Only one side of each transaction on the exchange will prove profitable.

There is so much emphasis on the buying end of the investment equation that there is plenty of available evidence to monitor how overheated a market is becoming. Bullish pressure can be palpable if an investor looks and listens, and that is useful and valuable input. If one can sense when the clamor to buy is getting out of hand and out of touch with reality, then he or she is recognizing a classic contrarian signal.

Master and Practice Contrarian Principles

To succeed as a contrarian, you need to understand the emotional position of the market, and wait until it becomes palpably fairly extreme. So always look for telltale signals. Many can be detected by observing events in the world outside that of daily quotations and trading:

◆ Is the market front-page news in the general local media?

◆ Do TV programs or movies use stock market jokes or plots?

◆ Are people talking about stocks at the water cooler or over lunch more than usual?

◆ Are you receiving more broker calls offering exciting opportunities?

◆ Are there numerous initial public offerings (IPOs), many doubling or more right away?

◆ Is corporate or personal prosperity widespread; are expectations of continued expansion the norm?

◆ Are many more investment advisors and letter writers bullish than bearish?

◆ Is the percentage of mutual fund cash in equity funds low or fast declining (see ICI.org)?

◆ Has there been an historically very strong net inflow of money into growth-oriented mutual funds?

◆ Do investors commonly expect historically unrealistic annual returns such as 20 percent to 25 percent or more?

◆ Are people fixated on potential rewards and ignoring or downplaying risk?

◆ After a major rise, when skeptics pose troubling questions, are bulls saying: It is different this time?

These signs of a major long-term top tend to accumulate gradually over a period of months; therefore, they never appear as sudden, shocking cluster. No one rings the bell and declares a bull market over. It happens, literally, when people least expect it. So the would-be winning investor's job is to out-smart and out-think the other players. It is impossible to hit the exact top (that perfectionism issue covered in Chapter 3), so stop worrying about that or trying it. Almost all major market tops occur as rounding-over patterns when viewed on a chart, not as one-day flagpoles. (Chapter 21 will list a few signs of short-term exhaustion tops, but our focus now is on the big picture rather than on tactics.) The losers have absolutely no idea that they are helping to create a top by their classic overenthusiastic behavior. They miss selling at top by a mile, just as they grossly miss the bottoms as buyers. Savvy investors catch the greatest percentage of the move by cashing in somewhere near the top and are entirely content to sell to a potentially greater fool who tries to hold for the top.

But make no mistake: It is not easy to lean against the tide. It is unfashionable to be a worrier near the top; if an investor starts selling early (the best time), she is written off by others because she looks wrong for a time. She may suffer regrets (seller's remorse) and second thoughts against selling more stocks as they get increasingly overvalued.

In the short run (usually quite near the frothiest point before a top), one is tempted to reverse field and jump back in to chase just one more hot one while it looks inviting. That impulse should be resisted above all: it is a classic final signal to cash in rather than buy more. In the long run, one proves right with a disciplined contrarian attitude.

The key to success is to do what is not easy. What seems very easy will probably prove a mistake. Almost invariably when a buy looks compelling and overwhelmingly obvious, the investor actually is getting in too late. The best bargains are purchased when the investor has to struggle and debate, afraid even to tell his broker about an idea under consideration. When he loves the stock because it has treated him so well and wants to stay on board longer to maintain that highly comfortable association, he has overstayed the market. Thomas Herzfeld, a

Florida-based brokerage executive and closed-end fund money manager, told a reporter at The Wall Street Journal in 1993: "We buy [on] wars, earthquakes, coups, assassinations and devaluations. We sell on peace, free-trade agreements and all that other good stuff."

Buying and selling that way is how to succeed, but it always feels like facing into a 100-mph head wind at the time.

Remember that the majority always feel that they are right, even when they are not. The crowd can be correct during much of a long trend, but always overstays and proves itself wrong at turning points. When the feeling of bullish rightness becomes universal and powerful, a top is immediately at hand. Being successful in trading means leaning against that powerful tide, which then creates psychological, financial and social stresses and strains not everyone can handle. Humans banded together for mutual protection for centuries, so our learned natural tendency is to feel uncomfortable when deliberately walking alone, to a different drummer.

If by nature an investor is passive, a follower, he may lack sufficient courage to do what is required for trading success. But if one can stick to contrarian principles despite probable early suboptimization of profits, he acquires a bucketful of cash near the top (plus some interest) for use later when the panic phase arrives. Perhaps the most forceful statement on the need to act in the contrary mode appears in *Confessions of a Wall Street Insider* by the self-named C.C. Hazard:

> (T)he stock market is built on a necessary foundation of error. You make money on the market mainly by living off the errors of other players. You become a predator, in fact, a carnivore, a beast of prey. Others must die that you might live... (T)he stock market requires an endless supply of losers.

By refusing to act like and with the crowd in either its manic or panic phases, an investor immensely raises his or her chance of not being part of that pool of losers. Bernard Baruch, who enjoyed impressive Wall Street success, summed up his most important advice in a mere four words: "Never follow the crowd!"

CHAPTER 12

Rethink That Old Buy-and-Hold Religion

Keys for Successful Selling

◆ Understand That Fundamentals Change, Driving Revised Values
◆ But Recognize That Investor Psychology Drives Prices
◆ Realize Why Selling Is Important
◆ Think of Advanced Price as Advanced Risk

In numerous other areas of our lives, change is assumed and a rational person would be considered foolish not to adapt. We would scoff at anyone giving advice to stay irrevocably with our first declared major in college, definitely to marry the first person we date, to keep our old car despite it obvious failings, to live forever in the first home we buy, to stay faithfully with our first chosen employer and even to stay in a clearly failed personal relationship. We understandably change our personal wardrobes by fashion and season. We abandon politicians and their parties when they prove no longer suitable. But in investments, we are told to stay the course no matter what! How curious.

A large army of investment advisors and media commentators preaches the mantra of buy and hold. Just buy great stocks and hold them for the long term, they counsel. Prominent among them, perhaps not surprisingly, are mutual fund management companies, which benefit most if shareholders deposit their money for a permanent ride. This chapter takes the heretical position that following that old-time buy-and-hold religion will lead an investor to essentially average performance at best. Growing capital faster than merely average is the main reason investment books are purchased and studied, why analysts pursue their craft and (beyond merely to rack up fees) why advisory services and investment managers exist. Investors who would settle for average performance over the long term should abandon direct ownership of individual stocks (which carries risks of adverse selection and lack of diversification); index funds with low expense ratios but with zero chance of outperforming average are designed for those folks. The next several pages will develop a distinctly contrary proposition, namely that buying and selling has valuable benefits, can result in outperforming the averages, and actually reduces risk. The reason selling is necessary is really quite simple: Things change!

One reason the buy-and-hold admonition has gained prominence lately has been a recent run of literally extraordinary market circumstances. From the depths of summer 1982, U.S. stock prices rose without any lengthy interruption for nearly 18 years, driven not in small part by declining interest rates reflecting lessened inflation. The new generation of market pundits and, disturbingly, young portfolio managers, had not known a bear market: As of 1999 the most recent declines lasting two calendar years had been in 1977-78 and 1973-74. So it was no surprise that investment managers lacking long experience or a sense of history believed naively in buying every dip and never selling. They and their unfortunate clients were destroyed by the 2000-2002 bear market. The prior upside excess was corrected with a vengeance, and not for the first or the last time.

High on the list of buy-and-holders' arguments is the assertion that one cannot time the market. It is true that many computer simulations and models have been created and tested, with most failing to outperform the averages when they attempt to implement market-timing rules. Results of those tests do not conclusively prove the theory. Rather, such failures should be attributed to one of two possibilities: first, that the models (constructed by experimenters with a strong anti-timing bias) used bad rules and omitted safeguards that rational live investor implement and second, that markets that constantly change obviously cannot be dealt with profitably by any set of rigid or unchanging rules. Investing is an art and not a science!

Of course, mere identification of an extreme trend will not guarantee selling at an exact top or buying at precise bottoms. But selling above the long-term trend when markets are buoyant will produce returns above those from selling on average at the long-term trendline. (Buying well, namely when fear pervades, gives another advantage to those derided as timers.). Thus, the evidence supporting a faithful buy-and-hold approach is skewed when viewed in longer history as a more valid context. Investing is not as easy as the period of 1982-1999 (or the bull recovery of 2003-2007) made it appear. Market moves are driven by an ever-shifting combination of fundamentals and psychology; to be successful, investors need to seek to understand both rather than ignore them.

Fundamentals, Which Change, Drive Value

Undeniably, fundamentals drive stock values over the long term. Earnings, dividends and cash flows form the numerator of the value equation while inflation rates drive the required rate of return (interest or discount rate) that makes up the denominator. A company whose earnings and dividends grow at an average rate of 10 percent annually will see its stock price rise, over the very long term, at that same pace on average. The long-term buy-and-hold camp makes some key assumptions. First, they assume that a company that has historically grown will continue to do so. Second, they assume that its growth rate will be constant. And third, they assume an economy with little or no fluctuation in interest rates and without periodic recessions, implying only minor wiggles in price on the long upward climb. Those are brave suppositions indeed! In fact they are fantasies.

This mechanistic mind-set of the modelers is again where the buy-and-hold idea breaks down. Companies do not continue growing just because a least-squares trendline of prior earnings points ever upward. They continue to prosper only because of excellent management, keen attention to costs, improving technology, and superior marketing skills—and the absence of serious external (uncontrollable) events. They continue to lead only if some other company does not come along and do the job better. And, in case those theoreticians missed it, capitalist economies go through expansions and then recessions in which very few companies feel no effects on their growth and profitability. The grand buy-and-hold model is based on an assumed average growth rate of all companies, calculated based on perfect 20/20 hindsight. In the real world, investors buy individual stocks rather than averages, and those companies and their stocks stray from that smooth mathematical average as they navigate into an unknown but certainly non-constant future. Those willing to settle for the average should buy an index fund and abandon any efforts at excelling in their investment lives. But their precious index funds will fluctuate too!

Table 12.1: Five Identifiers of Trends Primed for Reversal

1	Above-average longevity
2	Acceleration of price velocity on high volume
3	Extremely steep slope of price movement
4	Virtual unanimity of opinion; downplaying of risks (at tops) or opportunity (at bottoms)
5	A loud media drumbeat praising or bemoaning those above conditions

While prices for individual securities and major overall market averages swing from over-optimism to the depths of despair and back again, the sizes of successive movements cannot be predicted with great accuracy. Mechanistic models that base predictions of one cycle on the size and length of its predecessor (or on theory based simply on prior averages) are doomed to failure. Live, proactive human beings, by observing psychological conditions in the market, can successfully identify areas of temporary extreme valuation, both high and low (see Table 12-1). That is the essence of contrarian investing. No pretense is made here that exact tops will be identified and sold nor precise bottoms bought.

But reasonably intelligent investors, observing market moods and press headlines and keeping an eye on price charts, can usually tell a pure academician when the market is frothy and when it is afraid. Those areas are near tops and near bottoms. Those are times when market psychology and fundamental reality have diverged significantly. Such areas cannot be predicted accurately in advance, but they are quite readily identifiable in real time. Taking action in the opposite direction of an extreme trend will not guarantee selling at an exact top. But selling above trend when markets are palpably too buoyant will produce returns exceeding those from selling on average at the long-term trend's midline. (And when deep fear clearly pervades, buying will give another advantage to disciplined so-called market timers derided by the buy-and-hold zealots.)

Table 12-2 lists twelve companies viewed as great growth vehicles and industry leaders—in their heydays. They were accorded elite status on Wall Street and were presumed to be destined for unending prosperity and market leadership. Interestingly, all provide or provided consumer goods and services, a characteristic statistically associated with lower risk than the heavy industrial and transport sectors. And yet, somehow, their fundamental trendlines stopped projecting ever upward. Those that now remain in business have become troubled or have proven cyclical rather than perpetual growth engines. Who can say that any one or several of today's revered leaders might not suffer similar fates? One need only look back to the story stocks of 1999 to find widespread carnage. Buy and hold?

Table 12.2: Companies Once Known as Growth Blue Chips

Winn Dixie	Four Seasons Nursing Homes
L. A. Gear	Polaroid
Memorex	Franklin Mint
Levitz Furniture	Tucson Electric
Equity Funding	Kmart
New Process	Winnebago

A look back at one major growth industry is startling. Arguably the most important industry of the 1980s was computer technology. Of the seven largest U.S. computer firms of 1984, only one (IBM) remains intact in its prior form and even it has gone through a widely chronicled painful transition: It entered and left the PC business, reduced its dividend twice, and has turned heavily to consulting instead of box building. Before the great bull run of the late 1990s, its stock price was net flat from 1971 to 1995! At one point it had suffered more than a 75 percent drop in share price. Burroughs and Sperry merged as Unisys, which survived but struggles for marginal profitability. NCR was bought by AT&T and subsequently totally written off. Digital Equipment suffered major reversals, changed to a network solutions company, and was bought by Compaq (which itself was later swallowed by Hewlett-Packard). Honeywell's computer business was sold to France's Cie. des Machines Bull, which has downsized ever since. Control Data has changed name and survived as only a minor factor. Things do indeed change, a lot!

Calendar 1995, when Alan Greenspan spoke of irrational exuberance, provided an interesting, and incidentally periodically repeating, illustration of how prices move to temporary extremes. Excluding shares priced below $5 at year's end and excluding closed-end funds, the average NYSE-listed stock traced a price range of 60 percent from low to high during the year. Earnings per share rose about 10.5 percent, coincidentally equal to the long-term average rate of return on common stocks as noted by Ibbotson Associates. Major market averages showed gains exceeding 30 percent for the year. Thus, 1995 represented a time in which a bull market in prices was strongly outrunning stocks' underlying fundamentals, while, as usual, individual stocks also were fluctuating much more widely than the overall net price change itself. Those passively holding for the long term into 1996 were assuming that corporate earnings would catch up with the recent 30 percent-plus price gains, and that interest rates would move permanently lower—or were setting themselves up for an inevitable fall. Markets rise and fall; they do not proceed smoothly on a path of long-term mathematical average growth. The period from 1998 through early 2000 took major market indices to unprecedented P/E highs. As of mid-2007, the S&P 500 P/E has been virtually halved while price has finally just recovered to its 2000 high. Could the buy-and-hold zealots not see that P/Es in 2000 were silly—even granting that no one could tell exactly when the music would stop? But they counseled buying and holding, and lost seven-plus years until mid-2007 while patiently waiting to recoup their losses.

Why Selling is So Important

Buying and holding for the long term assumes that one is willing to settle for whatever long-term average return is generated. Buying and holding for the long term also assumes that one can successfully select a stock, or group of stocks, whose fundamentals will continue intact. Technology is moving ever more rapidly, and for most corporations the relevant competitive context has become worldwide, whether or not they wish it were so. These facts imply that selections of companies likely will not remain valid as long as they could in the past. In a dynamic world, a static portfolio is by definition a fatally flawed strategy.

By way of example, the United States now has become transformed into primarily a service economy, as contrasted with its smokestack industrial nature of 50 or 100 years ago. The Dow Jones Rail Average was forced to substitute several truckers and airlines and become the Transportation Average. Well more than half of the 30 components of the broadly followed Dow Jones Industrial Average have been replaced since 1961. Bottom line: One year's favorable and seemingly stable fundamentals are not a given that can be assumed in perpetuity, much as we might wish they could. The price of investment success is constant vigilance!

Fundamental trends do not continue undisturbed, much as academics or we actual investors might wish for such a simple landscape. Thus, the advice to buy and hold long term begs a critical question: buy and hold what? And, amusingly, if the answer is that one should buy good growth mutual fund, it should be observed that many of these engage in 50 percent to 100 percent or faster annual turnover (rather than buying and holding.) in their continuing efforts to stay atop the best holdings.

Investor Psychology Drives Prices

While fundamentals do drive value over the long term, the path of value for any firm's stock is neither smooth nor forever necessarily sloped upward. But even if it were, stock prices do not inch along with the regularity of interest compounding in a bank CD. Stock prices fluctuate sharply in response to significant swings in investor psychology. Prices reflect changing collective moods of optimism and pessimism. Bull and bear markets wind around the long-term upward slope of national output and personal income. Intermediate price swings punctuate those bull and bear markets. Daily and weekly fluctuations provide ripples around those swings.

A logical, although very disturbing, challenge to the long-term buy-and-hold advocates would be this: Assuming you are not willing to abide a possible 100 percent loss of capital due to your sworn passivity, how much adversity would you endure before finally concluding that a failing stock should be sold? Our long-term holders, if indeed they ever abandon their faith and do sell, would be doomed to exit below the slope of the formerly healthy average fundamental projection. Their sales if any would come very late, only after possibly fatal corporate decay was totally obvious and well after many more-nimble investors have perceived trouble and exited. Our long-term holders will therefore sell below the former trend and thus will actually achieve below-average (and below their theoretical) returns. They forswear trying the voodoo exercise of timing the market and so will never try selling high. Thus they predictably will let their successful positions run to an eventually average result but will realize below-average net results, possibly including significant actual losses, on their less fortunate selections. This is not a rhetorical, theoretical argument. Studies by mutual funds tracker Lipper Inc. have confirmed that at major market bottoms even the holders of S&P 500 index funds (the true believers in randomness and long-term passive holding) are actually scared into becoming net sellers on balance. This defeats their chance of actually achieving the market's long-term net average return. When things get really rough, even the declared long-term faithful fail to hold.

The opposite of holding is selling. Buying and selling allows an investor flexibility that buy-and-holders deny themselves. Those willing to sell are capable of capturing excessive returns as market cycles develop, rather than settling for (at best) long-term average results. Logically, an investor either should surrender the battle of active stock market participation and buy a low-cost index fund or should adopt buy-and-sell as his or her modus operandi. Those who retreat to buy-and-hold as a credo either assume they cannot beat the average and/or accept it as given that they would sell badly if they tried to sell. Selling well is the subject of this book and, clearly, is one receiving too little attention. Buying badly and selling badly are symptoms of succumbing to crowd psychology. Buying well and selling well reflect independence of mind and action. Buying and selling, as contrasted with holding long term, is a mind-set designed to capture profit opportunities that markets provide routinely. Selling above the central (average) trendline captures abnormal profits.

Figure 12-1 presents a stylized version of major market swings, powered by emotions, driving prices successively to considerably below and then well above value as defined by fundamentals. (For simplicity, fundamentals here are assumed to improve smoothly and dependably over time.) Those pursuing a buy-and-hold approach accept two risks to their capital when markets are in an above-trend area near point A. First, they are exposing their capital to some subsequent decline into a depressed region near point D and requiring that they will neither panic at the worst of times nor need their funds at a very unfortunate point in the cycle for such uses as education, housing, medical emergencies, etc. Second, they are allowing their capital a lazy period from the time of A to the time of B, when fundamentals will presumably catch up with the temporarily excessive price levels that prevailed around time A. By holding resolutely for the long term despite the interim favorable selling opportunity near A, the investor is accepting a remaining long-term average return slightly flatter than the slope of the presumed fundamentals, namely, an unplotted return from the A area to the right-hand endpoint of the fundamentals line. That point might represent retirement or death, arguably the logical ends of long term. The only way a long-term holder who eschews the benefits of selling near A can capture a return equal to the fundamentals' slope is to convert from buy-and-hold to buy-and-sell near area C or one of its later cyclical equivalents.

Opportunities for capturing excessive profits are not, however, limited to selling near major cyclical tops such as were represented in Figure 12-1 by area A. In Figure 12-2, the fad-driven trend or cyclical advance is the major slope that is rising away from a longer term, fundamentals-justified value trendline. This fad-driven trend here is a blow-up of the latter half of an advance from a low area like D to a high area like C in the original plot. Not only is the cyclical or fad-driven move generating a major medium-term divergence above value, but interim ripples up to areas such as near point X provide multiple short-term opportunities to sell and capture excess prices. In this second graph, areas near points E, F, G and H represent short-term situations analogous to the longer term ones posed by A, B, C and D in the longer context of the earlier graph. This figure in practical terms represents what happened to stocks in the 1997-early 2000 period as prices sharply exceeded value.

Figure 12.1: Market Timing Versus Holding Long term

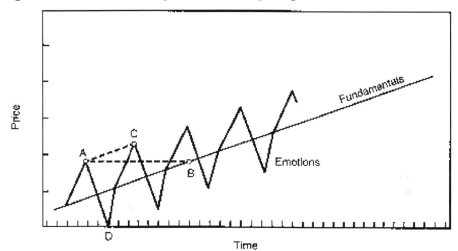

Figure 12.2: Ways of Viewing Risk

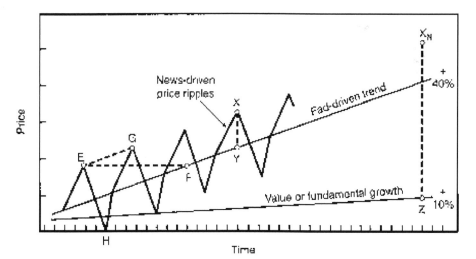

Think of Advanced Price as Advanced Risk

Focus now on a time period in which a bull market is pushing the price level cumulatively farther above true fundamental value. Here, in Figure 12-3, vertical distance between the long-term fundamental line of value at the bottom and a point on the cyclical trend such as Y or Z can be thought of as not just advanced price but also extended risk. For this reason, the scale on this graph has been relabeled as risk rather than price. Given that prices will fluctuate, high price is also high risk. On this graph, areas near points E, G, and X represent doubly risky times when short-term rallies in a bull market push prices (and thus risks of giving back gains) temporarily above the bull trend, which itself is increasingly far above value.

Figure 12.3: Deflate Trend for Change in Value; Change in Price Is Change in Risk

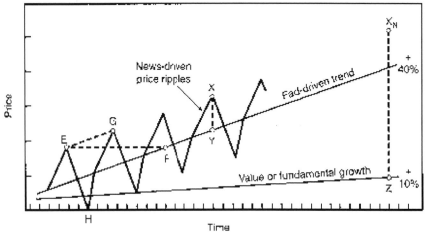

Figure 12.4: Fundamentals and Discounting Rate Determine Value

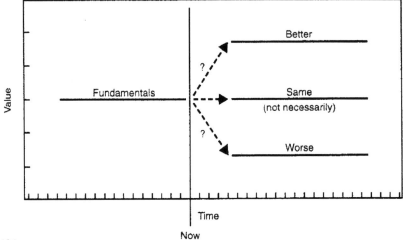

The virtue of selling well is even greater when one considers Figure 12-4. Underlying our measures of perceived risk in the three prior graphs was an assumption that fundamental value could be accurately assumed. But the world is not that simple. It is possible that your company might develop an important new technology or that tax-law changes might raise the value of corporate earnings or that interest rates might permanently shift downward, thus fundamentally raising a company's value. But, of course, equally important and opposite changes can also occur. A court could set a precedent holding smokestack utility companies more liable for environmental effects; corporate tax rates might rise; oil prices might rise above $80/bbl, perhaps driving sharp inflation; a new competitor may leapfrog a former industry leader's product position. The FDA can force recalling a major drug. Any such shock can radically shift the position of that fundamental line. If that shift is to a lower position, the risk as previously measured will prove to have been a vast underestimate. Thus, advanced price poses hidden risk in an unquantifiable amount—a difference that means that the vertical distance between fundamentals and point Y or Z on the prior graph was a vast understatement of exposure to capital loss.

With the significantly increased amount of institutional domination in the market and the faddish chasing of high earnings and price momentum, even a single earnings disappointment (which may have no special long-term significance) can suddenly shift the position or slope of the perceived fundamentals line. An extremely unpleasant and immediate loss of capital can result. This is illustrated by the accompanying price chart (Figure 12-5) of Department 56 (later acquired): Its quarterly earnings grew a mere 31 percent in the quarter reported on February 1, representing a vast disappointment (to greedy trend chasers) after the 42 percent growth of the prior quarter. A $38 stock became a $22 stock in one day. Viewed in this context, selling in areas above trend and above value is a form of risk reduction at the same time it captures abnormal profits. What a pleasant double bonus for the good seller, providing all the more support for buying and selling rather than passively holding long term. Especially in large-cap stocks heavily held by institutions, the type of risk recorded here is magnified to such an extent that open-ended holding is virtually waiting for some time bomb to go off.

Figure 12.5: Significant Revision of Expectations

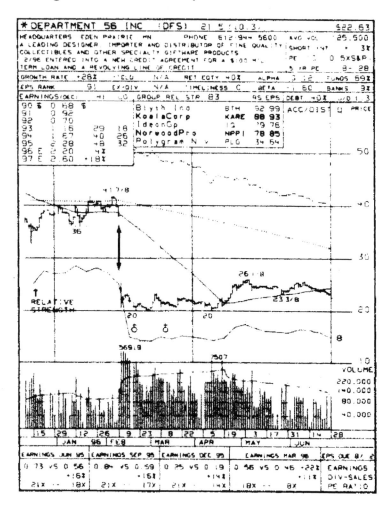

Figure 12.6: Sideways Price Movement after Downside Spikes

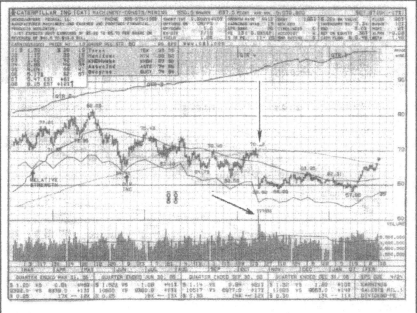

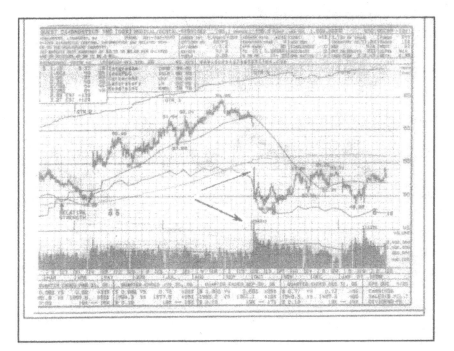

Another and less dramatic pattern can occur in which a more modest percentage slam is felt, to be followed by a lengthy period of dead money as investors wait to see if other shoes might drop. Why be patient and hope there is no further bad news? That is not a positive investment strategy. And if a policy of regularly selling holdings when they rally is followed, it is possible that the sudden news-driven loss might be avoided. Advanced price is indeed advanced risk. This pattern is illustrated in the two price graphs in Figure 12-6, for Caterpillar and Quest Diagnostics.

Successful selling requires an investor to manage his or her own emotions in a disciplined manner at exactly those times when most other investors are letting psychology ruin them. While this chapter's major thrust has been selling versus holding as related to fluctuating prices against values, selling has another advantage over holding: It helps with respect to one's mind-set regarding taxes.

All too many investors have frozen themselves into never selling stocks that have treated them well because their large long-term gains represent huge tax liabilities. Selling periodically along the way, paying the resulting tax, and then buying another stock or the same stock on a dip rids one of psychological lock-in from taxes. That lock-in can skew decisions in harmful ways. IBM is a classic example of this problem. For decades its stock had been a great performer; it was a core holding for most institutions. Earnings began faltering in 1985. The shares traded above $160 (pre-split basis) in both 1986 and 1987. Thousands of investors had locked themselves in with perhaps tenfold gains over many years. At $160 they could not sell because of the taxes to be paid. Likewise at $120 in 1990-1991 or at $90 in 1992. Taxes on their long-term gains were locking them in, they felt. Perhaps when the stock fell below $40 in 1993 that problem had been cured. Only then, with earnings at a deficit and after two dividend cuts, was the threat of taxes on their gains small enough to allow them to sell (at the bottom). Being emotionally and intellectually prepared to sell any holding at any time will free investors from the tyranny of tax lock-in. Potential price change is by definition larger than potential taxes. As this was written before the 2008 elections, it seemed possible that the advantage of selling sooner rather than later night become urgent. Rates of capital-gains taxation have been a volatile and jagged line over time; lowered rates since May 2003 had fueled part of the recovery to 2007 levels.

To summarize, this chapter has challenged, in prototypical contrarian's manner, the generally espoused merits of long-term buy-and-hold orthodoxy. We have noted significant questions about that approach's underlying assumptions. We have come to view advanced price as a measure of risk. We have started to focus on the emotional condition of the market as one that can be accurately perceived, and certainly as one that can be graphically observed in the form of price charts. We have seen that the challenging art of planned active short-term market timing is not the only possible alternative to passive holding but that taking advantage of major periodic positive and negative emotional excesses when presented can be of great advantage and a means of reducing risk, even though the timing of such events cannot be predicted.

The long-term holder's problem of psychological tax lock-in was also exposed. If the reader still harbors any tendency to hold passively, Chapter 10 has challenged that from another important vantage point: money's time value. Again, passive holding (the opposite of occasional opportunistic selling) is proven suboptimal.

CHAPTER 13

Calibrate Decision Making to Personal Emotions

Keys for Successful Selling

◆ Recognize the General Warning Signs

◆ Know Your Personal Warning Signs

◆ Act in a Contrarian Mode

The worry threshold can be avoided in most investments by limiting buying size and by selling when emotional concern rises. Most investors fail because they sell from worry when a market bottom occurs—not at market tops when their buoyant emotions should act as a signal to worry.

For example, the presence of gloating and smugness should signal concern about pending buy decisions that most likely are inappropriate. Gloating can consist of such behaviors as uncharacteristic celebrations, self-congratulation, bragging or an unscheduled counting of the chips—all of which typically propel unwary but overconfident investors into putting more cash into the market just when they should be selling.

To be successful, you must lean into the wind of market emotions, observing and thinking as a contrarian. The harder the winds are blowing, the more firm must be your resolve-at just the time when temptation to join the crowd is greatest. Recall that, by definition, a major bottom occurs in an atmosphere of fear and gloom, sometimes panic. Remember 1987, or July and October of 2002? Major tops (such as early 2000) form when investors are at their most euphoric; when all the newer buyers have already come in and all the older players have exhausted their buying power, the balance literally must shift to the downside because there are no further buyers' dollars to create further net buying.

This point of maximum collective over-optimism defines a top. When the euphoria gets to him, the investor must do exactly the opposite of what his emotions support: He must sell. Once that critical psychological signal that a top is at hand is received, he must not rationalize inaction, tell himself he can get another few percent, chase just one more hot story or current fad, or get swept away by the excitement of his peers and the media.

Recognizing the General Warning Signs

Each investor tends to have her own pattern of emotional reactions as a top arrives. Because such responses are predictably recurring and serve as the single most telling personal indicator of the need for action, we describe them carefully here in order to identify and catalog the most common personal signals.

Self-congratulation usually occurs gradually when an investor has a single huge winner over time (or several large winners) and no offsetting losers. These occurrences should signal taking profits because multiple major winners at one time indicate the market has performed well for a lengthy period and odds are (based on mean reversion) that the market is likely nearing a high.

Smugness can occur when there is a spectacular success in the portfolio or a run of several consecutive heady gains. Psychologists would call this a feeling of grandiosity, meaning belief in one's superiority or indestructibility. When an investor starts to feel he or she has finally learned the secret formula for winning that cannot miss, it is an urgent signal to sell. No one believes there is a secret formula near the lows.

Strong confidence—even the quiet, self-contained person is not out of the woods emotionally when, secretly savoring her success, she notes that things really have been going extremely well lately. The contained person usually does not recognize her feeling as a danger (sell) signal because it is so moderate. But it is nevertheless important despite its moderation. If, by nature, you are a person of moderate emotional swings, you should not expect to experience total euphoria before the market tops out.

Smugness and related emotions are danger signals because ultimately they produce two behavior problems for the investor, and, paradoxically, those are opposites: One is hyperactive buying and selling (driven by overconfidence in a frenzied market atmosphere) and the other is inaction on selling resulting from complacency (precisely because everything is going so well).

An example of excessive or hyperactive play is the investor who after a major advance has finally created a comfort zone, and now drains his savings for the big plunge. The suddenly massive (record) net flow of money into equity mutual funds in January through April 2000 was a classic collective example, following as it did a sharp market advance in 1999. March 2000 proved to be a top for seven years. Other patterns of excessive late-bull activity are people who open their first margin accounts and use this added buying power to the maximum or to speculate in situations that have an uncharacteristic high-risk/high-reward profile compared with past personal patterns. Multiply this unnaturally aggressive behavior by a few million individual of investors and a classic overheated market is created. Historical charts will show that market period as a top.

Such aggressive trading behavior requires that the investor have a feeling of overconfidence, which can be experienced only following highly successful recent history. Some investors increase the number of positions they hold, open added brokerage accounts (for wider exposure to hot initial public offerings [IPOs] or more expected good tips), raise their frequency of trading activity, take on higher-than-typical risks, or become so satisfied and happy with their success that they raise their targets and hold their stocks stubbornly for imagined further gains. In each of these instances, the investor is doing the wrong thing: either buying or holding just when selling is the right course of action. Therefore, take the first sign of any of these impulses as a strong warning flag, and do some selling. Tactical success require doing what feels unnatural.

For many investors, feelings or hunches alone are not a sufficient signal that the time to sell has come; for them, overt action is the key indicator to watch for. Investors who try to control and override their own feelings must examine past and current actions in relation to the stock market as a gauge to help them discover what works as a true signal.

It is unlikely that any one investor exhibits all of the symptomatic behaviors of overconfidence; no one behavior is by nature more right or wrong or more valid a signal than another. The key is to identify which ones apply to you and then take selling action when those behaviors or temptations crop up.

This process of definition and discovery can lead to a second-level problem: an intensified need to become alert and ready to act (i.e., to sell stocks) as one watches oneself in self-observation. This is because once an investor becomes aware of what personal triggers signal trouble, he or she begins to block or suppress those actions when greed kicks in. The desire to deny that the very enjoyable game is about to end creates irrational behaviors. When reaching this stage of awareness, one must use a more sensitive screen by beginning to interpret the mere impulse or intention to act, even if it is overridden eventually, as a strong signal.

Knowing Your Personal Warning Signs

Common actions that should act as danger signals range from subtle to bold; whatever your personally relevant signals, you must remain aware of them and not become judgmental or self-righteous in comparing your self with others. Seven actions are typical key indicators:

◆ quietly confiding investment successes to others;

◆ spending increased time in market study;

◆ openly bragging about winners or a hot streak;

◆ celebrating in unaccustomed ways;

◆ counting the chips more frequently than usual;

◆ adding more money (including use of margin); and

◆ playing the new-issues or options game

These signals are listed in approximate qualitative order of increasing severity. If these behaviors are absent from an investor's reaction repertoire, he should not necessarily take comfort in noting their absence; most people practice some variation on one or more of these themes.

In crossing the dividing line between feeling responses and taking actions, probably the most restrained behavior is the quiet confession of successes. This is, of course, not a case of bursting into a colleague's office and announcing that XYZ stock just jumped six points for a 50 percent profit. It merely means letting others know how it is going in the market. It may be an unpretentious comment when someone else mentions his own success or frustration with a recent trade or investment or an opportunity missed in a roaring rally. It may be as innocent or intimate as mentioning how well it is going if that is not something the investor typically divulges. The point is, for any investor not regularly in the habit of sharing personal financial affairs (or other confidential matters) with others, breaking that usual taboo is noteworthy and should be considered a signal.

Spending an increased amount of time studying the market, devising systems, surfing financial databases and chat rooms on the Internet, researching companies or reading advisory reports also can be a signal. Although serious study is good, uncharacteristic attention to trading gives evidence that the investor is excited; this occurs only when the market has run up quite a distance already, not when markets are dull or depressed. Collectively, advisory services reach subscription peaks at or just after market tops. So does trading volume. So does the number of people deciding on a career in brokerage or in professional money management. And likewise the creation of new money-management firms, hedge funds and mutual funds.

An investor paying much more attention than usual should watch out. It may be time to direct that energy toward stocks that should be cashed in rather than towards new buys. But beware: Brokers are very unlikely to comment disparagingly about new-found investor interest. More frequent calls to a broker can lead to more trading, usually in the form of buying.

More toward the overt end of the reaction scale is actually bragging about trading successes. This usually means going out of one's way to inform others about remarkable investment conquests or airing financial affairs in the presence of outsiders. When the investor behaves uncharacteristically in this way, it is a selling signal. Remember that bragging in any form occurs not after failure, loss or price decline but after one or (usually) more heady successes. And contrary opinion predicts a reversal after a series of rises. The fact that a series of investments performed beyond normal expectation suggests that a bull market has been running for a while. Therefore, assume that a top is much closer than a bottom.

Joseph Kennedy, father of President John Kennedy, is reputed to have avoided the October 1929 bloodbath because he used the too-much-talking signal on the part of others as his indicator to sell in the summer of that year. Why? He noted that even cab drivers and newspaper vendors were talking about their market conquests and dispensing advice. He accurately concluded that there was too much good feeling about the market for it to remain in an upward trend much longer, and that virtually everyone was already in. This was a classic contrarian observation of the tendency of tops to develop when the market is a frequent front-page story in the national media and even in local non-financial media.

An even more overt behavior is celebrating market success uncharacteristically. Although most everyone goes out to dinner to celebrate a raise or a promotion, it is a change in typical celebratory behavior that should be considered significant enough to take action on. One example is taking the whole office out to lunch instead of a just your spouse or one best friend. When the impulse to make a grandiose, sweeping celebratory gesture occurs, cash in some of the chips without further delay.

When the game has become so pleasant and profitable that an investor wants to total up his or her holdings, an intermediate or final top can be directly at hand. Naturally, the impulse to take an inventory is absent when the market and personal fortunes have declined or when a listless period of sideways action has occurred. But let the market roar for an extended period or let an investor make several consecutive great trades, and that desire to stroke the ego, covered by curiosity, is stirred. This is not to imply that investors should fail to track how they are doing. Keep a regular tracking inventory in the form of historical tables and/or graphs. One very easy way to do this is by keeping securities in street name so that your monthly brokerage statement includes a computerized valuation. Be sure to note all cash infusions and withdrawals promptly so that the tally is kept on a fair basis.

The key point is to heed excessive chip counting because such counting is never done at market bottoms. Valuation normally should occur every three to six months. In fact, some investors use even a conscious curiosity or semi-serious intention to count their chips too frequently as red flags. Calibrate your own typical pattern: If you usually count monthly and now start looking weekly, that is your signal. Another and even more dangerous indicator of a market top based on one's individual response patterns is the decision or serious temptation to add a chunk of capital to one's equity account (or mutual funds portfolio) after a significant market rise—precisely as occurred on a massive scale in early 2000. This takes place because the investor observes that the bullish trend is well established and therefore erroneously decides that it is foolish not to increase exposure. Or he may perceive an excess of attractive new ideas; anticipating price strength to continue, he will not want to sell any existing holdings to fund new purchases. In effect, he is acting like the proverbial child in a candy store, coveting one of everything. The predictable result (fairly soon) will be an adult-sized bellyache when the feeding frenzy is over.

A good antidote to the adding-money warning is the substitute practice of selling any time when overconfident behavior arises. Not just incidentally, if your broker refuses to help actively in such an arrangement, says conditions are different this time than in the past, or tells you it is unnecessary because the market is in no danger, consider that to be a strong, even an urgent, signal to sell (and to change brokers). Brokers are human beings, and you can watch their behaviors, in addition to your own, for emotional signals of the time becoming ripe for selling. There are some conscientious brokers who have the moral fortitude not to pander to a client's overexcitement when they personally believe it is time to sell. Get help from this kind of broker by asking one to give a loud warning as soon as they see top-typical behavior from you or some of their other clients. This would be one of the useful services that could make paying the higher commissions of a full-service firm worthwhile, if you are indeed getting that valuable service.

Ideally, and as discussed in more detail in Chapter 16, each sale should be timed and made on its own merit. Over time as a market's cycle matures, a diversified portfolio should gradually be liquidated as an increasing number of stocks reach or exceed reasonable or targeted price levels. Unless the investor has identified truly counter-cyclical issues to buy at that time, the series of multiple sales she makes based on discipline should act as a signal of topping out rather than as a ready source of funding for new buys. Sometimes an over-stimulated investor with too many apparently attractive ideas can become frustrated in a strong market, especially when there is no more available cash to add to the account. Therefore, to satisfy the urge to buy into the new ideas, an investor liquidates one or more existing positions, not on their own merits, but to raise money to pay for greater excitement. This substitute behavior is a good example of how the failure to exercise a specific red-flag behavior should not be excused. If the investor seriously considers adding to her stake after a long rise but instead ends up merely selling in order to buy, the danger signal is just as validly in effect.

A wary and circumspect investor should be especially suspicious if there is the urge to sell existing positions to move funds into recent new issues or actual initial public offerings. Even if one eschews the IPO games, moving to more risky (e.g., recent-fad, high P/E ratio, high-technology) stocks late in a rise is a similar symptomatic signal. It is very likely he has become psychologically bullied by an overheated market environment, seeing so many stocks doing well and hearing so many friends bragging of their successes.

Typically, investors will be getting virtually no encouragement from brokers to sell at a time like this. Brokers, too, are enjoying the ride and are in a very positive frame of mind. Their training, dependence on trading commissions, and refusal to rain on client parades by suggesting that even bull markets come to an end all point to no talk about selling. This means that, on their own, investors will need to lean against the tide and should expect to feel lonely in order to sell in a timely manner. Just as at such times you will be getting a lot of unsolicited broker suggestions about new ideas to play, so too the temptation will feel overwhelming to put more chips onto the table.

Any or all of these phenomena should suggest an extended or overheated market that threatens to top out soon. Heed such signals and sell. Selling at the time will be a lonely exercise, but the reward comes from quiet knowledge that the crowd is usually wrong and the contrarian usually correct at turning points. So, when tempted to add money, sell instead. In this type of market circumstance, it is important to keep emotions under control. Remember that in seeking psychological gratification from the market (moving towards comfort or away from discomfort), an investor is sowing the seeds of financial discomfort. Comfort at the top is holding and buying more (late); comfort at the bottom is getting into cash (late). Move towards discomfort.

CHAPTER 14

Adjust Sale Targets Rationally

Keys for Successful Selling

◆ Have a Price Objective with Three Key Elements

◆ Make Reasonable Downward Modifications to Expectations

◆ Always Remain Tactically Nimble as Key Facts Change

Most investors inevitably wonder if the market plays fair; this chapter demonstrates that stocks go where they want to despite what any participants think is justified and despite what we might wish would happen. An investor over time attaches some validity to his initial price objective, meaning that modifying that expectation becomes difficult for reasons that are totally contained inside his head alone. But what any single investor wants is irrelevant, so it is important to avoid developing a set-concrete mind-set about price objectives. The rest of the market may be thinking different thoughts, and facts are constantly changing, so mental flexibility is required.

Be prepared as well to let go of original price opinions, if or more likely when events warrant a change. Remain flexible and realistic rather than unreasonably optimistic and/or obstinate. An investor unable or unwilling to change—to become right in a world that itself does change—is doomed to lose. There are two primary ways that investors get into trouble when setting price objectives:

◆ The initial idea, including the selling-price objective, may have been wrong from the start.

◆ Although correct at first, the original idea can become outdated and therefore inaccurate as subsequent events transpire.

In both cases, original thinking can be either overly optimistic or unnecessarily pessimistic. It is important to reexamine the market environment constantly in search of inputs that warrant adjusting one's scenario on proper price expectation, in light of both fundamental metrics and shifting market psychology. When analyzing the environment, exercise extreme care not to be selective—not to credit only those factors that support the direction and extent of your starting thesis. An approach that merely seeks to validate original thinking is worse than valueless because it misleads us by neglecting to prompt valid questioning and cautions. It strokes the ego (with either validation or consolation) while allowing the brain to run at idle speed—or worse, on cruise control in a wrong direction! Such an exercise deals in less than full reality.

A Price Objective with Three Key Elements

Price objectives, both when set initially and when reconsidered later, should have three elements. Failure to include them indicates a purchase or a holding decision not well thought out. Such holdings will become permanent relics through the mental back door. Absence of the three realistic assumptions signals probable rationalization.

When a stock is purchased, it should be with a target sale price in mind. Buying merely because a stock is acting well or represents a great company is the beginning of trouble since those mind-sets imply no clear exit path, no sell discipline. A proper sale target includes a combination of three parts: a price, based on a story and in a time fame. This can easily be remembered conveniently as PST, like the whispered voice of reminder or conscience. Such a script or scenario for a stock purchase might say, for example, that XYZ shares should trade at $39 because a certain new product (or expanding market share or improved margins or cost cutting, etc.) will produce EPS of $2.60, and a justifiable price/earnings ratio is 15; those earnings should occur in 15 months, so the stock should sell at $39 by that time.

If any element is missing, the story is too loosely conceived, and the position will become open ended, resulting in financial drift and wishful thinking and probably leading to a loss. If there is no story, or driver, the idea is probably nothing more than a chase after current momentum. If there seems to be a story (e.g., a great research and development program) but it has no clear date or goal for accomplishment, the true story may amount to no more than admiration of reputation. A biotechnology company should have a specific drug due for approval by a predictable date. If not, you are buying merely on vague hope or general corporate aura. If there is a clear story with a related time frame, it still must be quantifiable. Just generally seeing the market as being excited over that new drug approval or an expected granting of a key patent is not enough. Current (buy) price, having been established by the consensus of many other investors, may already discount that expected future excitement. Your scenario should have clear reasons for a given price target. Your target probably will not prove precisely accurate, but your thinking should be sharp lest your money be in trouble from day one.

One must be able to project a future climate in believable numerical terms: The earnings will be X and the P/E reasonably will be Y, or analysts will then project a product market of Z dollars and say the company should sell at so-many-times sales, which represents its realistic attainable market target. Failure to have a concrete price goal allows you to fall into the trap of celebrating already-expected good news while having no disciplined intention of asking whether a resulting price jump is high enough to justify sale.

Successful investing requires correctly anticipating change. Projecting merely an extension of the present is lazy thinking, and a changing world is likely to prove such soft scenarios off base. The market, meaning the crowd, is now paying (in today's price) for what it can already see! Your buying, and your sale-price target, should be based on a specific something additional or different. That might be changed facts, more generous valuation or improved psychology—or some combination of those.

When reconsidering a price objective, be careful not to become greedy and turn into a cheerleader for your stock. Only new and positive information that previously was unanticipated should prompt an increase in your price target. If good news—a new product, a contract won, strong EPS, a higher dividend or even a takeover proposal—is in line with earlier reasons for buying the stock, note merely that one part of the projected scenario (i.e., your story) is coming to pass and that the stock may begin to achieve your price objective. Do not double count such positives by upping your target.

If good news does occur, it then becomes important to remain calm; excitement over the good news should not overwhelm judgment just because everything is going so well. The investor who counts positive factors twice is engaging in self-delusion. There are both positive and negative factors that legitimately prompt a reassessment of price objectives and they should be studied in light of two strong caveats: (1) as noted in Chapter 7, your price paid does not matter, and (2) while realistic reasons may arise that lead to cutting the price objective once a stock is held, do not allow those changes to prompt lowering a stop-loss order.

Except to protect against possible panics in heavily institutionally owned stocks, it is generally not a great idea to use stop-loss orders. This heretical position is expounded in Chapter 23. But if entered, stops must not be pulled or lowered, or they become useless. They may actually become worse than useless by temporarily providing false comfort while they did exist.

When examining a potential equity investment, an investor makes a number of assumptions; any could be unconscious or wrong. Some buying assumptions are as follows:

- ◆ information sources are accurate and disinterested.
- ◆ some specific good thing actually will happen fundamentally.
- ◆ that event will be big enough to move price meaningfully.
- ◆ that event is not already anticipated in the price.

- interest rates will be at a certain level and moving in a favorable direction, supporting the general level and P/Es of future stock prices.
- the psychology of the market, irrespective of fundamentals such as earnings and interest rates, will be in at least a neutral state.
- the projected price is not out of line with demonstrably reasonable valuation standards such as yield or P/E ratio.
- major developments in the industry or in relevant sectors of the economy will create or allow the expected stock-price climate to exist.
- political and/or geopolitical factors will be as expected.
- the projected scenario can reasonably happen in the time window used.
- the investor is not oblivious to important factors that, if known, would temper his enthusiasm or make him think the stock is not undervalued.
- he has not been misled deliberately.
- the world will go on as it is now.
- there will not be positive or negative wild cards in play.

A technically oriented trader (probably unconsciously) also assumes many of the steady-state supportive fundamental factors noted above. This participant substitutes a key market-price buying trigger and technically derived price target for he fundamentalist's positive new event.

Modifications to Expectations

As indicated earlier, each, or at least very many, of these factors should be in place when a buying decision is made. But they cannot be expected to remain static. Therefore, set a reasonable selling target for the stock at the outset, but understand that any target becomes subject to immediate and ongoing modification because the world does not stand still. Assume that change will occur; to do otherwise is operating in a bubble of fantasy designed to justify your mental inertia.

Suppose, for example, that an investor is attracted to a certain company, perhaps a drug firm that has a good record of increasing earnings and that occupies a leading position in prescription preparations for diseases of the elderly, a growing population sector. Stocks in general have been soft lately, so, as a contrarian, she senses an opportunity to buy a fundamentally attractive stock at a good price. She checks several sources of earnings estimates and projects that, at an historically realistic relative P/E ratio, the stock could sell at $38 in 18 months, despite a current $28 quote. She then buys, setting $38 as the objective. (Actually, she should be prepared to sell out a bit below that exact level so that a 100 percent perfect analysis is not required to generate acceptable locked-in profits.)

Each of the factors in that extensive list given above is subject to sudden or gradual change, so our investor must always be ready to adjust the price objective for cashing in. Here are just some things that could go wrong:

◆ product tampering on an over-the-counter medicine could hurt the company or cast a psychological pall over the whole drug group; in another industry scenario, an airplane crash could raise safety concerns about all small or discount airlines.

◆ management could signal upcoming fluctuations in earnings due to product testing/approval cycles and R&D costs, whereas smooth earnings had earlier been the prevailing expectation.

◆ analysts and portfolio managers could become considerably less tolerant of even minor changes in sales growth or earnings trends, particularly in high-technology or high-P/E groups.

◆ the value of the dollar could fluctuate, changing translations of foreign costs or earnings.

◆ a strike may disrupt production, or supplies of materials.

◆ federal deficit-reduction pressure could intensify, putting a tighter squeeze on medical reimbursements and/or raising interest rates (the latter implying a lower P/E as realistic).

◆ a competing firm could come out with an exciting new product or technology.

◆ generic equivalents could gain market penetration faster than earlier expected.

◆ tax or antitrust legislation could dampen takeover appeal across the board, causing an industry's stocks to lose attraction.

◆ the company could be sued by a competitor for patent infringement, by the government for poor testing procedures, or by a competitor or the Justice Department for antitrust violations.

◆ the market could become speculative, abandoning traditional growth stocks in favor of short-term concept plays; it could change emphasis from cyclical to growth stocks or vice versa. Preferences between small- and large-cap stocks could flip.

◆ tax-law changes (such as seen in May 2003) or merely the aging of the investing population could make dividends more attractive than growth.

◆ margin regulations could be tightened (although this has not happened for many years).

◆ fund managers could decide that other industries are more interesting.

◆ on further reading, the investor could discover that some of the good things projected were already predicted by a major brokerage analyst, implying that the remaining upside is smaller than thought since those ideas are already in today's price.

◆ wild-card trouble of some sort could develop.

Here are some unexpected good things that could happen, thereby implying upward-revising a target:

◆ management could announce an unexpected but promising new drug (or other new product type in a different industry).

◆ major magazines could feature this stock as one of the top 10 to buy for the next year or as some star portfolio guru's favorite, broadening investors' awareness.

◆ tax laws more favorable to research and development (R&D) or to offshore manufacturing could be proposed or enacted.

◆ economic forecasts could shift positively, implying that stocks are due for a more extended rise than had earlier been thought reasonable.

◆ mild recession talk could develop, cutting interest rates and moving investors toward defensive industry groups such as drugs, foods, supermarkets and utilities.

◆ a change of party control in Washington could occur, implying more spending on health or reduced regulation.

◆ an existing company drug could be discovered to have positive effects in the treatment of a second major disease.

◆ the company could have a breakthrough in research on a hot drug type for treating AIDS, Alzheimer's, or cancer.

◆ the company could announce a restructuring plan designed to enhance shareholder value, or could announce that directors have authorized exploring strategic alternatives (corporate code for saying the company is up for sale).

◆ a well-known corporate raider could take a position in your stock or in another one within its industry (e.g., this occurred with Kirk Kerkorian for GM in 2005 and MGM in 2007).

◆ earnings could rise above estimates for sustainable reasons.

◆ favorable foreign exchange fluctuations could occur.

◆ an actual or rumored takeover proposal could occur for the company or in its industry.

◆ positive wild cards could develop.

Now think about a few possible types of negative jolts. The negative reverses of many of the positive events listed above are possible. But in addition, a major externality, as economists like to call them, such as a regional war or a new worldwide oil embargo threatens to disrupt the economic expansion or to boost inflation sharply. Bonds and stocks will fall across the board, regardless of the attractiveness of specific companies, their newest exciting products, or their present relative under-valuations. Revisit Figure 12-4. In this suddenly changed scenario, P/E ratios, driven by rising yields, generally will fall, forcing the investor's relative P/E-derived target lower. The stock remains undervalued, but at a lower price and with a lowered future target. And the time frame for a possible realization of one's original scenario is considerably lengthened because inflation takes a long time to quiet down. Targets must be lowered and very likely the stock sold immediately regardless of the existing paper gain or loss. One's old target literally has become an irrelevant relic of a past time.

Therefore, analysts cut EPS estimates. Investors trim their levels of tolerable risk. On seeing signs that a major shift is occurring among institutional investors, you must assume that— right or wrong—this new opinion or perception trend will take some time to play out; it will end with prices lower and attitudes less favorable towards the growth drug company (or whatever else is the case) than they are today.

In this scenario, one's earnings forecast may still prove entirely correct, but the expected actual or relative P/E ratio has been rendered too high for the time frame originally established for cashing in. The psychological damage may take a long time to repair. On a market-wide scale, our investor is looking at the longer-term or bigger- picture equivalent of a company announcing good news on a day when the Dow is down 160 points on heavy volume. The positive fundamentals are swept away by the negative psychological tide of the time. Thus, expectations must be adjusted downward to account for the emotional damage sustained, or one will in fact be holding the stock to reach a now-unrealistic goal.

Other major factors, not even related directly to the company, can force a lowering of targets. For example, companies in other high-technology or growth industries such as computers and software (does this sound like middle 2000) start reporting disappointing earnings. This happened in housing stocks in late 2005. As a result, the bloom comes off the rose for many favored stocks or those with traditionally high multiples, even though their specific fundamentals may be unchanged.

Tactically, only the introduction of important new factors should serve to increase previously established estimates of reasonable value. A near-term jump of two points on good quarterly earnings is not a reason to raise a long-term target by $2. If truly important new information arises, expectations must be adjusted up or down.

Here is an example of truly important changes in the scenario. Suppose that, in the preceding example, the initial judgment of fair value is $38 and the target for cashing in is $35. Suppose time has elapsed and other factors have not changed (unlikely), or there have been offsetting pluses and minuses that leave the target unchanged. Our holder has been lucky, and the price is now at $33.50 due, primarily, to a rising overall market. Suddenly, a bid is made for another drug company by a major European or Japanese conglomerate. This opens a new round of potentials on the upside. The valuation numbers may get historically full, but the market senses that a phase of bidding up is just starting. Our holder might suspend temporarily her resolve to sell at $35 because the sights for all drug stocks are going to be raised. Suppose instead that a hostile bid comes in for this company. The offer is $40 and the stock goes to $41 in hopes that another shoe will drop. The investor thinks $40 is fundamentally full or even excessive, and she may well be right. But if management, normally circumspect and credible, advises shareholders not to act hurriedly and to anticipate a possible company response that could raise prices further, our holder should very temporarily suspend that standard of reasonableness by a few points and sell on the next concrete positive news. One must remain fluid but totally logical, reacting realistically to major new items in the picture but yet not getting carried away with enthusiasm. The question, Would I buy it now? is always a highly useful focuser of one's thinking.

Three Classic Case Studies

Here is an actual case history illustrating the need to modify targets. An investor in late 1989 could buy Long Island Lighting Company (LILCo) in the $17 to $18 range. Under an agreement with the state of New York, LILCo scrapped its costly Shoreham nuclear plant in exchange for needed rate hikes for several years. It then publicly committed to dividend rates of $1.00, $1.50 and $2.00 for the years 1989, 1990 and 1991. The implied original downside scenario for late 1991 was that, even if no more dividend hikes were in prospect, the stock could sell on an 8 percent current-yield basis, or at $25, which implied a very attractive total return over 24 months from a buy price in the $17 to $18 range.

Although dividends actually grew less sharply than originally projected or desired, only the temporary surprise of the Gulf War kept interest rates from declining faster than earlier hoped. By late 1991, with a dividend rate of $1.70 in place, a reasonable discounting yield was down to 6.5 percent rather than the projected 8 percent, allowing an increase in the investor's original target, to $26.25. The stock actually moved to above $29 in 1993.

But then during 1993, directors sharply decelerated dividend growth, raising the payout from $1.70 to just $1.78. Having been given a gift in the form of unexpectedly low interest rates, and therefore raising his target, the investor would be foolish to ignore a second negative dividend signal and should have been happy to accept $26.25 (a modified target) on unexpectedly low interest rates. That the stock overshot by three points was not to be regretted since a second negative fundamental red flag had been raised. Had one not sold out at the target price (through placing an above-market order well in advance), the dividend deceleration would have been a sell-at-market signal in 1993, in effect representing a sharply reduced price expectation. This situation involved first an upward revision (due to lower-than-hoped interest rates) and then a downward shift of sale targets (due to negative dividend-growth signals). Eventually the company was to strike a partnership with nearby Brooklyn Union Gas, and the combination was later acquired by a British company, but that goes beyond the scope of our study.

A high-tech example of changing targets is also of illustrative value. Lotus Development Corporation suffered an earnings downturn due to product development costs with Lotus Notes. Its earnings quickly rebounded, with estimates of $2.20 per share for the following year. If one had estimated a reasonable P/E of 20 times, based on growth for a software company, the price target would have been $44. However, as soon as IBM was rumored to be interested in acquiring Lotus, that target would have been suspended. IBM's decision would have been the sell trigger either way: If Big Blue walked away, figuring it did not want to pay a premium above $44, what investor should have doubted its judgment? A sale would be in order at market. When IBM decided to pay $66 in a preemptive strike, that also became an immediate sale signal well above the original $44 target. Why wait around for any possible trouble like a not-inconceivable Justice Department inquiry, perhaps a disappointing earnings surprise quarter to make IBM rethink its decision, or anything else? Take the gift. (As later history developed, Notes would be swamped competitively by Excel and thus IBM would be proved to have vastly overpaid, but again that is another story.)

Curiously, another IBM decision stands as an example of a reason for changing price targets: its decision not to acquire Apple Computer. Apple had lost its founding chief, Steve Jobs. Its penetration had begun slowing, and its market share was slipping. Stock-price objectives were being lowered until both Sun Microsystems and IBM were named as possible suitors. As events had it, both passed on the opportunity. In such a high-technology industry, when two leaders demur on acquiring a company, the revised target should immediately become sell at market. Apple stock was soon sliced in half, from $40 to $20. Later events would give the company a rebirth, but they could not be foreseen at the time those two rumored suitors walked away!

Summary Thoughts

Sale-price targets must be set from the start, or there is no focus and no discipline. But those targets must be written in pencil because circumstances in the real world will almost always change. And we must work hard to keep our ego firmly under control so that changing an original price target is not a psychological problem. The mind should remain fluid, looking for important factors to add to the equation as plus or minus adjustments to that original price objective.

It is critical, although by no means always easy, to sort out in real time the truly important from the passing and trivial. Even though they are the hot focus of financial TV's buzz, quarterly earnings almost always fall under the latter description. It is crucial to resist emotional tides and take action only after the mood of the crowd has abated. The market moves to manic tops as well as to panic bottoms, so the investor must adjust targets and risk tolerances for such extremes. And at all times, one must be mindful of the need to remain dispassionate by resisting the temptation to become a holder turned loyalist or cheerleader. Again, the critical question should be asked: If I did not own this stock already, would I buy it today, knowing what I (and the market) do now, at the current price? If the honest answer is not strongly affirmative, it is time to cash in and move on.

There is no need to be loyal to any stock; it is an inanimate object without feelings to be hurt. You can change your mind and sell. If you are wrong, you can always buy back. The lower your commissions expenses, the less it will cost to buy a little distance and risk insurance, even if you later do change your mind and buy back. Keep your price targets fluid and realistic. The market will always have its own way, without regard to what your old opinion was. No need to lock in on that opinion forever, because the market will not.

CHAPTER 15

Try This Exercise in Forced Discipline

Keys for Successful Selling

- ◆ Let an Options Trade Teach Discipline
- ◆ Take the Tutorial for Options Novices

It is said that there is no substitute for experience. In the real world (of investments and otherwise) where decisions are required in a real-time mode, experience picks up and fills in where theory ends. In making decisions to hold or to sell stocks, reality is a great teacher and disciplinarian. In fact, all too commonly the decision to hold a stock is not conscious; usually it is an inaction by default. The hidden purpose of such a non-decision to hold is to spare the investor the tension of making a decision to sell and of actually executing that decision. Taking action to sell is more challenging that ordering a buy, so a forced exercise in selling should help.

Letting an Options Trade Teach Discipline

What follows is an exercise that will help investors learn the discipline necessary to make the selling decision consciously. In this exercise, your author suggests that investors buy some options—worse yet, short-term options. This experience, carefully defined and timed as outlined here, carries a good deal of educational and psychological value that does not exist in any paper market-following experiment. An imaginary scenario theoretically involving options cannot teach the lessons of urgency and discipline that are required for real market trading because there is no money involved in a fantasy. So no emotions are involved—including the pitfalls, and the tactics to use against greed, fear, pain and elation. Fantasy paper profits are not real, so they are not vivid enough to drive strong emotional responses that tend to cause mistakes.

In a similar way, there is no artificial way to create true-time urgency. One of the aspects of selling that subtly but so often strongly leads investors to fail is the lack of any forced closure point: the market opens up again tomorrow morning, so the game continues if an investor does not take action today to stop it. It will continue until he takes action. If he never takes any action, the game will go on in spite of him (and because of him); he has become a passive collector rather than an investor.

Options have a unique characteristic making them ideal for teaching discipline: they have a finite life. There is an absolute end to each option's trading life: the Friday afternoon before the third Saturday of the month. Calling a time-out is not an available choice. Option holders must sell or exercise, or lose whatever value remains. (Some brokerage firms exercise at the close on the expiration trading day for the option holder if he fails to respond to expiration notices and if there is enough value to cover round-turn commissions.) When owning options, taking the attitude that you will come back and think about it some more at leisure is just not an option.

Although this exercise entails probable cost (which there is a way to minimize), consider that expense worth the opportunity to learn how to make a decision to sell in a real-world environment. We will assume that the options involved are calls because people usually think in bullish terms and because understanding value in these contracts is easier than with puts, especially if the reader is an options novice.

To limit the possible net cost of this exercise, buy options that have a very short period of time remaining to expiration; about two weeks is a good choice for this purpose. Further, choose a stock whose trading price is at, or very slightly above a multiple of $5.00, which is the most common multiple of striking prices in listed options. Finally, select a stock that is relatively stable or nonvolatile and that provides a good dividend yield. All three of these suggested criteria—short remaining life, proximity to strike price and low underlying stock-price stability—will contribute to a low risk exposure in terms of dollars.

A good example might be an electric utility stock not in the path of a coming hurricane. Choose a company with a record of ongoing annual dividend increases to avoid falling into a dividend-cut snake pit by accident. Also, be sure that the stock does not go ex-dividend during the remaining option life. And do not purchase in a month when the company reports quarterly earnings (i.e., the month after the fiscal quarter ends). A good example of the relatively low volatility of mature utility stocks is provided by Consolidated Edison, (NYSE:ED). In each of the years 2003-2007 its shares traded in about a $7 range around a middle price in the 40s, or less than 20 percent year around average price.

For illustration, assume that on or about September 1, we buy ten calls on a mythical XYZ Electric Service with a strike price of $25.00 and expiration on September 16. Suppose the stock is trading at $25.20 at the time and that $0.35 per share ($35 per 100 shares) is paid on a limit order for those options, plus commission.

For 10 calls, which gives the right (but not the obligation) to buy 1,000 shares, $350 plus commission has been put on the line. (You could cut this in half by using five options, but the emotional impact will be softened in that case.) Thus, a game is created that must be played actively. The first goal is to make money. The fall-back positions are to break even or at worst to minimize any loss. In either case, learning by doing is actually our most important purpose. Consider the clock as both an enemy and a helpful goad.

A Tutorial for Options Novices

A trade group called the Options Industry Council provides a fine website, 888Options.com, which offers booklets, tapes, videos and even podcasts to help people learn about options. It is an excellent resource recommended for in-depth options learning. Our purpose here is only to provide a very brief tutorial that will enable understanding of the discipline exercise being suggested.

For options novices, the following is a description of our suggested purchase: A call option is a contract that allows its owner the right (but does not impose the obligation) to buy 100 shares of the underlying common stock at a specified price (called a strike price) up to and including a specific date of expiration.

In this case, each call entitles an investor to buy 100 shares of XYZ Electric at $25.00 per share, right up to market close on September 16. In options-market lingo, you are long ten XYZ September 25s. Once September 16 is past, the option will have expired with zero value if it was not exercised. It can be sold at any time before it expires, thereby transferring the right (and the time pressure) to a new buyer. With the stock trading above the strike price, namely at $25.20 per share, the option clearly has some intrinsic value: It can be exercised now and the stock would be worth more than the $25.00 paid to exercise. The option is inherently worth the difference, or at this moment 20 cents per share. But the option actually trades somewhat above that intrinsic value because it has some remaining life. It has a time value, although in this example there is only minimal speculative value to that time. Therefore, probably $0.35 per share as a total price is realistic, including both the intrinsic value (at this moment) and the remaining time premium.

Gradually between your purchase date and expiration date, the time-value premium of $0.15 will essentially disappear, and the option finally trades at intrinsic value alone. But a total disappearance of premium for time happens late in the game—so late that the slight premium mentioned above should be paid in order to buy a remaining game that will take enough time to be useful as a learning laboratory.

Back to Our Trade as Teacher

The objects are to come out of this trading experience with as much money as possible and, more importantly, to gain a newfound sense of urgency and decisiveness about all choices of whether to hold or sell. As noted earlier, nothing forces an equity investor to make a decision about selling. If you hold a stock today, you can think about it again tomorrow. If you hold tomorrow, there always is another trading day after that. With a stock, there is no imperative closure, no deadline. Option rules are, however, critically different. There is no escaping that looming September 16 expiration date on your calendar; you must make a decision. Playing this option-trading game greatly intensifies, on a daily basis, all those feelings normally experienced when one owns a stock; a sharp and growing sense of urgency is overlaid because of the approach of expiration (see Figure 15-1).

If an investor buys a two-week contract, 10 percent of his possible-profit time window of ten remaining sessions disappears the first day. With just four days left, 25 percent of the remaining time horizon evaporates the next day. With two days left, it is 50 percent. One must then decide to act today or accept tomorrow's verdict, which will be final. Time value within the total option price is evaporating with each trading session!

Normally when an investor owns a stock, he feels good when it rises; he wants more but also fears giving back the paper gains. When it goes down, he resents the loss and fears the price may evaporate further, causing more loss. But because he owns a stock, he can stretch out his time horizon and let the stock and the general market do what they will, or what he hopes they will. He is under no requirement to sell at any time. The option, by contrast, dies at a known time. Therefore, choices are defined within a very specific time window.

This tension is unpleasant. Often, passing time generates such pressure that an option holder makes a mistake in sale timing that he would not make ordinarily if he were selling a stock. By actually doing this exercise, an investor will learn that he can pull the sell trigger and that doing so is not as frightening or as unpleasant as imagined. Our brave learner then owns the experience of having done it, so selling will be more familiar and less difficult the next time. But most of all, the pressure of time forces him to make a decision rather than postpone it—a highly valuable experience. While the financial result may be less than fully pleasant, one useful lesson learned will be that selling in not a huge, life-changing act.

Each day our utility stock may fluctuate by well less than a dollar. Unless something surprising happens to the overall market (perhaps caused by shifting interest-rate expectations), expect the stock to wiggle only a little. This relative stability helps backhandedly: Because of its low volatility, the stock is unlikely to move much on any day or two. Therefore, with just a few days left until expiration, the investor realizes that further movement is likely to be minor and that therefore there is not much to be gained by hoping for a lucky upside run. That sobering perspective should help tilt the decision between holding and selling. If the stock starts by going up, there is little reason to let greed take over: this is a stock that typically makes only narrow moves. So, to be realistic, do not expect much more upside gain inside just two weeks.

Figure 15.1: Market Value of an Option: Intrinsic and Time Components

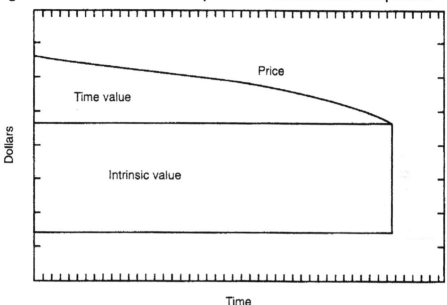

Time

Even if the company is strong and releases no new news, the overall market could go down tomorrow or the next day for some reason, taking away any gain swiftly with only an even shorter opportunity remaining for possible recovery before expiration. If the stock instead begins by going down, our investor lacks the luxury of being a trader-turned-collector: The game will end on the appointed expiration date, and one's job is to salvage what one can. The point is to try to get the reasonably best execution in the remaining days. Early in the game, there is a time premium that can be sold to someone else. But as the days wear on, you will have consumed that premium as a payment for having stayed in the game. Note that the emotional effect of each fluctuation is intensified. For example, a mere 25-cent rise (one percent) in the stock's price nearly doubles the option quote. An investor might start thinking that if it would go up just a dollar he could make several hundred percent. The press of time should, however, curb such expansive hopes.

What if the rally reverses and he starts giving back what he earned? He must be tighter on the trigger than if he owned the stock itself, which he could keep holding for months or even years in hope or in stubbornness. If he owned the stock, a 25-cent rise would cheer him little if at all because he would know the stock is typically stable and might give it back in a day or week just in normal fluctuation. And just by owning the stock rather than the option, he would be signaling a probable long-term relationship which he has no intention of terminating for a mere quarter point in hand today. He is holding for the dividends anyway.

But with the option, he is in a damage-control mode in which he must pay a second commission to get the best price in two weeks' time. Should he hold and take another dime's risk, or cash in now? What if he cashes in to end the risk and tension and the stock then runs to $26 but corrects back to $25.25 a week later? How will he feel then?

No matter whether the stock rises, falls or holds steady in the first week or so, if he is still holding the options he will have come to rue the meaning of the phrase, thank goodness it is Friday. The Friday deadline will be a sword of Damocles hanging over his head, forcing him to make a decision. If he holds, each day of no change or fractional loss leaves him less time for potential gain or for recouping losses. He starts looking at each nickel or dime of fluctuation as a big percentage against his stake. And it is. The looming time constraint allows him no chance to relax, however, because all could be lost with one wrong decision to hold too long. The option could go to a nickel a share, or it could be five cents offered, no bid, so he must decide not to allow himself to forfeit everything he has put on the table.

Expect that the decision will not be perfect. Unless sale occurs extremely late into the two-week period, the underlying stock and the option itself will probably have time to tick up above the exit level at some point before the final bell tolls. That is just the way the market is and always will be. Therefore, learn to accept imperfection as virtually inevitable. Do not expect to beat the market for all the possible profit it offers—for that proverbial or literal final nickel. Learn to live with your choice and move on to the next situation.

This exercise in decisiveness, if applied as suggested using a full ten contracts, may cost at most a few hundred dollars. Consider it tuition well spent. You will own dozens of stocks in the future, and a little extra learned decisiveness could save you many thousands in wealth. You must learn to sell, to commit that act of accepting closure in the face of uncertainty. A little well-bounded options-trading exercise such as this one could prove a valuable teacher of that reality and of better selling skills.

CHAPTER 16
Separate Selling from New Buying

Keys for Successful Selling

◆ Expect Rotational Group Leadership

◆ Beware of the Simultaneous Switch

◆ Keep a Seller's Checklist

There are several reasons why investors should not sell one stock to raise funds for buying another. A stock sale transacted solely to fund a new purchase frequently turns out to be a double mistake: The sale can be badly timed and the purchase can be badly chosen or poorly timed. Based on a matrix of relative post-switch performance, the theoretical odds are more than 2:1 against a successful transaction (see Figure 16-1).

In general, the odds are more favorable if an investor is buying but not selling, or selling but not buying, at any given time rather than doing both together. The exceptions to this guideline require having pinpoint accuracy in detecting rotational group leadership in the general market or knowing something that borders on inside information—or just plain blind luck. Smart investors dismiss blind luck. Luck is something pleasant to accept when it happens but not something to count on, which leaves rotational group leadership to consider.

Figure 16.1: Relative Post-Switch Performance Results

Action of Replacement Bought

		Up More	Equal Move	Down More or Up Less	Flat	Down
Action of Old Stock Sold	Up	Good	Out commission cost	Bad	Bad	Bad
	Flat	Good	Out commission cost	Bad	Out commission cost	Bad
	Down	Good	Out commission cost	Bad	Good	Out commission cost

Rotational Group Leadership

Significant stock market movements tend to carry the majority of stocks with them in one overall direction—either up or down. In fact, market historians and technicians use a tool called a diffusion index (see Chapter 17) as an indicator to detect the end of an overall advance. By that definition, a top occurs when a majority of stocks are no longer moving up within the time frame studied.

Because the majority of stocks move in the same direction most of the time, mathematically the odds do not favor an investor or trader who buys one stock and sells another simultaneously unless it is done because the sold stock, independent of the market, has fundamental or technical problems or has reached a technical price target without obvious help from the overall trend. If the market is in a period of broad advance, raw random odds indicate that both the stock currently held as well as the proposed buy candidate would be advancing. Conversely, if a declining period is to follow the switching action, the odds favor both the stock currently held and its proposed replacement moving lower at the same time.

Naturally there are exceptions, as in any case in which mathematical probabilities are operating. But the odds exist as described earlier. Over time, an investor fares better by playing on the side of the odds rather than against them. Good advice would steer investors toward seizing opportunities where probabilities of winning are above average.

As previously mentioned, the single exception to not selling and buying at the same time involves successful timing of group rotation. During a period of market advance, not all stocks rally at the same pace. While the overall bias for a majority of issues is generally upward in a bull market, some individual stocks or entire industry groups push ahead for a while even as others seem to lag behind and rest. Then a rotation of leadership takes place; some prior laggards come to the front of the pack while some recent leaders rest. In early 2007, for example, oils and metals led while homebuilders and banks trailed.

At the bottom of a major market cycle, those investors who have the courage to buy at all tend to concentrate in blue-chip stocks. At the top, when optimism reigns supreme for weeks or months, speculative fever takes hold and-lower quality or smaller-capitalization issues provide most of the action and the leadership for the rally. This is a very broad, or macro, description of rotational leadership. Industry-oriented rotations take place as well. The group that leads at any given time depends to some extent on what industry has been lagging lately and so becomes more attractive. This pattern has become even more apparent in recent years as money managers widely use computers to monitor market movements more closely and comprehensively, in real time, than was the case several decades ago.

Another factor that affects rotational leadership is the national (and world) news environment. Depending on what news dominates the media at a given time, certain industry groups lead and others lag. For example, if inflation is quiet, the expectation of lower interest rates is likely to develop. Interest-sensitive industry groups then get an upside play, including banks, savings and loans, insurance firms REITs, and utilities. Housing and automobile manufacturing stocks may move up in this phase in the expectation that lower interest rates will encourage consumer purchases. If the dollar is low or falling in international value, the idea of a boom in basic industry stocks, supported by favorable changes in export/import trends, could take hold. Steel, machinery and chemicals issues do well in this phase. The point is that in a sustained advance, one group leads for weeks or months only to be supplanted by another. News developments might be the trigger, or in other cases computerized monitoring by leading hedge funds might (with no public announcement, of course) decide relative value is better in one industry than in the one that has recently run up nicely.

In such rotational scenarios, simultaneously buying one stock and selling another makes statistical sense only if the one can identify the leadership changes and time such changes accurately. This is very difficult to do; unless one can do that successfully, the statistical odds of winning in a simultaneous buy-and-sale are low. The likeliest probability is that both stocks will move up or both will move down.

Thus, except for the possibility of a much greater percentage move in one stock versus the other, there usually is insufficient justification for a sale-purchase switch. To recap, if most issues are dropping or seem poised to decline, execute the sell but postpone reinvesting the proceeds. (One makes invisible and pleasantly untaxed profits by standing aside and not buying too high; these are not as exciting but add every bit as much to capital as the visible gain that comes after a successful purchase.) When stocks are generally running or seem about to rise, it is better not to sell at the time of another purchase. Buying may be more profitably accomplished with added funds or even through using margin. Such choices should come only in a contrarian mode.

Beware of the Simultaneous Switch

There is a dangerous psychology underlying the sell-to-buy of a simultaneous switch. If an investor is buying a stock and is already fully invested, it is probable that he has begun to indulge a prevailing bullish frame of mind to overrule cold logic. Presumably if he is already so fully invested that a sale is required (to generate funds) before he can make a purchase, the market itself might be well into an advance. One of course is typically not invested fully at the bottom because of fear.

As the market moves higher, particularly for a stretch of a few years or at least many months, investors begin to see more success stories and to feel some strongly performing stocks are passing them by. The game seems to be easier, the odds more in one's favor. When this scenario develops, it seems a time for the investor to retain what he already owns. Although he also wants to grab for a little more gusto and ride the bull full tilt, he should consider it a warning signal if he feels himself getting into this frame of mind: falling prey late in the game to prevailing psychology instead of leaning against the trend. (That general subject was covered at more length in Chapter 13.)

Elsewhere in this book is the suggestion to keep a notebook in which to record market movements, stock actions, personal emotions about the market, the nature and timing of one's own transactions, personal gain/loss performance and focus of personal attention. If these notations are correlated with past market action over a period of time, such a personal notebook can serve as a useful way to calibrate one's habits and patterns against the emotions of the marketplace. The object, of course, is to discern when a good feeling is too good (more on that in Chapter 19) and when a depressed or scared feeling signals that a bottom is close. One easy way to track market phases for later quick reference is to write in red ink on down days and green on up; use blue or black for sideways.

It is a natural human tendency to study the market and individual stock opportunities more intensely as an advance becomes broad and mature. We just feel that the process and the results are going to be fun. That spreading of enthusiasm is why bull markets occur on rising trading volume over time. So, if an investor is caught up in the predominant optimism of the cycle, he is studying possible purchases. Being focused on this intense study of buy candidates when one is already fully invested signals a problem. In the middle to late stages of an advance, our investor should ideally be examining all currently owned positions to identify which stocks should be retained and which need to be sold. If he is fully invested and has not identified sale candidates, he has been devoting insufficient attention to the selling side of the equation and is neglecting proper sale discipline. Fully committed investors who think about additional buys literally are working on the wrong problem. Therefore, develop an innate sense of contrarianism to serve as a warning signal against the seemingly natural, easy thing to do.

Given such a discipline, selling a stock as a forced activity driven by a need to raise funds for a new purchase reflects an ill-timed or overly optimistic purchase. A surefire way to detect this investment pothole is to note frame of mind and very recent short-term trend action. Is there real excitement about the new buying idea? Does it look more like a sure thing than any other that has come around in a while? Is your fear focus on missing a major chance by not getting on board right now, rather than on any possible risk of loss? (Fear of missing a profit is greed. Buys made without some accompanying true fear, i.e., of loss, usually prove to have been done late, in a high general market or high in a swing for the individual stock itself.)

If your answer to any of the preceding questions is yes, then back off and postpone buying because it is too late in the current game. In this kind of environment, the buy side of the simultaneous sell-to-buy is poorly timed. It is time to sell but too early to re-use your funds. The time to re-deploy funds will come later; best buying times occur in the absence of excitement—when there are doubts about the market's ability to pick up and rally again. Lean against the tide. Do what feels uncomfortable. If you really feel you must own this stock, at least have the discipline to enter a limit buy order somewhat below today's price!

Turning now to the mechanics and psychology of the sell side of this proposed simultaneous sale/purchase, how or why is the sell side likely to be a mistake? As stated earlier, if an investor is focused on the buy side, sale questions are getting short shrift, so one needs to refocus on selling, giving it at least equal thinking time. Forced sales probably are not well chosen because they are likely to be done in haste. Each sale should be done on its own independent merit and timing.

Visualize here the random walkers' favorite cartoon caricature: a blindfolded investor throwing a dart at the quotation tables and buying whatever stock is hit. In a similar way, a sale forced by a proposed purchase is equally foolish. In effect, our selling investor is throwing a dart—not at the price page but at the calendar. He sets up the sale's timing randomly, without due consideration either for the reasons behind sale or for current price. He is forcing himself to sell not to benefit from the performance or revised prospects of an owned stock. That lack of attention is being driven by a completely unrelated factor: a need for capital to make a proposed purchase. It is possible, even probable, that a sale made to raise cash on an emergency basis for funding a purchase is a sale poorly chosen among the available alternatives. A quick decision might be dominated by flat-price-induced boredom or recent short-term frustration rather than by more sensible considerations such as fundamental value or near-term price movement potentials based on close chart analysis.

Whether a stock is trending upward, downward, or sideways in a channel, the best time for its sale is when price trades near one of its periodic high points along the continuum of fluctuation. If an investor chooses a stock to sell from frustration or boredom, it is likely that the stock has not been acting in a positive way lately. Therefore, it probably is nearer a bottom than an interim top of its price channel. A frustration sale may then turn out to be a disadvantageous transaction.

A Seller's Checklist

If an investor needs to sell to fund a buy, he should acknowledge that he may be revealing a serious problem, and he should step back to impose self-discipline. An exercise of general virtue at any time will also serve nicely here: make a thorough and logical inventory of all stocks currently held, writing down for each stock the answers to such questions as the following:

- What is a realistic technical-analysis price target and over what time period (and what is the implied return per annum from today if that projection were correct)?
- Is the stock now fundamentally undervalued, fairly valued or nearing fully priced?
- How does the stock fit against today's market tastes and group leadership patterns?
- Is this a volatile or a stable stock, and what does that imply if the market should correct and move lower?
- If stocks literally could not be reviewed again for three months, how high in your comfort list for continued blind holding would this one be?
- Does this stock overexpose in the portfolio one sector of the economy or one industry without a deliberate decision to do so (for example, starting in 2003 one could logically have decided to significantly overweight energy issues)?
- Would you buy this stock again today? If yes, why?

A comparison of the well thought-out and written answers across one's current holdings will usually reveal which are the best candidates for current pruning and which still have most merit for retention. This is one of many instances where the self-imposed discipline of standing back, taking a mental deep breath, and committing some unbiased factual items to paper will serve any investor well.

Two very specialized exceptions to the odds against simultaneous switches as described above are worth noting. This exists when takeovers or Dutch auctions occur in large-cap stocks. Institutions tend to adhere to deliberate industry allocation guidelines. Therefore, if a major stock they own is taken over, they will very likely re-deploy that money into other stocks in the same industry. For example, a takeover of Exxon Mobil (highly unlikely) arguably would redirect money into Chevron and other major integrated oils. The happy owner of XOM should sell it shortly before the actual transaction and move that cash into other oils of choice—perhaps ones that seem most likely as next takeover candidates. Somewhat similarly, when a Dutch-auction tender offer is occurring, the stock involved is temporarily elevated by arbitrageurs. Selling into that strength and at the same time buying another stock (perhaps in the same industry) would tend to be a good practice.

CHAPTER 17

Use a Personal Diffusion Index

Keys for Successful Selling

◆ Understand Advance/Decline Oscillators

◆ Understand Broad Market Diffusion Indexes

◆ Make a Personal Diffusion Index

This chapter presents quantitative indicators to use as actual selling signals. It introduces as a useful indicator a personal diffusion index, which falls under the broad category of technical indicators and, specifically, overbought/oversold timing oscillators. The chapter's beginning describes such indicators generally; subsequent material shows how to personalize this kind of analysis.

Advance/Decline Indicators

The simplest and one of the most widely used overbought/oversold indicators is an easy, 10-day total of net daily advances less declines. This market statistic is tracked by subtracting daily individual-stock decliners from advancers (usually on one exchange such as the New York Stock Exchange or NASDAQ) to arrive at a net figure for the day. Then the last 10 days' individual figures are added, resulting in a number that generally ranges from a few thousand positive to several thousand negative. While precise buy-and-sell signal ranges vary over time depending on the market's emotional intensity level, following this indicator for a few months is a useful way to time sales (and purchases) to short-term swings within about two days. One can readily see where the high and low ranges of readings are, and ranges are good enough.

A daily overbought/oversold indicator is a short-term measurement and is useful for only limited purposes. So is the weekly net advance-decline measurement used by some market analysts. In contrast, many market technicians consider a measurement called the cumulative advance/decline line to be one of the more powerful indicators of changing intermediate-term direction in the market. This line is calculated in very much the same way as the 10-day line, except that a cumulative total (rather than one for 10 days) is kept from the time one starts the project. The current plot of every investor's indicator has exactly the same shape, no matter the data-collecting start date, but the net total for each differs (by the same net amount) ad infinitum into the future. The absolute total has no meaning; relative position and movement over time are the keys to watch.

Technicians use cumulative advance/decline (A/D) figures to detect divergences in market behavior. They plot this indicator graphically against a popular market measure such as the Dow Jones Industrial Average or S&P 500 and look for differences in the shapes of the lines. Because the cumulative A/D total is much broader (encompassing all stocks on the exchange(s) studied), it is considered a more valid signal of market direction than is a narrower index such as a 30-stock or even 500-stock average.

Technicians look for times when the two lines move in different directions. As a selling signal, they watch for the cumulative A/D line to move down while the Dow moves sideways, as occurred in rather classic form in late 1989, prior to that October's mini-crash. A major warning also occurred in early 2000 since for all of 1999, which was considered to be a roaring market, more individual NYSE stocks fell than rose! The leadership had become very narrow. The theory behind divergence readings is that a longer list of stocks tells more truth than the mathematical average of a few, which can be skewed by only one or two individual components' performances. or example, within the Dow 30, one high-priced oil, or a high-priced IBM or 3M or P&G, might carry the others that are collectively no longer advancing.

Figure 17.1: More Stocks Join the Party

This year's advance-decline line (cumulative total of advancing stocks minus decliners for the year-to-date) has turned up since April. It has regained about half the territory lost in the first four months of the year.

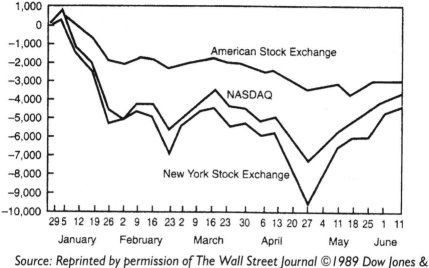

Source: Reprinted by permission of The Wall Street Journal ©1989 Dow Jones & Company, Inc. All Rights Reserved World Wide.

Figure 17.2: Fewer Gainers

Running total of weekly number of NASDAQ issues advancing, less those declining, Dec. 31, 1987 =0

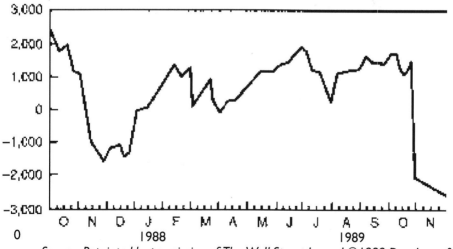

Source: Reprinted by permission of The Wall Street Journal ©1989 Dow Jones & Company, Inc. All Rights Reserved World Wide.

The Market Diffusion Indicator

Another useful indicator based on advance and decline data, which has even longer term implications, is the market diffusion indicator. This is constructed somewhat differently; because of that difference, it tends to reflect more profound changes. Surprisingly, it seems not to be tracked by major charting services these days, probably because of the short-term-oriented methods by which computers have been programmed to store data.

Most chart services focus on very short-term data, typically programming their computers to plot daily closes (and maybe highs, lows and volume), showing the largest day-to-day percentage price changes or maybe the largest weekly net changes. Market diffusion indexes look at a much longer period than a day or week and, therefore, they give big-picture signals. In the 1940s through 1970s, a Boston-based advisory firm (which is no longer in business) published a weekly stock market advisory service called the *Spear Market and Group Trend Letter*. Its editors performed extensive research on industry price movements and also on major technical indicators. The advisory service was conservative and longer-term oriented.

What few indicators it used were designed to identify significant long-term market trends, not to wiggle every week or every day. After back-testing decades of data, the Spear editors found that the most meaningful basis on which to plot a long-term market diffusion index was a nine-month window. (Interestingly, and perhaps not by total coincidence, nine months contain very nearly 200 trading days, and of course 200-day moving averages are among many technicians' most revered indicators.)

A diffusion index takes time to compile, but the work was less mathematically intense than that supporting advance/decline indicators as described earlier, since daily readings are not involved. The analyst simply compares each stock within the defined universe with itself as of a fixed earlier time (adjustments are of course made for stock splits). Using the 9-month convention, October 10 is compared with the prior January 10, October 17 with January 17, and so on. The number of stocks up in price, net, over that period is plotted as a simple percentage with no adding or accumulation. Each period's calculation is an end-point snapshot.

Market diffusion indices, when plotted, tend to be shaped somewhat like the mathematical first derivative of a simple plot of the overall market level. Well before the market makes its top in a major cycle, the diffusion index tops out and heads down. The diffusion index falls through the all-important 50 percent level quite close to the time

when the overall market makes its top as recorded by major averages. (A fall to near the zero- percent level indicates exhaustion on the downside and signals that selling is far too late because a bottom is very near.)

What any long-term diffusion index records is the tendency of a market's leadership to narrow as a bull market matures. Fewer stocks continue to make new highs over a period of months. More seem to be consolidating (but hindsight will show they were actually forming distribution tops). See Table 17-1. If the percentage of net advancing stocks is dropping in the later stages of a bull-market advance, it follows that the odds of making profits on the long side, or even of achieving increased profits in positions already held, are decreasing before overall market averages hit their final cyclical peaks.

This is a very important observation to understand and heed when you are considering holding versus selling. The urgency of diffusion data and the importance of heeding its warnings are all the more critical for another reason: It is precisely during those late stages of a major advance that excitement builds and the temptation to jump in (or to commit more cash, or even to use margin) is greatest. That is exactly when the odds are starting to swing against holding and toward cashing in because, while some issues make spectacular advances, overall fewer stocks still are going up. A diffusion index tells that tale.

Unfortunately, it appears that none of the popular hard-copy chart services currently track this indicator. The explosion of on-line technical analysis packages makes such a statement in that realm risky, however, so doing some exploration may prove worthwhile. But an investor can follow diffusion data relatively easily if he or she is willing to invest the time. Use a chart service such as *Daily Graphs* by William O'Neil & Co. (see the reference list at the end of the book), or use the *Monthly Stock GuideHandbook* by Standard & Poor's in your local library (perhaps your broker may be willing to supply a used copy). Or follow prices in Barron's or The Wall Street Journal if you are willing to save the back issues: Post them in a tracking ledger, perhaps a spreadsheet program.

Visual chart inspection is faster because it requires only quick eyeball comparisons. Only a few stocks trade so close to nine-month-ago levels that an analyst would need to look closely.

A way to accomplish the same result without subscribing to charts is to keep a list of diverse stocks (it should be consistent over time, with changes due only to acquisitions or leveraged buyouts or the like). Tally these once a month in a vertical column. Compare the price at the latest date with the price nine months earlier, and score one for each up stock. Divide the total count of ups by the size of the universe, and plot the percentage result on graph paper. One can readily create a macro in Excel that would plot such a graph based on the data. With stocks now traded in pennies since 2001, very few literally zero-change issues will be found. A good way of capturing an unbiased and broad sample across the market with even less intense effort would be to track a number of the Fidelity Select (sector) funds as if they were individual stocks. One caveat if using funds: adjustments must be made in October and December when annual capital gains distributions arbitrarily reduce per-share net asset values of funds.

Some market students reduce the workload required to use a diffusion indicator by narrowing their universe further. To do that, follow the 30 Dow Jones Industrials.

Table 17.1: 9-Month Diffusion Index: DJIA 1996 Components

	Mar 95	Apr	May	Jun	Jul	Aug	Sep	Oct	Nov	Dec	Jan 96	Feb	Mar	Apr	May	Jun 96
AA	41.50	44.88	46.50	50.13	57.00	57.13	52.88	51.00	58.50	52.88	55.50	56.88	62.63	62.38	61.63	57.38
ALD	39.25	39.63	40.38	44.50	46.75	44.38	44.13	42.50	47.38	47.50	49.88	55.63	59.13	58.00	54.75	57.13
					Example for ALD: Up/even/down vs. 9 months earlier:					+	+	+	+	+	+	+
AXP	34.88	34.75	35.50	35.25	38.50	40.38	44.38	40.63	42.50	41.38	46.00	45.88	49.38	48.50	45.75	44.63
T	51.75	50.75	50.75	53.00	52.75	56.63	65.75	64.00	65.88	64.75	66.88	63.63	61.13	61.25	62.38	62.00
BA	53.75	55.00	58.88	62.63	67.00	63.75	68.25	65.50	72.88	78.38	77.50	81.13	86.63	82.13	85.25	87.13
BS	16.13	14.13	14.75	16.25	15.75	14.63	14.13	13.13	14.00	13.88	15.13	13.75	13.13	13.63	12.75	11.88
					Example for BS: Up/even/down vs. 9 months earlier:					.	.	.	.	.	.	.
CAT	55.50	58.50	60.25	64.25	70.38	67.13	56.88	56.75	61.38	58.75	64.38	66.75	68.00	64.13	65.63	67.75
CHV	48.00	47.38	49.13	46.38	49.38	48.38	48.75	46.75	49.38	52.38	51.88	55.63	56.13	58.00	59.75	59.00
KO	28.19	29.06	30.81	31.88	32.81	32.13	34.50	35.94	37.88	37.13	37.69	40.38	41.38	40.75	46.00	49.00
DIS	53.50	55.38	55.50	55.50	58.63	56.25	57.38	57.63	60.13	58.88	64.25	65.50	63.88	62.00	60.75	62.88
DD	60.50	65.88	67.88	68.75	67.00	65.38	68.75	62.38	66.50	69.88	76.75	76.50	83.00	80.25	79.75	79.13
EK	53.25	57.50	60.38	60.63	57.63	57.75	59.25	62.63	68.25	67.00	73.38	71.50	71.00	76.50	74.38	77.75
XON	66.63	69.50	71.38	70.63	72.50	68.75	72.25	76.38	77.38	80.50	80.25	79.50	81.50	85.00	84.75	86.88
GE	54.00	56.00	58.00	56.38	59.00	58.88	63.75	63.25	67.13	72.00	76.75	75.50	77.88	77.25	82.75	86.75
GM	44.00	45.13	48.00	46.88	48.75	47.13	46.88	43.75	48.50	52.88	52.63	51.25	53.25	54.25	55.13	52.38
GT	36.75	38.00	42.13	41.13	43.38	40.00	39.38	38.00	42.38	45.38	47.88	47.38	51.00	52.13	50.50	48.00
IBM	82.13	94.63	93.00	96.00	108.88	103.38	94.50	97.25	96.63	91.38	108.50	122.63	111.25	107.75	106.75	99.00
IP	37.50	38.50	39.31	42.88	42.25	40.94	42.00	37.00	38.25	37.88	40.75	35.75	39.50	39.88	39.88	36.88
JPM	61.00	65.63	70.88	70.13	73.25	72.88	77.38	77.13	78.50	80.25	81.25	81.88	83.00	84.13	86.88	84.63
MCD	34.13	35.00	37.75	39.13	38.63	36.50	38.25	41.00	44.63	45.13	50.25	50.00	48.00	47.88	48.13	46.75
MRK	42.63	42.88	47.00	49.13	51.63	49.88	56.00	57.25	61.88	65.63	70.13	66.25	62.25	60.50	64.63	64.63
MMM	58.13	59.63	60.00	57.38	56.63	54.63	56.38	56.88	65.38	66.38	64.50	65.13	64.63	65.75	68.25	69.00
MO	65.38	67.75	72.88	74.38	71.63	74.63	83.50	84.25	87.75	90.25	92.75	99.00	87.75	90.13	99.38	104.00
PG	66.25	69.88	71.88	71.88	68.88	69.38	77.00	81.00	86.50	83.00	84.00	82.00	84.75	84.50	87.88	90.63
S	26.91	27.35	28.49	30.00	32.63	32.38	36.88	34.00	39.38	39.00	41.50	45.38	48.75	50.00	50.88	48.63
TX	66.63	68.38	68.50	65.63	66.38	64.75	64.50	68.13	73.88	78.50	80.88	79.75	85.75	85.50	83.75	83.88
UK	30.63	32.13	29.13	33.50	34.75	35.50	39.75	37.88	39.63	37.50	42.13	45.00	49.63	45.50	43.13	39.75
UTX	69.13	73.13	75.88	78.13	84.00	83.38	88.38	88.75	93.75	94.88	102.63	107.38	112.25	110.50	109.38	115.00
WX	14.13	15.00	14.50	14.63	13.63	13.63	15.00	14.13	16.88	16.38	20.75	18.50	19.38	18.88	18.38	16.88
Z	18.50	16.00	15.38	15.13	15.63	13.38	15.75	14.63	15.00	13.00	11.25	12.00	15.63	19.13	20.50	22.50
Diffusion index: percent up vs. 9 earlier:										93	97	90	93	87	90	87

This list changes pretty infrequently, so it holds consistent over time. Tally the total of up components and divide by 30. Plot the result. When components do change, go back and capture the old data.

Because the difference created by one Dow Jones stock equals 3.33 percent in the result, be sure to score unchanged stocks as ½ each to refine the reading a bit. Once your tally reaches extremely high percentages, the process of a rounding top will begin, with progressively fewer stocks moving ahead. The key change in momentum and the all-out sell indicator is when the index reading declines below 50 percent after hitting a high of about 90 percent.

Another handy source for this kind of tracking exercise is your local Sunday newspaper. If such a weekly source is used, go back approximately 39 weeks or take the Friday prices closest to the end of the calendar month. In the Internet age more and more newspapers are dropping even weekend stock-price tables, so you may need to use one of several free online chart services such as StockCharts. com or BigCharts.com. Manual posting from newspapers takes longer than chart inspection, so be careful to adjust for stock splits when major drops in price appear from month to month. Whichever compiling method is used, the signals that a market diffusion index provides are as follows:

Table 17.2: Personal Diffusion Index Based on 5-Stock Portfolio

	Dec-06	Jan-07	Feb-07	Mar-07	Apr-07	May-07	Jun-07	Jul-07
Stock (cost)								
Stock A (45)	41.33	46.02	45.67	49.31	48.55	57.75	44.66	44.33
up/down?	-	+	+	+	+	+	-	-
Stock B (105)	91.38	108.51	122.64	111.25	107.75	107.92	105.73	99.44
up/down?	-	+	+	+	+	+	+	-
Stock C (35)	37.13	37.69	40.36	41.38	40.75	46.01	47.33	42.26
up/down?	+	+	+	+	+	+	+	+
Stock D (82)	80.55	80.23	79.83	81.47	84.22	84.03	85.21	82.94
up/down?	-	-	-	+	+	+	+	+
Stock E (15)	13.02	11.84	12.76	14.24	16.27	17.18	16.44	14.89
up/down?	-	-	-	-	+	+	+	-
Total Up	1	3	3	4	5	5	3	2
Percent Up	20	60	60	80	100	100	60	40

Personal start-selling signal occurred April 2007 at 100%

◆ A move up to the 90 percent range is an early sell warning; stop buying and start weeding out stocks and build cash.

◆ A decline from about 90 percent to 50 percent is an immediate final sell signal—this is the market top. Do not delay.

◆ Below 10 percent tells you not sell because it is already too late. A major panic-type bottom is forming.

The market diffusion method is much better as a selling indicator than as a buying tool. Why? Tops in the overall market form gradually even though individual stocks may display exhaustion peaks; bottoms are violent. At bottoms, an oscillator-type index such as an A/D line or diffusion index can appear numerically oversold, but the final and usually most violent decline can take a few days or a couple more weeks and still result in severely lower prices. Therefore, as buying indicator, a diffusion index is an imprecise tool-as (briefly) are most other technical indicators when severe panic psychology governs the market.

Making Your Own Personal Diffusion Index

Creating a diffusion index can be a highly personalized exercise. Investors not only can choose a (diversified) universe to follow to customize a market diffusion indicator, but they also should keep a tally on those stocks they actually own. As an indicator perhaps that latter is more crude and subject to statistical imperfection because the sample is small and may not be fully diversified. And the list itself is subject to revision over time as one's portfolio changes. However, it is a useful exercise if done in the following manner (see Table 17-2 as a sample.)

Keep a log to record the periodic closes of each stock held. For personal diffusion-index purposes, use the last Friday each month or the one closest to month-end rather than the actual last day of the month. Using Friday data lets weekends conveniently allow more chance for real-time data recording and for prompt study. Record each stock's current close, and compare it with a past period's price.

With a personal portfolio list, use a three-month rather than a nine-month span for your time window. There are two reasons: Portfolio turnover, combined with a nine-month start point, reduces the number of stocks in the sample at any time quite significantly and the shorter window is more sensitive. The indicator should be designed to say something soon, when in fact a significant upward market move has occurred and some selling is in order.

Also consider this guideline: When a personal list shows all winners over a three-month or longer period, do some selling. Such a reading means that the market has been extremely strong and/or the investor has been hot (probably aided by the overall trend). This probably will not last for long. Because the market makes just a few meaningful wavelike swings per year on average, a three-month window is likely to help catch roughly a full wave.

Note also a likely need to make mental adjustments about one or two stocks in the list. For example, one stock in a list of 10 took a bad tumble several months ago, but was retained anyway. If there are problems with this company and the investor remains stubborn, he effectively must forgive the index for including that stock because realistically he cannot hope for a 100 percent reading (the usual signal for selling) while this laggard remains in the list.

One final caveat: Be sure to look at price performance over a fixed time interval for all current stocks, not net price performance since the dates they were bought. It is obvious that a hugely successful, long-term growth holding would always give a plus reading on the latter basis, providing no useful guidance as part of the percentage reading. Therefore, track changing intermediate-term momentum, and use a three-month comparison window.

Again, not only should some stocks be sold when there are all winners (because momentum arguably cannot get any stronger), but also you should use a fall through the 50-percent level as the trigger for serious selling. This means that either the market itself has rolled over and lost momentum or that your individual feel or judgment about stock performance and prospects has lost contact with current market tastes. Always consider contrariness as a virtue in investing. When an investor feels the most confident, that is exactly a time to lean the other way deliberately and sell. A diffusion index is a powerful mathematically objective guide to use when contrary selling should be implemented. A personal diffusion index, as described in this chapter, both tailors the signal to personal holdings and provides an excellent disciplinary tool for portfolio reviews.

CHAPTER 18

Overcome Greed: Stop Chasing That Last Nickel or Dime

Keys for Successful Selling

◆ Learn to Walk Away

◆ But Also Beware of Rushed Sales

◆ Know That Hurried Thinking Breeds Impulsive Sales

Investors, and particularly traders, all too often succumb to the temptation to seek what is virtually impossible: the legendary last dime, both in a literal (micro) and in a figurative (big picture) market sense. In the literal sense, logical investors realize that the odds against selling a stock at the highest price—on a short-term swing or in a major bull market move—are overwhelming. For example, a seasoned blue chip, exchange-traded, low-beta common stock might trade in a range between, say, $30 and $50 over a 12-month period. Examples of such names might include General Electric, Home Depot and Merck. Elementary mathematics indicates that a 20-point price range consists of 201 dimes or 2001 pennies, so the random odds are hundreds or thousands to one against selling at the exact top price. From the technician's viewpoint, volume peaks before prices in a bull market; therefore, on a volume-traded basis, the odds are that fewer shares will trade at the top penny than at prices somewhat lower. So those stated long odds against hitting the exact top are actually a bit understated.

Even if an investor watches a quotation machine or PC screen all day long with an uncanny, intuitive sense of technical action, she still needs terrific luck to catch the top tick. What kinds of things can go wrong even if she is that smart? Her timing, indeed, may be perfect, but her broker may be on the other line and cannot call back for several minutes. Or, with the stock trading at its absolute high for the day and the year, she enters a market sell order and it is executed down a few cents at the bid, while someone else's buy order at market is transacted at the offer, coming in perhaps just a few seconds later.

Contrast those two traders' feelings: One buys at the exact top and the other's worst failing is to sell perhaps a nickel lower! Or say a seller somehow catches the top one day. But overnight the dollar is up against the yen and the Federal Reserve chairman makes a speech that Wall Street likes. Program trading opens the market ahead 85 DJIA points, and yesterday's high price is now eclipsed. Clearly, by any objective standard, the chance of getting out at the exact high is slim.

Despite these odds, a surprising number of investors and traders get trapped into trying for at least the figurative last nickel by ego, fantasies of wealth and an unbridled need to win. These people literally want to go for it all. But going for that last fraction of a dollar can be very costly. Or, all too often, it can really be just an excuse not to act at all.

Learn to Walk Away

The old, pre-decimalization expression "the last eighth" (now we say the last penny or nickel) is probably too literal. In the industry it means the attempt to squeeze out just a little bit more, or it can mean staying around too long. Either way, the basic notion is getting too greedy when reason, near-term timing logic, or one's predetermined target price says that right now is the time to sell.

When that time to sell arrives, it takes tough mental and emotional discipline to pick up the telephone and call a broker with the instruction to sell at market—or pull the trigger by mouse click after watching successive trades move the latest price up or down every recent minute. Even when having the discipline and good sense to take action promptly, an investor can confound his own good sell decisions with poor tactical execution. Any number of factual inputs, hunches, or emotional reactions can induce him to enter a limit order just a little above the market. Target limits should have been entered long ago and well above then-current prices, not now when one is feeling giddy or greedy.

He may muse that, after all, the stock has been strong enough to land on the 52-week high list, so why not let nature take its course and allow the momentum to give me a couple of extra up-ticks just for being a little more patient? Surely sometime today or tomorrow the stock's current strength and natural fluctuation volatility will net me just a little more rise.

Such thinking is ego-centric and often overly optimistic; selling a stock near its top is a difficult exercise that requires tremendous discipline, a contrarian's mentality, an updated feel of the tone in the particular stock and the overall market, and a strong dash of luck as well. Holding for that little extra also assumes no surprise adverse company, industry, economic or geopolitical news.

When a stock has reached or exceeded an investor's objective or especially when new market/industry/company developments prompt a reduction in price objective, the most prudent course is to enter a market sell order. An even more judicious action, which would avert the entire emotion-laden situation that will crop up at a later time, is to have entered a good-until-canceled (GTC) order at one's target price when the stock was originally purchased. Knowing that he is out on a market order, our investor can move on to some other selling or buying ideas, freed of the distraction of waiting or worrying. He can feel less exposed to a possible drop in the overall market because he will have lightened up his position.

When a stock is peaking, an investor runs a very serious risk of missing the top area altogether by trying to stretch winnings too far. Once a stock stops rising and starts declining, psychologically the difficulty of selling it becomes even greater. Giving up points that have already melted away is more painful than imagining giving up points of paper profit that have not yet been created. As veteran observers will all attest, it is easier to sell on the way up than on the way down.

Usually, an investor's tendency is to remember each high in a successful stock rally. Each further advance to a new price peak then establishes a new mental plateau to which revised perspective is anchored. We begin to view that level as an entitlement and to assume or at least believe that pleasant great height is attainable again.

If, in fact, the real lasting high has already been reached (a fact the investor will not know for some time, and then only with frustrating hindsight), his efforts and hopes for just a little more already are doomed from the beginning. His mental state heads south with the stock's price, weakening his decision-making abilities. Thus, when a predetermined price objective is reached, the best policy is to sell at market and walk away (or better, to have been taken out on a GTC order).

When an investor has made the decision and has actually walked away by selling out, he should just keep walking: unless there is a specific reason to continue watching the sold stock. Do not look at its quotes or chart for awhile. Count on not getting that final dime, or point, or two points. Move on without regrets and without looking back. If your stock reached its sale target, those who bought it higher—even if they now have a small profit—are among the greater fools who just do not realize it yet. Do not worry about them getting the extra point because it was not obvious in real time that the stock would go any higher; such self-second-guessing is not only useless but self-defeating.

Beware of Rushed Sales

Ironically, the flip side of the error in holding on for the proverbial extra dime or two is departing instantly when actually there is no specific hurry. Here, sale is done instantly at market once the decision is made. This is not the macro-level problem of failing to let profits run; it is the micro-tactical tendency of many investors simply to throw in a market sale order to get the mental decks cleared. Emotionally, having endured the self-imposed stress of coming to a sell decision, one wants to ensure closure since an immediate sale will end the experience with certainty.

When a trade is to be closed in a generally stable or rising market environment, bypassing a market order and making other reasonable efforts over the very short term might net a better execution without unnecessarily exposing the holder to a nasty downside erosion. The objective here, at the margin, is to increase overall profits (through good micro tactics) over time from many positions as they are sold out. The way to do this, in defined circumstances, is to slow down and take what the market allows instead of insisting on the immediate gratification (hooray, look at my nice profit and relief afforded by an immediate sale.

This advice applies best when the sale is made in response to achievement of a fundamental target rather than as a technically driven action designed to avoid danger or as a response to changed news. It must be emphasized that if a stock's sale is being made for more urgent tactical reasons, say, to avoid declining prices caused by important bad news or a failing general market, slowing down is not the right action. But if an investor is selling a stock because it has reached her objective on a fundamental basis, why should she be in a hurry? Suppose her studies indicate that a stock is likely to be fully priced when it reaches 120 percent of the market's P/E multiple, two times book value, eight times cash flow per share or a dividend yield of two percent. Those exact targets are not likely to be shared universally by other holders. So there probably will be no sudden huge rush of sell orders entered (or even a large cluster on the specialist's book) when the stock hits our hypothetical seller's exact fundamental target.

Nor is she a market guru like Miller, Cramer or Garzarelli, whose publicized targets and known actions create headlines and move stocks. Bear in mind that just as the market does not pause to note an individual's purchase, it has no knowledge of your fundamental target prices.

If your sale is being made based on fundamental measures, barring the bad luck of sudden bad news or a slumping overall market, be in no special hurry to get out. Do not let ego rule your exit tactics. Take a little more if the market will allow it, but never expect perfection. Always recall that the odds of selling at the very top price (for the year, for the move or even just for the near-term future) are very long. A perfect exit is nearly impossible to execute, so do not burden your intellect or your overall mental state by seeking one or by missing one.

Hurried Thinking Produces Impulsive Sales

Several subtle sources of emotional baggage are carried by investors who jump quickly and get bad executions in what should be unhurried sales. Not all past sales closed out profits, and some closing trades later were regretted (whereas all buying decisions are made in an upbeat frame of mind). When an investor decides it is time to sell, earlier patterns and experiences pop up from the subconscious or unconscious; they define the way he or she feels about present sales and influence current actions unless such forces are consciously recognized and controlled. This is important to remember for fundamentally driven, non-urgent sales, especially presuming your sale proceeds are not being recommitted the same day. A tendency to get it over with when selling is supported by one or more of the following six excuses to hurry:

◆ selling to raise funds for a new purchase (note the warnings given in Chapter 16);

◆ wanting to end an unsatisfactory experience;

◆ selling mainly based on frustration or boredom;

◆ being accustomed to instant gratification in life;

◆ wanting relief from uncertainty or stress; and

◆ false (externally imposed) urgency over shifting market expectations, probably from watching financial TV.

On the other hand, some fundamentally driven stock sales—even though they are not this-minute urgent—are caused by reassessing prospects and lowering expectations:

◆ the company has not been reaching that accelerated sales pace you had projected.

◆ interest rates have risen sooner or more than you expected, putting a squeeze on P/Es.

◆ the general market feels like it is topping, implying some near-term need to prune

◆ group rotation seems to be moving elsewhere, implying that your hoped-for P/E is now less likely to be achieved.

A revision of expectations, although not a sudden disaster, often carries a touch of personal disappointment when compared with original hopes for the stock position. Thus, investors rush to sell this mildly under-performing investment (to push away the source of bad feelings) when actually there is no solid reason for hurrying.

Selling a stock out of frustration or boredom has similar results. For example, an investor may hang in with Dullsville, Inc. stock when it has not lived up to expectations instead of riding Whiz-Bang Spiffycorp. Belatedly, he now awakens to the fact that he has wasted the time value of his money and that his snoozer is going nowhere fast. But this late dawning of the light does not mean that the smartest way out is an immediate market-sell order. If there is no reason to suspect the stock will crack over the short term, at least one can try to do better on the exit than he did on the entry. The best course is to control the desire to move impulsively away from the frustration; to proceed more slowly toward a good tactical execution. Perhaps you can get an extra 25 cents in just one day's random fluctuation!

A subtle reason for making unnecessarily impulsive sales is the nature of life in the 21st century. This is an age of instant gratification and computer speed. In just the past generation, our concept of speed has changed radically. Computers churned on big problems for many minutes in the mid-1970s; today, if spreadsheets take more than seconds to recomputed or the GPS map does not appear instantaneously, we become annoyed and impatient or we suspect they are broken. We operate business at Internet and FedEx speed, not by USPS. With our mind-set shaped by so many experiences of speed in daily life, traders or investors are subconsciously programmed to reach for an instant confirmation when it is time to sell. But if there is no valid fundamental or technical reason to rush, they pay in needlessly lost dollars for irrational, habit-driven impatience.

When an investor finally decides to sell a stock, the conditioning created by uncomfortable past experiences with waiting and uncertainty comes into play. He feels, even if perhaps only subconsciously, that he can at least take control in one aspect of life by selling immediately. One thus may jump instinctively for the market order without any compelling reason. By becoming aware of this unconscious, ingrained tendency, one can take conscious steps to control it and then usually can get more profitable results on the margin.

All an investor has to do in these circumstances is slow down. Stocks have a natural tendency to fluctuate—over a week, day to day and intraday. If there is no immediate deterioration in fundamentals or in overall market psychology, on average a seller can presume to do moderately better than the randomly priced last trade or the current bid by exercising slight patience and entering a smart order on a limit instead of a market-sell order.

Distributions of returns, and therefore of micro changes, are statistically shown to vary with the square root of time. Thus, for example, an exchange-traded stock that typically fluctuates within three points in a week's span might be expected to wiggle by a bit more than 40 percent that much, or $1.25, on a daily basis. Starting from a randomly selected price such as yesterday's close or the morning opening, and assuming a trendless but normally fluctuating market, one might thus project variations of as much as 62 cents higher (and lower) during today for such a stock. That makes entering an immediate market order seem a bit shortsighted, assuming a fairly sideways market for the day.

Over the market's long history, prices average a small net gain per day—not a small loss. Thus, on average, waiting can gain a fraction if there is no bad news in immediate prospect and if one is not clearly in a bear market or interim downdraft. Learn to take advantage of natural random fluctuations instead of ignoring them. Be satisfied with a quarter, half or point's improvement over randomly determined current market. In many instances, improved exit tactics can thus at least pay for your commission cost. But do not let brief calculated patience in hope of a small, marginal exit advantage morph into an open-ended (long-term) hold-and-hope.

CHAPTER 19

Sell Just When It Feels Real Good

Keys for Successful Selling

- ◆ Evaluate How Fast a Stock Can Rise, and for How Long
- ◆ Ask Yourself What Further Good Things Could Drive More Price Gain
- ◆ Know What to Do if Good News Does Not Move a Stock

Every stock has its own peculiar behavior patterns. These can be triggered by news, by psychological or technical conditions in the general market, by the enthusiasms or phobias of momentum-chasing institutional investors or by the movements of other stocks in the same industry group. Fortunately, sometimes the ways in which stocks behave actually provide signals to exit.

This chapter focuses on how fast a stock can reasonably be expected to rise and for how long. Such information should discipline investor thinking regarding successful positions that are so good that a temptation develops to fall in love with the stock and marry it for the long haul. Because nearly all good things do come to an end—or at least simmer down—the most successful investors are those able to step off before it becomes obvious to the greater majority or crowd that the market's direction has become overdone and due for reversal

How Fast Can the Stock Rise: For How Long?

When a stock starts acting heroically, that in itself is a pretty good sell signal. Refer to a set of charts, preferably online so you have a totally updated view. Detailed technical analysis is not the purpose; simply study wavelike movements in broad terms.

Take, for example, a growth stock such as PepsiCo, McDonald's, Johnson & Johnson or Lowe's. Over the very long term, such persistently successful companies achieve growth in EPS of perhaps 12 percent to 15 percent per year. Over the long term, of course, a stock's price cannot be expected to move faster than in proportion to its EPS and dividend growth. To ask for more requires a secular increase in P/E ratios, but such changes tend to reverse cyclically when interest rates rebound or during recessions and bear markets. All a long-term, buy-and-hold investor can reasonably hope for is price growth in line with long-term fundamentals.

But even the stocks of established growth-machine companies do not climb a steady, slight incline from day to day or from month to month. (A $40 growth stock with a 13 percent growth rate should advance, net, by $5.20 per year, which works out to just a dime per week; yet virtually any stock moves much more widely than on such a narrow track.) Prices gyrate up and down in waves at percentage rates well in excess of the fundamental growth rate of the underlying company. In the process, a stock swings from being ahead of itself or overpriced to being oversold. If only an investor had perfect foresight, he or she theoretically could catch each top and bottom and thereby become wealthy rapidly. If only.

Reality demands that we not attempt to catch tops and bottoms of each swing perfectly because failure in that endeavor is certain; aiming or hoping for 100 percent perfect execution will only create self-defeating frustration and tactical second-guessing. However, it definitely is readily possible to track the multiple wavelike movements that stock prices exhibit while swinging around their long-term growth slopes, as described in Chapter 12. Within these movements, and well short of their extremes, lie opportunities for above-trend returns as well as for useful, practical investment education.

Look at the accompanying price charts of Colgate Palmolive and Sysco in Figure 19-1, for instance. While the earnings momentum of these two companies historically has been fairly steady at about 15 percent per year (and, therefore their stocks tend to mirror that net pace over the long term), there are both large and small wavelike upward price movements at a much more rapid pace (interspersed with corrections). Even in a 12-month period when the stock might rise by its net theoretical average of 15 percent, one can easily spot three or four quick price moves of 10 percent to 15 percent each, each taking only several weeks to accomplish. Those moves present price vectors that are fundamentally unsustainable over the longer term, but they provide very profitable opportunities for the nimble investor. The trader tries to catch most of the move over the short term. But even the longer-term-oriented investor should also see such moves as unsustainable and use them as timing opportunities to cash in; one can always re-enter later. The stocks presented in Figure 19-2 were making several wave-like upward moves on the order of 20 percent each, which clearly exceeded their likely annual potential price gains. Recall that Chapter 10 laid out the mathematical and psychological reasons for cashing in frequently (higher net returns and lowered risk), while Chapter 9 warned of a heightened risk of giving away pleasant paper profits when institutions suddenly

Figure 19.1. Chances to Take Oversized Gains in Steady-Growth Companies' Stocks

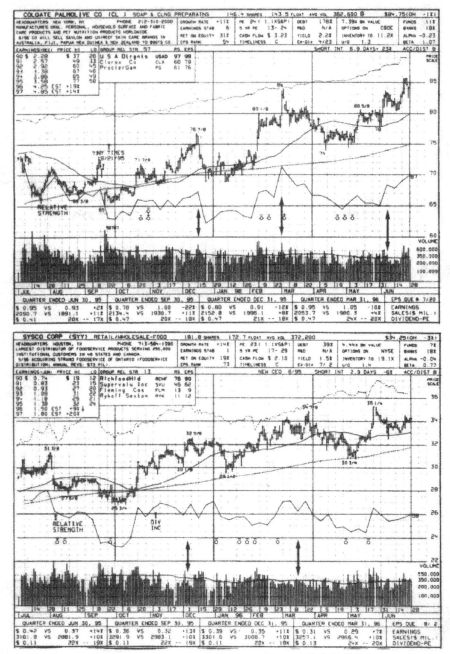

Courtesy of Daily Graphs and Long Term

Figure 19.2: Stocks Showing Excess Gain Potential in Recurring Waves

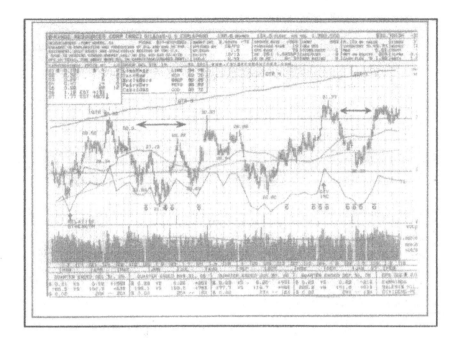

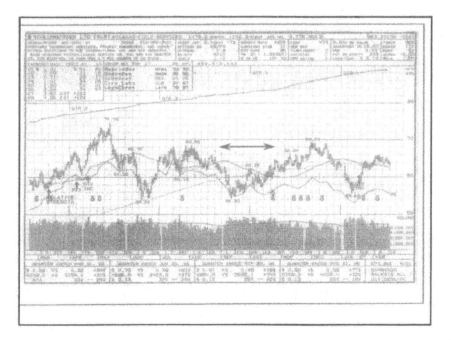

abandon a stock. Both of those factors are reasons one should capture unsustainably sharp, brief run-ups rather than lazily let capital ride for the predictable correction or lengthy pause.

Because this is not a study of technical analysis, we make no attempt to quantify the number of moves per year per stock or the average percentage slope that can be expected. Such parameters differ for each stock, and they tend to change over time for any one issue. The phenomenon of unsustainable upward movement is described here, however, because it offers an opportunity for well-timed sales. In fact, some of the best selling opportunities occur when things seemingly just can't get much better. The three graphs in Figure 19-3 illustrate very pleasant but clearly unsustainable asymptotic or parabolic rises. Do not fall in love; sell and buy back after the short-term adulation for such stocks simmers down.

After a very strong short-term advance, one is quite likely to be virtually in love with the company, fundamentally for its presumed long-term virtues. But suppose that just now an analyst's recommendation envisions a 25 percent increase in price over a 12-month period, driven by good fundamentals and rising awareness of the company's strengths. If your broker calls after the stock has just risen by multiple percents in perhaps less than a month, tell that broker you refuse to chase strength. You must resist that temptation to buy what feels most obvious and comfortable—just look at how well it has been acting. Instead, if you like this stock, the proper course is to place a below-market GTC limit buy order for the next reaction. This requires patience and guts for both broker and investor, but it pays handsomely in the longer run.

Bear in mind, also, that a brokerage recommendation in itself is contributing to the current price strength, but this source of buying will be exhausted in a matter of days. Do not join that artificially created temporary crowd. The same principle applies when your already-owned stock is running ahead pleasantly and sharply. Omitting the occasional spectacular move on rumored takeover offers, when a stock moves several percent in a week some very exciting but unrealistic annualized growth rates will begin to dance in your head like sugar plums. Just three percent per week is 156 percent per year! But each stock and its moves are unique. And the tone of the general market affects each stock differently on each movement. Thus, there is no universal formula or meaningful average measure that can be applied. One approach, although it cannot be counted on precisely over short time periods, is to compare a stock's actual percentage move with the market's percentage move times the stock's beta. For example, suppose in the past two months the Dow is up 5 percent and your happy stock, whose beta is 2.0, has risen 15 percent or more. Statistically, any net move beyond 10 percent (2.0x5) is excessive and not long sustainable.

Another highly useful way of deciding in the short term that enough is already enough is this: If your stock percentage has moved a full year's worth (its fundamentally sustainable annual growth rate) in a month or two, give it a rest. Viewed in realistic perspective from a non-owner's distance, such a stock has done

Figure 19.3: Stocks Showing Unsustainable Parabolic or Asymptotic Rises

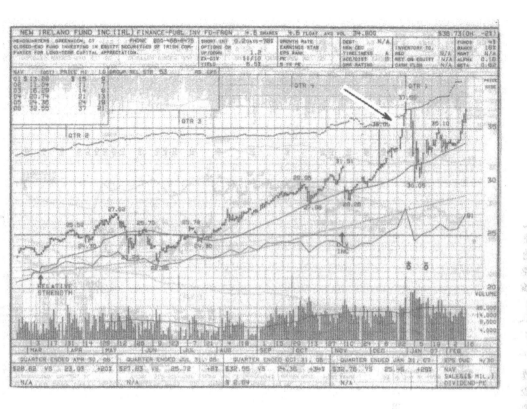

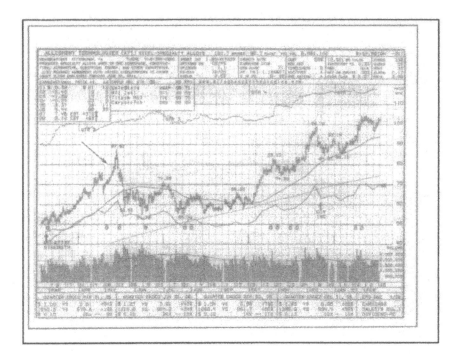

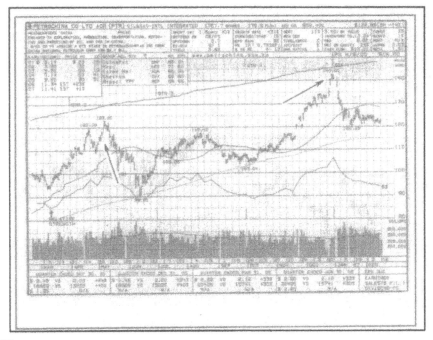

more than its share of rising for the short term and should be logically avoided until it cools off. An example is McDonalds: Its EPS growth rate may be about 12-13 percent, but its stock will run ahead perhaps 20 percent two or three times per year, literally getting way ahead of a sustainable level. Such rises are simply too much based on both fundamentals and technical-analysis patterns.

In an orderly market, each stock—and particularly one traded heavily by institutions—tends to form its own patterns. Some technical traders notice these patterns and assume they will repeat. Their buying and selling tends to make such expectations somewhat self-fulfilling, but precise percentages or point moves should not be expected to be exactly equal each time.

Therefore, look at each individual stock's chart and see how large the past moves were. For example, use rules of thumb such as these: For stocks like McDonald's or a Home Depot, be a seller rather than a buyer after a rapid (two week or less) 10 percent price move, or after a 15 percent move in two to three months. In a slower but still dependable grower like General Electric, 5 percent to 7 percent in a week is a major move that should be sold on a short-term perspective unless it occurs immediately off the bottom of a major bear market. Discover the typical patterns in each stock you own, and lean against the overly happy tide when such fast moves occur. You may love the stock now, but you can buy it back lower later on.

The charts in Figure 19-3 illustrated climactic but unsustainable rallies. This pleasant experience is somewhat different from the several-a-year undulating trading rally described earlier. The patterns here showed a sustained gradual rise followed by a curve seemingly accelerating almost straight upward. Such culminations of moves usually occur on high volume and, in fact, with frenzied trading that cannot be maintained for long. Sometimes short sellers are being squeezed, adding temporarily to the obvious buy-side pressure.

Often such a pattern occurs after a concept has been prominent in the news for some time and after virtually everyone finally becomes convinced. Examples here include prison privatization, the Internet/telecommunications frenzy, pharmaceutical merger fever and resurgence of oil-price (or other commodity) inflation. It is usually impossible to predict an exact top in such emotionally charged phases, just as one cannot tell precisely how deep a panic sell-off will go before reversing. Two clues are usually helpful, however: (1) a decline of trading volume on a rising-price day or longer and (2) a general market upset (perhaps economic data drive fears of slowed retail sales or Federal Reserve Board tightening) that is likely to find portfolio managers scrambling to nail down profits in their most recent and hottest winners. When a stock has taken you for a giddy ride, the temptation to get greedy is extremely strong. At the first sign of hearing yourself say, just one more day or just so many more points, sell out immediately.

Stocks Entering the S&P 500 Index

On rare occasions, the market provides a true textbook example of how to know when (but not at what level) a price rise will end. Figure 19-4, charting Fidelity National Information Services and Terex, illustrates this. Both issues were added to the Standard & Poor's 500 Index: FIS in November 2006, and TEX the following month. Nearly a trillion dollars are invested in index funds by individual investors and institutions that have given up trying to beat the market. When a new component enters the S&P 500, all such mutual funds literally must buy it. Technically, they should buy it at the close of trading the night before it becomes a component (but a few cheat and buy on the announcement). The resulting cluster of buy orders is monumental, and its timing is precisely known a few days in advance since S&P discloses such changes in news releases. In the two cases cited, volume topped 10 and 20 million shares on the appointed day. The charts indicate that at least temporary important price tops coincided exactly with those volume explosions. Why this type of event created a top is literally answered by asking what could possibly create a greater concentration of buying orders; answer, nothing short of a surprise takeover announcement. The only logical action in such cases is a sell-on-close order or a sale at the next morning's opening. Note that similar but less dramatic patterns occur when stocks go into other S&P and Russell indices, but the dollars involved are considerably smaller Actually experiencing on a lucky occasion the positive reinforcement of timing a sale almost perfectly in such a case (regardless of the exact dollar profit nailed down) is of benefit to one's future confidence in pulling that sometimes-rusty sale trigger. Always take such profits.

What Further Good Things Could Drive More Price Gain?

Once a stock stops rising briskly, the change in supply/demand dynamics of traders alone implies that its price almost never levels off calmly at its new higher level. And value investors become profit takers as the new higher quote seems full to them. Rather than hold steady, price will pull back. Get out of the way rather than risk exposing your capital and your mental well-being to the negative emotions and darker imaginings that take hold once a price pullback gets underway.

Another important cue for assessing how much better it can get lies in fundamental developments. In the same way that a stock can get so technically strong that there is no near-term encore possible, company news can cluster very positively. When that happens, it is a signal at least to become extremely cautious; at most, it acts as a direct signal to cash in. This observation is more than an extension of the old admonition to buy on rumor and sell on news. At issue is fundamental exhaustion on the

Figure 19.4: Stocks Rising Briefly on Huge Volume When Entering a Major Index

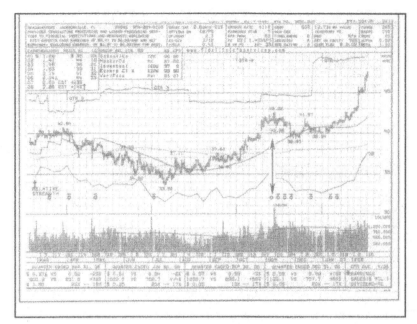

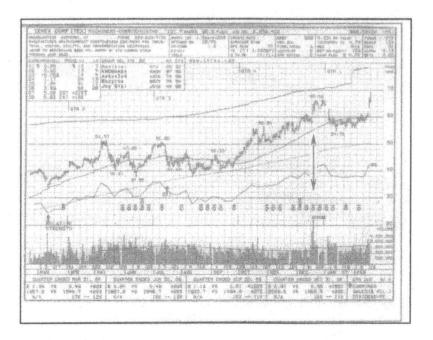

upside. Sometimes there simply is nothing left that has not already gone right. The quarterly EPS beat consensus; directors upped the dividend and declared a stock split. What else can you hope for, this week? At some point in time, investors collectively expect everything to continue positively, so there can then no longer be any further price impact from good news. All the good news has already been anticipated and told, and everyone interested is already on board. There literally are no buyers or buying reasons left untapped; the stock can only retreat. Think not in terms of how good the news is but instead focus on the near-term supply/demand realities for the shares once the crowd has already acted!

Once again, this rough measurement is more an art than a science. Point values cannot be assigned to dividend increases, stock splits, contracts announced, earnings gains, important new technology, clustered analyst recommendations or patents awarded. Simply observe a number of situations and from them develop a sense of how good it gets. From that rough measure, which changes over time with general market moods, project approximately when the party will wind down. It is usually a matter or one or two days, because in the Internet era news and ideas travel very fast. So do not let seeking the prefect become the enemy of achieving the good.

It is extremely dangerous to try to sell at the very top during an emotionally charged market period; be resigned beforehand to the certainty of missing tops in a spike-shaped move by quite a bit. Be content to come out a decent winner, to avoid the sure decline that follows, and to learn a little each time from the micro experience in which you participated in making your exit.

The following is the story of one company that illustrates the boundaries of the possible on the upside and what good news can and cannot do for a stock. A micro-cap U.S. electronics company had good products and a smart management team that kept overhead expense low. Quarterly revenues fluctuated noticeably as big orders came and went, so the stock moved in a wide range. Soon it appeared that big developments were afoot: The company was developing highly significant new markets for its key product and started hooking some very impressive customers. The selling cycle was predictably long on these deals because they involved enterprise-wide technology decisions by the buyers. But the array of pending and rumored deals, across a number of new customer industries, was exciting.

The stock was trading at below $2 per share. When management hinted briefly in quarterly reports about important orders, the stock perked up to more than $3. Pending deals involved a first-echelon bank, two major oil companies, a major foreign government agency, a leading retail organization and a top regional bank. Two individual potential orders (likely units times price) each exceeded the company's highest previous total annual revenue. The prestige of capturing industry leaders as customers would have spillover effects on sales. Predictably, brokers and investors started asking the only analyst following this little stock how high it should be expected to go. The proper reply was that market conditions would dictate that at the time announcements were made. Given a decent overall market climate, each of the two most important awards, when and if actually received, would probably be good for a point in the stock almost overnight. The scenario was to wait for the number of anticipated contracts to be won and announced and then exit with good profits.

Some brokers, appropriately trained to think in terms of fundamentals, asked what the company's earnings stream would look like and what P/E would be likely. The analyst's response, to their surprise, was that it did not matter. Once the company was actually delivering on the orders, the peak of excitement would have passed. The hottest news would already be known: the contract award itself. The critical task was to identify when the sizzle was so hot that it could not get much hotter. The prospect was for blockbuster contracts compared with the company's previous contract history. The earnings probably would follow, but mere actual future quarterly EPS releases could in no way top the impact of a string of contract announcements for excitement. The revenues would be episodic, as in the past. Therefore, the market would not assign a high P/E when the actual earnings would become known. It literally was a classic illustration of just how good can this get?

An investor, like a seasoned analyst, who thinks ahead in scenarios harbors no illusions about divining the exact peak of excitement in such a stock. But after a nice string of positive announcements, she does feel confident that the news can hardly get more exciting; at that point, prices probably will have reached a level when staying for more is greedy. It is, therefore, impossible to quote a price objective or a time frame in advance. (In this actual case, the stock moved to $8 before the game was over.)

Without knowing the exact inside details of what is really going on at a company, investors can create mental scenarios about what is realistic; they can make up a wish list. When a few of those wishes come true, especially over a short period in a generally up-trending market, investors then must ask themselves what more could realistically go right. Because at that point, any of those happy workouts of the company's plot is a signal to sell. The psychology becomes incapable of further improvement. Fundamentals drive value, but the collective investor mood drives prices.

The idea of acting early before the whole world sees the story, and then learning towards taking profits later upon the actual good news, can readily be applied to industries and sectors as well. In the summer of 2002, it was becoming obvious that the Bush Administration was tiring of bureaucratic U.N. delays and forgiveness regarding Iraq's blocking inspections. The U.S would attack sooner or later. War means higher oil prices. Does one need the full details in advance? No. Oil stocks at the time were by no means everyone's favorites and thus were conceptually great buys without knowing the future details. By 2006-2007, oil and oil-stock prices were way up and the game was comparatively late.

Remember, too, that it takes rising volume to take stocks to higher price highs, which requires increasing doses of fundamental news, investor excitement and (especially) sponsorship. An investor may not know exactly what the upper limit will prove to be, but she can develop a good intuitive feel of approximately when enough is enough by observing a number of these situations carefully over time. Once again, take written notes and record personal feelings at the time. Keep a chart of the stock and date the observations, keying them to price history on that chart. This helps you develop a documented record that is useful as a model for parallel future situations. Also track major concept stories in stocks which you do not own that are in the news. See how long they take to play out. Never expect things to be exactly the same twice; do look for clusters of events and for general patterns.

What if Good News Does not Move the Stock?

Now what happens if good news does not move the stock? This requires only brief treatment: the bottom-line answer is that selling without delay is in order. One of the hallmarks of a bear market is its being a time when investors just do not care about good news. Applying this logic to individual stocks, if good news fails to elicit positive stock price action (in a reasonably hospitable market climate), there is no longer enough unsatisfied buying interest in that stock to push it higher.

Here, the excitement has passed its peak, volume will be unable to build to new highs, and the price must erode. A sophisticated market observer can use this insight as a signal to cash in, while others less savvy use the latest good news as reason to buy the stock or perhaps buy what they think is a bargain on dips. Unfortunately, they fail to realize that they are buying into distribution and are starting to play much too late to be able to win in this game. Again a question of comfort arises: when it becomes obvious to even casual observers that fundamentals are wonderful, the big move (and perhaps the entire move) will already have been seen. Buyers are paid for investing while uncertain; sellers win by providing stock to the innocents who come late in the move and pay up for whatever is already grossly obvious.

What causes a stock to fail to react to good news (non-routine news such as big contracts, new technology or patents, or a good acquisition—not just positive quarterly earnings)? First, the general market tone may have turned so cautious that not enough investors are willing to buy to move the stock. Second, the news itself may have been anticipated (even though you may not have done so), so this item that appears like news is actually already priced in. Or the news may be less exciting than previous inputs, implying that the best is no longer yet to come. The stock already could have been sponsored heavily by brokerage recommendations and pushed ahead by institutional buying, so there is little untapped buying available. The story is, in reality, an old one. In any of these cases, project lower prices for the stock. The game has already been played out past its peak of excitement.

It is important to exit a stock promptly when your expectations are shown to be wrong. Holding a stock—dead sure the market is wrong not to be excited and after there has been a good upside move already—is a mistake. Doing so means that the investor has gotten too enamored of the stock (or of his own brilliance), has become greedy, or has misgauged how good things really can get. It is imperative to close out such a position to protect profits and to insulate oneself from severe later second guessing and regret.

PART IV

Using Smart Selling Tactics

CHAPTER 20

Use Appropriate Technical Indicators

Keys for Successful Selling

◆ Narrow the Field to Retain Your Sanity

◆ Focus on Indicators That Make Intuitive Sense

◆ Use Indicators That Point to Selling When Stocks Are Up

Investors' and traders' never-ending search for the silver bullet that will promise market-beating success is a well-known but sad story. Americans in particular want instant gratification with minimal possible effort. We fantasize in the age of Google that computers should somehow hold any possibly desired fact or answer. Numerous investment books, videos, audio tapes and software programs are published annually. A few are useful and have enduring value over many years; many pander to the hot or scary idea of the moment (recent examples as this was written are those focused on flipping real estate). Technical analysis is an area where computer power is able to crunch vast amounts of data and provide so-called answers that the average layperson could not derive in real time. So a number of dazzling black-box solutions composed of multiple complex and data-heavy equations blended in a secret formula to a master indicator are always on the market. Before paying for expensive market systems, technical-analysis or otherwise, one should seriously ask whether a guru actually possessing "the final answer would share that inside wisdom with other traders, and why someone who has the master key to Wall Street wealth needs to be selling copies for $2,995.

Narrow the Field to Retain Your Sanity

Technical analysis (TA) traces the price and volume information that result over time from the collective buying and selling decisions of all market participants. Many TA adherents say that the action of the market reflects all that is known or believed about a stock, and therefore it may be at least as important as the fundamental analysis that is part of that knowledge pool. There are multiple well-known TA indicators and systems, not to mention even more that are somewhat obscure. One very useful overview is provided by the book *Technical Analysis From A to Z*, by Steven B. Achelis. As its title implies, this compact volume provides brief descriptions of major TA systems whose names begin with every letter of the alphabet, at least one per letter. The beginning investor or trader interested in exploring the world of TA can quickly discover therein which systems make intuitive sense and are at an effort and intellectual level he or she might care to master.

Just as there are various approaches to fundamental valuation (e.g., discounted present value of earnings or cash flows or free cash flows or dividends; P/E ratios against EPS growth rates or against historical or industry means, etc.), there are many valid TA approaches. But in the real-time world of ever-moving markets and needs for actual decisions to buy or hold or sell, one cannot afford the time drain or mental confusion that result from trying to follow a dozen or more indicators. At almost all times in the market's march of history, a given mix of truly different indicators will probably give about 60 percent signals one way and 40 percent the other. That is hardly helpful to a person needing to make a decision, and arguably the frustration and uncertainty that such a collective split verdict renders may actually be of negative value by adding stress and reducing one's willingness to act. People instinctively dislike making decisions under uncertainty.

Arguably a market participant using technical analysis on a serious basis should choose his or her indicators with three requirements in mind:

◆ The number in use must be mentally manageable.

◆ Those chosen should make intuitive sense to the user so they will not be doubted when needed.

◆ The chosen few should be focused on identifying advantageous times and levels at which to sell.

Do the Indicators Chosen Make Intuitive Sense?

If you are using indicators that are so complex that you must take their calls on blind faith, sooner or later such an approach will become unacceptable—probably after you receive two or three bad verdicts in a row and lose money on a streak. Certain indicators likely will make much more intuitive sense to you than do some others, based on your understanding of the markets or your psychological disposition or your mathematical bent (or lack thereof). You cannot rely on a set of rules that you do not fully understand or believe in, nor should you rely on someone else's favorites. This is a major criterion that should guide your selection of technical indicators. For example, your author holds a strong belief that patterns of trading volume measure crowd intensity and manic/panic behavior. Therefore it would follow that a key component of at least one technical indicator must be the use of volume. For that reason, with all due respect to others who like point & figure as an approach, it makes little intuitive sense to me since it lacks a volume dimension. So I watch for volume crescendos and volume spikes, which are discussed in some detail in the next chapter.

Another area this writer finds of significant importance is overall sentiment in the market. Two intuitively useful indicators of that measure are a diffusion index (discussed in Chapter 17) and a cumulative advance-decline line. Both of these tell where the majority of stocks are relative to their recent past positions—and therefore how a large population of market participants is doing in terms of gains and losses, and as a result how they feel about themselves and about market at any important point in time.

Use Indicators that Point to Selling When Stocks are Up

Because the time value of money is so important (part of which is the idea of avoiding losing money), selling stocks when they are up (rather than after they have clearly proved that they are failing) is crucial in my view. Many people rely on moving averages to guide their buy/hold/sell decisions. And clearly those indicators have some value, if only because so many people follow them and will act on their signals. So one should not be ignorant of the relative position of prices versus their moving averages. In my view, using a 50-day moving average on a major market index or average is a useful way of knowing when the market as a whole is in acceptable medium-term condition or is in trouble. However, such information is primarily useful as a broad guide as to whether buying or selling or shorting or waiting is the currently appropriate tactic; for individual stocks of current personal interest a moving average just seems to give its signals far too late if you honor the time value of money.

Clearly, as is noted consistently in this book, it is not realistic to expect to get out at exact tops (or in at exact bottoms). In the neighborhood is quite sufficient as opposed to getting in or out at average prices (or worse). Three TA approaches provide useful signals as to when stocks (and the general market) are at a short-term top. These generally will not give contradictory readings, which is a plus in terms of lowering stress levels.

One of those three indicators is not published anywhere but is extremely easy to keep track of. It is simply the sum of the number of plus signs based on daily net changes of both the Dow Industrials and the Dow Transports. The time range is always the latest ten consecutive trading sessions. Therefore the range of readings is from zero to 20. Anyone can keep this on a piece of paper or in a notebook; the more computer-comfortable can easily track it in an Excel spreadsheet and even plot the data rather than read the numerals. This is a very simple oscillator of the overbought/oversold type. Its readings will very seldom reach the exact zero point (extremely oversold) or the exact top (20), but readings in either neighborhood are useful, and experience has shown that when the current reading becomes fairly extreme (high) and then turns down and crosses below the reading of ten sessions earlier, a top has been seen. This indicator is useful as a guide to the general market, and of course most stocks although not all tend to move in the short term with the major averages. So this simple oscillator is a first-cut gauge as to whether it is probably buying, or selling, time overall.

A very useful and widely followed major indicator for judging whether a stock is temporarily on the high (or low) side and therefore better to sell/avoid (or buy/hold) is Bollinger Bands, invented by John Bollinger. His books (at this writing in 2007, the latest (2001) being *Bollinger on Bollinger Bands*) are well worth reading. The system has been refined moderately over the years, so later works are more sophisticated in their explanations than is first book. This system is designed to measure the likely window of price volatility of a stock based on its recent past history. A stock's volatility shifts over time, and the bands capture this tendency. Charts are available free on the BollingerBands.com Website and on the EquityTrader.com Website. For those wishing to look at a stock and several desired TA indicators all at once in one place, the BigCharts.com Website offers Bollinger Bands as one of several options under the Upper Indicators list found by clicking on the Advanced Chart icon. For those to whom the concept of a stock being temporarily overbought makes intuitive sense, the bands will be comfortable as a source of measuring degree of price extremes. Because a large number of traders follow them, it is prudent to sell a stock when it starts to back off the upper band; as Bollinger devotees note, a stock is not necessarily an urgent sale when it first hits the upper band, as it can sometimes ride the band higher for a time period that cannot be immediately predicted.

Another very useful and heavily followed indicator is called Moving Average Convergence/Divergence, or MACD for short. This is available without charge at the StockCharts.com Website (the red and black lines below the price/volume plot) and as an option under Lower Indicators after clicking on the Advanced Chart icon at BigCharts.com. Conceptually somewhat similar to the Bollinger approach, MACD looks at the distance that stocks swing above and below their own moving averages. This clearly is not something that random-walk believers would watch. It is based on the idea that stocks move in trends but that trends become exhausted and then reverse. Each stock tends to have its own personality including volatility and strength of tendency to move in trends. If you think in terms of statistics, imagine a plotting of the frequency distribution of positive and negative differences (in percent) of each day's closing price against its recent moving average. This, not surprisingly, will resemble the classic bell-shaped curve, although it may have fat tails and be a bit skewed. What MACD does is to plot in real time the current net value of price less moving average. If you believe that when a value reaches the tail of it distribution it is likely to revert, MACD will appeal greatly to you. You can immediately see how far above or below zero the current reading is, and can compare that with any desired past time window. For this author, MACD is a strong indicator of when a stock is up—granting that an exact top is not a realistic exit target. As indicated earlier, the best TA indicators for each market participant will be those that make intuitive sense to him or her.

An honorable mention goes to the Equivolume Charting system pioneered by Richard W. Arms Jr. (also inventor of the famous Arms Index). This system is explained most completely in his latest book, *Volume Cycles in the Stock Market*. Conceptually, this type of chart incorporates elements of both candlestick ideas and the volume crescendo idea presented in Chapter 21 (see also *Trading on Volume* by your author). The Arms charting method tries to make reading a chart combining price and volume easy by changing the horizontal axis: that dimension or scale becomes trading volume rather than hours or days or weeks. The intuitive appeal of such charts is that they clearly display the appearance of unusually high volume after a price run-up, in effect making the chart look like price is forming a long and formidable top (Arms refers to that shape as over-square). An excellent and brief PowerPoint presentation of this charting method is available free at the Equivolume. com Website. These charts are a bit cumbersome to draw by hand; they can be had at a price in the MetaStock TA products suite at Equis.com.

In summary, this chapter encourages readers to focus their technical-analysis choices onto a relatively small number of systems that make personally intuitive sense. Clearly that latter judgment will vary among individuals. For the author, those that track volume and extreme crowd behavior are the most useful, and several have been named and described. A book named in the second paragraph may be helpful in saving time while sorting through numerous options. This caution is worth restating as well: There is no perfect system or magic bullet, so do not spend huge sums or years of your time seeking one. Settle on a few indicators that consistently point you to high areas (times and places to sell) in the overall market and in individual issues.

CHAPTER 21

Sell into Price-Volume Crescendos and into Long Runs

Keys for Successful Selling

- ◆ Gauge the Momentum by Watching Volume
- ◆ Take Advantage of the Occasional Upside Spike
- ◆ Know the Odds in Runs or Streaks

The central purpose underlying technical analysis of stock behavior is its attempt to identify, measure and act profitably upon changing relationships between supply and demand. Whether the specific technical approach is point-and-figure charting, the study of trends and channels, the identification of resistance and support levels or the price-volume methods popularized by several authors, at its core the real issue is supply and demand.

Most of the time, stock prices move in a primary direction—up or down—on heavier trading volume than they experience when making countertrend or sideways movements. The way to capture above-average profits is to sell when stocks are up rather than when they are at average or temporarily depressed levels. So this chapter focuses on two interesting short-term upside phenomena: crescendos and multiple-day runs. The purpose is to identify and describe high-volume tops and unsustainable rallies as they occur.

Gauging the Momentum by the Volume

Our first focus in identifying upside crescendos is based on the observation that volume tends to build when prices move in their primary direction; it tends to fall

206

during the countertrend, during corrections or during pauses in a stock's move. Volume cannot rise indefinitely over a short time frame. As it shoots progressively higher, crowd intensity of interest and therefore trading volume is nearing exhaustion. This has become increasingly true in recent years, when news and opinions circle the globe in minutes rather than days, and when thousands of traders' computers monitor short-term price momentum and can literally be programmed to mark apparent turns by ringing a bell. A look at historical charts can be useful in identifying roughly what the peak volume was when previous high points were reached. One-year daily charts, available from multiple sources. quickly show what the rough order of magnitude of the individual high-volume days has been over the past 12 months (about 250 trading sessions.) Likewise, online the BigCharts.com free Website allows quick views of daily price/volume charts for a user's choice from one to three years.

A major tenet underlying technical analysis of volume-price behavior is that a continuing price advance requires higher trading volume over time. Many technicians base their analyses and decision making on this important relationship. When they see a stock continuing to rise to new highs without ongoing strong trading volume, they refer to such a price move—even if it is to new 52-week highs or to news highs on the present move—as a weak advance.

The term weak advance has nothing directly to do with the money increment of rise (e.g., in the sense of $0.20 being weaker, or smaller, than $0.70). It refers to the cause, or the driving force, behind the price rise. As long as bulls who have been pushing the price higher continue to have strong conviction and remain unsatisfied in large numbers, they will still be active buyers, so trading volume will remain heavy. Price itself can also provide a clue. While the broad market averages very seldom reach a final high on a pattern of sharp acceleration called a spike, often individual stocks do, as was illustrated in the charts at Figure 19-3. This apparent anomaly occurs because averages are exactly that: they combine individual elements that sometimes diverge across time, so in the process they smooth the results.

Previous volume heights should be used as serious warnings, but do not expect them to be matched exactly or necessarily to be exceeded before you see current volume action as a valid signal of a price peak. When current volumes of daily trading reach into the general neighborhood of old highs or are several times average levels, be ready to sell without delay. You will never catch the precise high, but you may well be acting on the best day.

However, if interest shifts to other stocks in the same industry or if the market as a whole continues a strong advance but with other industry groups in the lead, your stock of interest may simply keep rising in sympathy with the trend. Because it has done well, there are many happy holders and few sellers (especially just before the tax year ends); such a stock can still rise briefly on lower volume. The shorts may be covering, and perhaps so many longs are happy that there are few urgent sellers, so mere modest net buying pressure causes an upward price tilt. This situation is inherently unstable and self-terminating. At some point in a price advance, more and more owners will view the stock as getting high on fundamentals or ahead of itself technically—and will want to sell. As there is no longer urgent or large buying power left to be satisfied, the sellers will begin to overwhelm the few remaining buyers, and upward momentum and price will crack. Stocks need strong current demand, not just a good story, to keep rising.

Not all stocks make their individual highs (or lows) on the same day or even in the same month. But when viewed individually, many do make highs on successive spike-like rallies accompanied by frenzied volume. What is happening in these stocks that causes them to change? For a while, successive price rises generate interest in a stock. Price starts to accelerate, rising by larger increments each day or week. But trends do not last indefinitely; acceleration itself begins to discourage new players as they perceive diminished fundamental value. At some point, traders begin to get cautious about owning, let alone still buying, this stock that has recently gone up so quickly.

The speculative bulls, seeing that excitement has at least temporarily halted, will pull back and wait for confirmation from other buyers that there is still some upside play left. Once upside volume is broken, price's faltering cannot be long behind. Typically, the most nimble owners sell their shares, causing the price first to decelerate, then to halt its rise, and finally to start falling. When the urgent speculative buyers finally are satisfied or go away, some sellers remain who have been waiting for one more good day or one dime or dollar. They will soon give up that hope and sell at market, driving the price lower.

Because of these supply/demand, volume/price dynamics, tops in stock prices tend to occur on high trading volume. In timing sales, you as a successful trader want to sell when they are hot, which is exactly when the trading volume is peaking on rising prices and in concert with general excitement about the stock. While each day's trading includes equal amounts of buying and selling, the personality and relative urgency of the players shifts as this scenario plays out. As price has risen sharply, more holders become nervous or satisfied by the newfound price levels, so selling volume is building. (And more owners are recent short-term buyers, often referred to as hot money; these are unstable holders ready to move out as soon as the action cools.)

Obviously, it is not always possible to know in advance exactly what day will see the height of volume or price. In general, however, there are two clues to watch. One is in the volume trend and the other is in price, and often they both apply. When they start to diverge, take it as an urgent sign to head for the exit door. Thus, when the price does stop rising, it can now suddenly fall sharply from its peak as those latest satisfied owners or nervous sellers fail to find enough interested buyers; volume, therefore, falls off. Note again that stocks can fall of their own weight, but it takes actual active buying pressure (not just general positive feelings) to boost them up.

Once some upside excitement is triggered and takes hold, volume tends to build toward a crescendo. Bar plots of consecutive daily volume resemble the shape of a mountain in which the slope becomes increasingly steep on the way to the pinnacle (some technicians refer to crescendos as parabolas). Not every single day falls perfectly in line, slightly higher than the day before and lower than the next. But the general shape is clear, and interruptions seldom exceed two days. Study the volume peaks on the charts in Figure 21-1 over the page. (Sometimes a discerning check at mid-morning can indicate that the prior day will prove to be the peak if today's action is clearly less intense.) In all cases the general volume-chart shape is clearly similar, and interruptions seldom exceed two days When current volumes of daily trading reach into the general neighborhood of old highs, be ready to sell without delay.

Careful study of past patterns in this intertwined pair of yardsticks—price and volume—will help you assess when a stock is close enough to make a sell decision wise. Trading volume is the driver; price change is the result!

While our intellect can see the evidence, there is something in human nature that makes it difficult to execute this maneuver on a prompt basis. One unscientific, but still effective, approach is self-monitoring. To calibrate yourself, you need to own a given, fairly volatile, stock and watch it closely on a daily basis. Record how many consecutive days the volume has risen and also whether a strong run in the major market averages is helping price. (Doing this exercise on paper while not owning the stock might prove interesting but would be somewhat sterile because of an absence of emotions.) As the stock crescendos in price and volume, observe personal daily reactions like the interplays among fear and greed and excitement; record these on paper, keyed with a letter, and mark that letter at the appropriate day on a price chart for future reference. When you execute a sale made during this flagpole run-up, mark it with an S on the chart and take note afterward whether your decision came prematurely or late—and, if so, by how many days the actual peak was miscalculated.

Note also what your best hunch was at the time the sell order was entered (past the top, or maybe still more to go). In effect, that is calibrating your own personal pressure gauge. Print out the daily price chart a week later, and attach it to your notes. Then next time incorporate your latest results into an operating plan. Naturally this is an imprecise art rather than a science, and your perhaps alternating or overcompensating (later/sooner) approaches may feel awkward. But after a few experiences, you will develop an improved sense of touch. Again, this exercise works only in real trading in the presence of actual risk and tension as real dollars and your self-esteem are on the line. It is also most effective if several observations can be made in a fairly concentrated period of time such as a few weeks or at most a couple of months. Otherwise, even with written notes, recall is not very accurate because of faded intensity.

A key point to remember in a rapid price run-up is not to expect to achieve a perfect exit. The stock's action will be very volatile from hour to hour; if an investor is typically busy at work, she probably has only one decision time per day via a broker call or online visit, perhaps two at most. Using on-line chart systems that

Figure 21.1: Price Tops Coinciding with Volume Crescendos

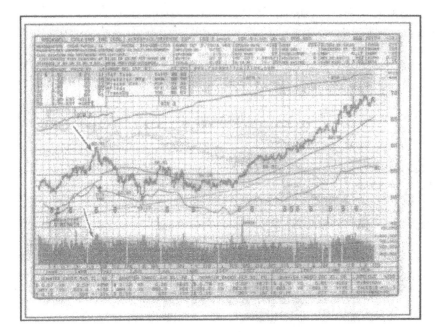

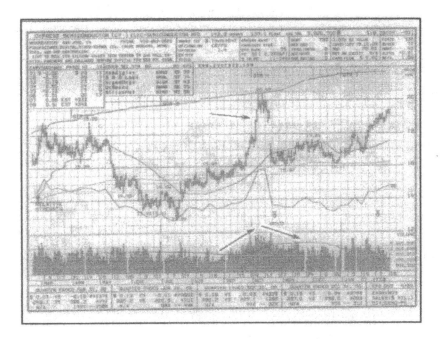

allow bypassing a broker conversation to monitor the current action serves as an increasing help. Even if there is more frequent (more than once-daily) contact, strive for the discipline of making only one choice (selling or holding) per day. That construct will impose a degree of structure on your sell decisions. Resist wanting to think more about it or to wait for just a little more (technical) information. Come to closure in one thinking session today, or force yourself to wait until tomorrow.

Once again, never expect to get the highest nickel or dime. Any investor able even to hit the best day, let alone the top price, is doing very well indeed: partly clever and perhaps a little bit lucky. Taking action within no more than one day on either side of the top is still quite laudable So keep a cool perspective: If a stock makes three high-volume price peaks a year, being within a day of the top when selling means you successfully identified and acted on one of the nine best trading days out of 250 in a year. That is besting odds of more than 25:1. Congratulations!

Both buying good stocks and selling them well are required for making profits. To trade successfully in up or especially sideways markets, one must sell into strong price and volume crescendos, that is, selling just as the buying crowd reaches its fever pitch rather than becoming part of that crowd. Do not worry about catching the top perfectly, so enter sell instructions in this circumstance at market rather than getting greedy.

Once having sold, walk away. Be content to look back again at that stock no sooner than a week or two later: If it was sold anywhere near the height of a mountain of trading volume, very likely you will be pleased to see that its price has fallen back and that your sale was a good (capital conserving) one. Your exit will not have been perfect, but you will have the great satisfaction of knowing how much better it is to have gotten out near that top than still to be in and be further away from it.

In summary, there are two aspects of selling on high volume to remember: Realize that volume will crescendo only so high, and use stock-specific past history as a guide to its reasonably likely upper limits. If volume starts to trail off after a buildup but price keeps going up, this is the weak, later portion of the price rise and time is running out fast. Figure 21-2 (over the page) illustrates the failure of volume build-ups to support further price advances.

Enjoy Spike but Act on the Special Case of an Upside Spike

In psychological terms, an upside volume and price spike is similar to a crescendo. But it is dramatically more forceful and shorter in time duration. Upside price spikes on huge volume are usually driven by some highly favorable sudden news development, whereas crescendos tend to appear when a new idea gradually takes hold or when excitement builds to a fever pitch after price already has had a pleasant upside run (a buying climax). An upside spike can be thought of as a sudden and

Figure 21.2: Lower Volume Defines Weak Advances

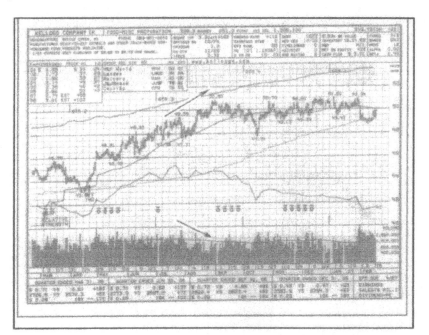

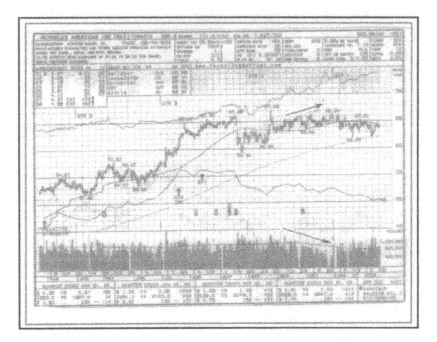

short-lived buying panic. A spike is defined by daily trading volume suddenly several or many times normal. Unless the new information that drives the spike has truly major longer-term import, the price rise will not continue into a second trading day, so selling immediately is the proper course. (Examples of news of lasting impact would be a takeover proposal or the finding that a company's existing drug has exciting new benefits in treating a second condition.) A shortening of news and opinion propagation times around the globe because of the Internet's role makes spikes more common than in the past and also tends to ensure that the price effect lasts no more than part of one trading session. Examples of volume/price spikes in three stocks are provided in Figure 21-3 (over the page), where the second graph of CompX International contains several spikes within one year.

You will be very happy with how your stock is treating your wallet when you own one that experiences a spike. But there is no time for celebrating, and no room for hoping that things will get even better tomorrow. The rest of the world that in the past would learn the news on evening TV or in tomorrow's newspaper is tuned in via Internet and financial TV and so has already acted if they are going to. Mutual funds that buy and sell on EPS momentum have already joined (and created part of) the crowd whose volume is so huge. In short, the party is already over on day one, and often this will occur by late morning. You should sell by that time.

A price and volume spike may (but does not always) cause an upside gap on the chart (see Wrigley), which further limits the interest of technical analysts in buying afterward. There will be renewed buying support once the stock eventually closes that gap and therefore investors and traders can then buy at the old price, where they wish they had done so before the great news. But there is nothing in terms of near-term demand for the shares that can hold them up. The crowd is finished buying. The usual pattern (Wrigley and Thermo Fisher charts) is for price to recede gradually or trickle down after the one-day upside burst shows no follow-on. So you as an unusually well informed seller will want to have been out on the first day.

Know the Odds in Runs

A second interesting and potentially very profitable upside phenomenon is the occasional but very pleasant long run of consecutive daily advances. In the real world, it is useful to isolate on examining such price runs in terms of their odds of continuing or faltering. In the same way that the emotions and momentum chasing described earlier will cause a crescendo to reverse itself once the volume rise stops, here the end of a long run of daily advances will be followed by price reversal as both short-term traders and observant, tactically nimble investors cash in. You should be aware of how the odds work and should take selling action accordingly. Our study of runs applies both to individual stocks and to the broad market as measured by widely watched averages, which can now be traded via ETFs. Tracking runs in major averages is helpful because it aids in timing one's sales of individual stocks. While

Figure 21.3: Examples of Extreme Volume Spikes

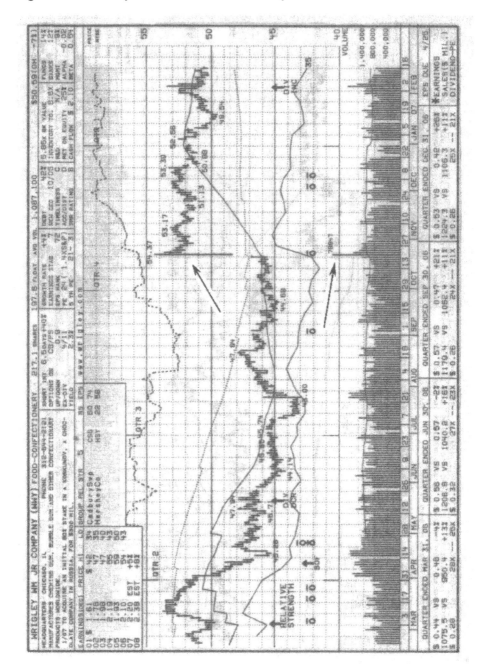

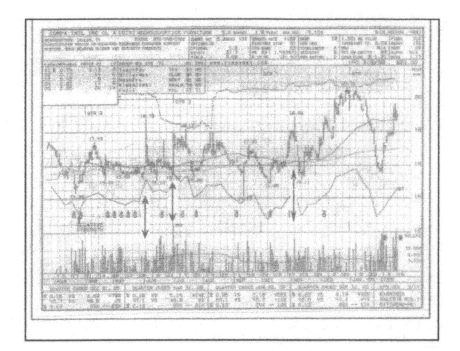

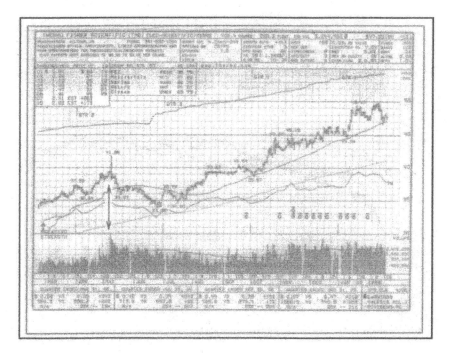

not every stock rises or falls on the same day as a major average, the general tone or trend of the market does influence single stocks' prices. During an upside run, market participants become increasingly confident and happy, regarding the whole experience of investing or trading as more and more pleasant. Once the string of positive daily reinforcements (rises) is broken, a return to reality sets in (free trading markets are, after all, a two-way street). An overly strong move on the upside can turn into a string of corrective days as momentum players depart and other participants become scared or disillusioned by the stock's newest action. So runs tend to be real.

If, as some academics not looking for patters believe, advances and declines actually were random events, and if the possibility of zero-change days were conveniently not a complicating factor, one could construct probability tables for predicting the frequencies of given lengths of price runs. For example, imagining that there were no unchanged days and that advances and declines were equal in number over the long term (like the two sides of a fair coin), following would be the pure statistical odds of various lengths of upside runs:

Days in a Row	Odds	Times per Year
One or more	0.5	126
Two or more	0.25	63
Three or more	0.125	31
Four or more	0.0625	16
Five or more	0.03125	8
Six or more	0.015625	4
Seven or more	0.0078125	2
Eight or more	0.00391625	1
Nine or more	0.001958125	0.49
Ten or more	0.0009790625	0.24

Thus, assuming all that was stated earlier, in a typical trading year of 252 sessions you might expect to see four times when an advance ran to six consecutive days and then just three times any longer; an eight-day or longer upside run would come but once or maybe twice a year. An advance extending to 10 or more consecutive days should be seen only about once in four years. Often, although not always, such a run is accompanied by rising volume. Moves into new high ground or moves to close a prior downside gap do not always need higher volume. You should expect that the longer the upside streak was, the sharper will be the pull-back once it starts.

Weeks in a Row	Odds	Times Per Year
One or more	0.5	26
Two or more	0.25	13
Three or more	0.125	6 or 7
Four or more	0.0625	3
Five or more	0.03125	1 or 2
Six or more	0.015625	0.8
Seven or more	0.0078125	0.4
Eight or more	0.00391625	One in five years
Nine or more	0.001958125	One in ten years
Ten or more	0.009790625	One in twenty years

Extremely long runs do occur, but tend to be rare, so do not count on them. In early 1996, the market as measured by the Dow Jones Industrial Average at one point rose for 10 consecutive weeks. Historians dug back and noted that this had last occurred in 1965, some 30 years earlier. The table of odds places the frequency of this unusually persistent kind of a rally at 1 every 20 years. A similarly rare strong streak occurred in April and May 2007, when the Dow rose in 24 of 27 sessions running, a feat last earlier seen way back in 1927. Such strings of happy news can only raise expectations to unrealistic levels and set up the market for disappointment.

The stock market is a free marketplace defined by human reality rather than one operating on pure statistical odds. News and emotions tend to get in the way of neat mathematically determined odds working out as perfectly as they can be calculated on paper. A week usually consists of five trading days; it is possible for the market to pause in midweek for a correction and then burst on ahead, showing a net plus for the week when perhaps three days showed losses. Similarly, the day consists of hours and minutes; the net movement for the day might be determined in the final 30 minutes. News events drive reactions by people. While government agencies release key economic statistics on a predictable cycle, a Kobe earthquake or a political assassination or a currency devaluation or a major corporate bankruptcy could occur at any time; such events will interrupt advances or prolong declines.

The preceding tables are based on a random 50 percent of days being up days. In actual fact, the stock market over the long run goes up more days than down, with the actual odds of a single daily advance being about 52.4 percent rather than just half. The tables also ignore the potential for unchanged days, which can serve as regrouping pauses that may actually extend advances (or declines). Obviously, in bull markets the odds of a rising day are a bit greater than 52.4 percent, while in bear markets the odds of declining days exceed 50 percent. And precisely because collective human emotions are involved, runs rather than random movement characterize stock-price patterns. Emotions switch from overly optimistic to cautious and then to overly fearful and pessimistic; stocks rise for a time, then fall back.

Because these and other real-world effects confound the theoretical mathematical odds, actual experience is a bit different from that in the tables. Actual observation is that for extended runs of consecutive daily advances (say, five days or longer), the real odds are about half those in the table. Thus, for example, a seven-day rally seems actually to happen about once a year and an eight-day upside run only about once every couple of years. Actual incidence of downside runs is a little more frequent than that of equally long rallies; logically this follows from fear being a stronger emotion than greed.

This perspective is potentially quite useful in a practical sense when an investor is considering selling a stock on a non-urgent basis. Suppose his stock has roughly reached its fundamental price goal and he is ready to sell, but there is no immediate news that inclines him to want to jump out immediately. If the market fortuitously gets into a run of consecutive days, that upside momentum and bullish state of mind will help move most stocks higher, including his sell candidate. As an informed and savvy seller, he now knows roughly the frequency or rarity of a run of consecutive days continuing once it reaches perhaps five days or more. He can cool-headedly use this background information to help determine when to make a graceful exit that would otherwise be unlikely for a non-contrarian.

Paying attention to such signals is important, for two reasons. First, as the advance gets going progressively longer, it is fun and an investor falls more deeply in love with his stock and with his own self-perceived brilliance in picking it. The natural temptation is to promise to sell after just one more day or just one more point, rather like a Las Vegas gambler on a supposed hot streak who plans to quit after doubling down just once more. The second reason that knowing these rough odds is useful is that remorse and stubbornness set in after a stock starts declining; there will then be a tendency to hold on for a return to the high, and our investor then does not sell at all, giving back all of the recent advance (and the time value of money) as a result. Knowing how long the odds are against a lengthy further advance, when the investor has already enjoyed a good run, should help give him the added contrarian's discipline to sell while things look most rosy.

In the cases of both price/volume crescendos and extended daily runs, there is no exact universal formula for precisely when to sell. However, this chapter has provided guidance regarding signs to look for in attempting to time sales on the upside very well, even if not perfectly. Being mostly right but less than perfect (selling near the top) is a lot better than being wrong and holding on into the next decline.

CHAPTER 22

Differentiate Market Stock and Loner Stock Characteristics

Keys for Successful Selling

◆ Know the Portrait of a Market Stock

◆ Contrast the Portrait of a Loner Stock

◆ Calibrate Actions to Stocks' Personalities

When considering whether to hold or sell, one of the determining factors is whether the stock is what is what can be termed a market stock. This is an important consideration because it can tilt investor judgment at the margin: if there is a forceful trend in the overall market (either up or down), this can affect the stock's performance in the short term, or it may not, depending on the stock's nature. The opposite kind of issue is characterized here as a loner stock. The following two lists differentiate characteristics for these two categories of stocks. Note that a stock need not fit all of the descriptors in either list.

Market stocks are:

◆ held heavily by institutions;

◆ consistently heavily traded and liquid;

◆ large-capitalization issues;

◆ stocks with very high betas, or betas near 1.00;

◆ among the Dow Jones Industrials or especially the S&P 100;

◆ in the trend-carrying or fad-leading industry at the current time;

◆ stocks in which options volume is heavy;

◆ non-financial and non-REIT companies;

◆ household names with multitudes of individual investors;

◆ outstanding fundamental achievers in their industries;

◆ not noticeably out of favor in a bullish period; and

◆ familiar and acceptable to non-U.S. investors.

Loner Stocks are:

◆ not widely held by institutions;

◆ small-capitalization companies;

◆ medium-capitalization but not always heavily traded;

◆ often listed on the AMEX or below NASDAQ's main list, with few market-makers;

◆ possibly but not necessarily in interest-rate sensitive groups;

◆ single-product or unique-concept or story stocks;

◆ high-technology companies in market phases not dominated by technology groups;

◆ low-priced issues;

◆ stocks with betas below 0.50 or negative (including gold);

◆ high-yield situations;

◆ not widely followed, if at all, by analysts;

◆ recent new issues outside the currently dominant fad industry;

◆ held heavily by insiders or parent companies;

◆ counter-cyclical-industry members;

◆ stocks that fall outside conventional industry descriptions (sometimes, conglomerates);

◆ regional or local companies not widely known elsewhere; and

◆ regarded as current or longer-term fundamental laggards in their industries.

Portrait of a Market Stock

What mainly typifies a market stock is a high coincidence of daily price moves parallel to the direction of the major market averages. Statistically that means perhaps seven plus days in ten on days of clear market direction, typically 60 plus percent of stocks move in the dominant direction. But such a high correlation of individual daily movement with the overall trend is not always something that can be checked readily when the need for a real-time decision to hold or sell arises. Prepared investors must identify in advance the personality types of their stocks.

A recent run of seven in ten 10 days could be just a coincidence or it could be driven by unusually sweeping and emotional trends in the overall market. Therefore, in testing whether an issue is a market stock, refer to the overall preceding lists of traits. The benefit of knowing these characteristics in advance is that they can be reviewed at any time before the pressure of a sell/hold decision actually arises. Make a mental or written note about which characteristics of the stock apply when your buy it, or even before.

Knowing whether an issue is a market stock or an independent one is important when making a hold/sell decision generally and also when it is time to cash in for a good sale in terms of short-term micro tactics. Under these circumstances, with a market stock one depends more heavily on judging the short-term trend or the likely action of the general market.

An advance personality assessment is important because, statistically, a market stock is likely to perform in line with the overall list direction and may move by a meaningful percentage. In this case, the consideration should be the merit of selling at market versus an above-market limit (or, conceivably, a stop-loss order) not only in the context of the stock's own action and chart position, but also in light of the overall market's dominant trend and probable near-term or daily action. Table 22-1 lists a few contrasting examples of market stocks and loners in several industries.

Consider McDonald's (NYSE:MCD), for example. It tends to move with the market on most days when there is a clear market direction. With the exception of not being in a trend-carrying group (restaurants have not been leaders for most of the past three decades), McDonald's fits the list of typical-market stock characteristics. If there is a broad market rally or a sharp sell-off in which major money moves the market, MCD is very likely to be swept along with the day's trend. Money flows into and out of MCD in part because this stock is in both the Dow 30 and the S&P500—and the related ETFs.

Table 22.1: Contrasting Examples of Market and Loner Stocks

Market Stocks		Loners
McDonald's	but not	Brinker's
Wal-Mart	but not	Family Dollar
Pfizer	but not	Perrigo
Exxon	but not	Pogo Producing
Intel	but not	Cypress Semiconductor
Southwest Airlines	but not	Mesa
Merrill Lynch	but not	Siebert Financial
Home Depot	but not	Pier One
Safeway	but not	Village Super Market
Hewlett-Packard	but not	Radio Shack

Except shortly after one of its periodic splits, McDonald's is usually highly priced enough that a change of a point or so is not unusual on a big-move day in the overall market. Thus, if a McDonald's holder has decided to cash in, she should pay more than a usual amount of attention to the general market's near-term direction. Suppose McDonald's has had a pretty good run to the upside lately and our investor, therefore, thinks MCD is getting overextended. If the general list is moving up or is likely to react sharply to some favorable overnight economic or geopolitical news, our seller ought to give McDonald's a little more running room right now because it is a market stock. Instead of selling outright at market, she puts in a limit above market (unless the stock is running into serious resistance or unless some company-specific negative news comes out).

However, if on its individual merit, the stock is not thought to be an urgent sell but the dominant market trend seems sharply down and/or the current day's direction is a real flusher, our informed investor should lean more heavily toward an immediate sale of a McDonald's or other huge-cap stock because of the market context. She assumes that the stock will move with the overall list because of its personality and because of the deep pockets who are likely to be trading in it.

In this case, the stock is unlikely meaningfully to fight the tape of the general decline. Because of the nature of the stock and its holders and especially its index-component status, it probably will drop with the list despite its own specific merits. Our investor is better served to sell at market rather than to reach for an above-market limit. It is better not to miss the market and give back a fast point or more of paper gains.

Market stocks can occasionally move independently, of course. Positive revenue or EPS surprises, or perhaps some beef health scare, or a rise in the minimum wage, for example, could easily move a McDonalds' independent of the overall list for a few days.

Portrait of a Loner Stock

A contrast to the large-cap and well known market stock is the typical non-market-influenced, or loner, issue. By any one or several of the listed characteristics, this stock simply is not in daily rhythm with the general list. Probably the most common keys to identifying these loner stocks are low daily trading volume, perhaps less than stellar fundamental performance within their industry, off-beat company natures, and regional rather than national or international stature. Conglomerates fit the mold, as they are not something quickly or clearly definable in traders' and money managers' minds. Some loner stocks may be perfectly fine companies but are simply not household names or analyst-followed issues.

These attributes make a stock somewhat uninteresting to big players, which can cause holders disappointment on the upside. There is a consolation: Except in crashes and temporary panics, non-market stocks probably hold well against a mild market downdraft lasting a day or two. The reason is that there is no hot money in them so they are not vulnerable to profit taking by active big players. When making a sell/hold tactical judgment about a loner stock, it is most important not to count absolutely on the strength of the overall market to move this stock in the dominant direction. In very weak general markets, however, loner stocks are likely to fall because of a lack of buying interest; in strong upside markets they are not among the first ideas traders have for participating in the rally and therefore may act quite independently The loner stock is not a leader in its group, nor a component of a major average/index, not subject to inclusion in program trading, and just generally seems to march to its own separate drummer.

In dealing with a loner stock, an investor might decide the overall market is so strong that all stocks should get some benefit; he holds on in the belief that the rising tide will raise all boats. But if he is dealing with a stock that acts independently, his mistaken logic is likely to cause disappointment. He is probably allowing the market's action to provide a subtle rationalization for postponing a sale decision or is allowing greed or stubbornness to rule his thinking. So it is important to know the differing personality patterns of market and independent stocks and to factor those traits into the hold/sell decision. On a short-term tactical basis, this added insight can often help investors realize better selling prices by adding a degree of key but often-overlooked context.

Once a high-volatility decline in the general market extends more than a few sessions, one must look hard at holding illiquid small-cap issues. When the market reaches a morning-panic stage, such stocks will have few or no bidders and can readily fall about 10 percent on a market order, particularly if traded on NASDAQ where no single specialist is charged with maintaining an orderly market. If you own such stocks and can see that they are thinly traded, during a calm or modestly bullish market period you should check the width of the bid/asked spread via your online trading platform. Anticipate that the spread will be twice as wide or more during some future scary market downdraft. This is one added part of understanding your stocks' individual personalities.

CHAPTER 23

Use Above-Market Instead of Stop-Loss Orders

Keys for Successful Selling

◆ See the Weaknesses of Stop-Loss Orders

◆ Be Careful about Order Placement

◆ Use the Advantages of Above-Market Sell Orders

Those few brokers and investment books that do provide any guidance to customers regarding selling almost always advocate using stop-loss orders as a selling tactic. This chapter advocates, instead, the use of above-market sell orders (except in very limited circumstances), which tend to be more profitable. Above-market or price-limit orders target a specific successful exit price and by selling temporarily above the fair-value range or into brief sharp bullish enthusiasm; stop-loss orders guarantee a lower price than exists at the time they are entered and they are executed only if and after something fundamental or technical has obviously already gone wrong.

Consider the old investment slogan: Cut your losses and let your profits run. The theory is that investors and traders should be relatively intolerant of non-performing or weak positions and should resist the temptation to pocket a quick, small gain on successful buys, holding on instead for a hoped-for major, long-term payoff.

This prescription sounds simple and obvious, but it is difficult to execute tactically. Needless to say, one can hardly quarrel with an objective like avoiding losses or with honoring the time value of money since time will prove to be either a friend or a subtle enemy. Obviously there is no argument with letting big profits accumulate. The problem is that we cannot fully forecast the future and so are not sure in real time whether an existing paper profit will run or will evaporate. What to let run is the same as the what in buy-and-hold.

The trick is choosing between these two kinds of standing price orders in real time. When there is actual money on the line and when emotions can cloud the decision-making process, it is difficult to discern which current, small-loss stocks will hibernate at recent quotes (or go south even further) and which others will turn into glorious successes.

If you use stop orders at all, these points should be kept in mind:

◆ Your entry point (purchase price) is irrelevant to defining a good exit point, as detailed in Chapter 7.

◆ Routine use of a fixed-percentage-width cushion ignores the inherently varied volatilities/liquidities across different stocks.

◆ Stop-loss levels should be set on the basis of support levels or trend lines, which almost always will be closer or farther away than some standard percentage method prescribes.

That first point's importance cannot be overemphasized: The level of your personal cost price has no impact on the overall market and therefore no relevance to the question of where to cut losses (or take a profit). Any reasonably experienced market participant not even professing to be an expert chartist can look at a price-history chart and make reasonable judgments about the prices at which a given stock will have proven something (on the upside) and at which it will have shown fatal weakness (on the downside).

Weaknesses of Stop-Loss Orders

Cop-Outs and Crutches

Stop-loss orders should be used in very limited circumstances because their success depends upon being implemented with near-surgical skill. Their most common usage is often a cop-out on the part of the supportive media writer, the broker and the investor implementing the tactic.

Brokers, as described in earlier chapters, are loathe to deal with money-losing positions. One simple way for any broker to avoid the inconvenient bind of discussing losses is to advise clients to limit their exposure by placing stop-loss orders a moderate percentage away from the buy point (recall the critique of that entry-point-based tactic in Chapter 7). If an account shows a mixture of profits and losses and if the losses are never drastic, the broker and his firm are safe from charges of incompetence or inattention when using a stops strategy. Almost always, they will be able to point to at least one major loss avoided—simply because stocks do fluctuate and sometimes some will go very bad.

If a chart analyst is told by a stock's owner: I should have told you that my cost price is 44. The only logical response is: So what? The point is, if a stock violates major support by breaking 43.50, that is a fact regardless of who the unlucky holders are and regardless of whether they paid 44, 21 or 55. A particular percentage down has no merit as a selling yardstick. If selling down 10 percent were always right, bargain hunting at a level that 10 percent defines would always be wrong. Entry points are particular to each investor and are scattered widely, as recorded history on each price chart will show. Today's market climate and updated company information and investor expectations are what will drive future prices.

While stop-loss orders routinely placed closely below the buy level do limit the size of individual losses, their main function is to relieve the broker and the investor of making a decision about selling, holding or doubling up on an underwater position— in real time, when emotions run high because money is on the line. Once a stop is placed, the market activates it automatically for the broker and the client, or it does nothing. The automatic pilot gets the credit or blame. If you have a terrible time operating under pressure or typically refuse to accept losses, then the crutch of a stop-loss order may be necessary for you.

If this book were focused on how to buy stocks, it would define how to buy to avoid the danger of being so close to the technical-analysis breakdown point. But here, our selling perspective emphasizes that cost basis is irrelevant to a sale decision. Therefore, using any specific percentage limit below the cost point is an irrelevant formula. It is about as logical as basing salary on age, eye color or height.

Bad Placement

The use of any fixed-tolerance formula relating to now-current price (e.g., X percent or Y points) is likewise not properly tied to the characteristics of the position. Stocks have inherent tendencies toward volatility, which may be defined roughly as percentage fluctuation within a day or week compared with the percentage fluctuation of a broad market index. (Students of market action and measurers of manager performance refer to this as beta.)

There is no need to know whether the price volatility of a given stock is caused by price level, floating supply, player emotions, institutional participation or other factors. Just observe that stocks fluctuate with their own amplitudes that generally tend to change only over long time periods. For one stock at $25, a daily range of plus or minus $0.25 is normal (check many utility shares as examples); for another stock at the same price level a dollar or even wider daily range is typical. (Look at biotechnology, Internet, semiconductor, airline, oil-exploration and computer-peripherals issues.)

In addition to this shortcoming, routine stop-loss orders have two other weaknesses: they are usually not placed at a logical price level, and, even more importantly, they necessarily cause a sale based on weakness rather than on unusual temporary strength—they predictably will get you out down, not up.

For example, many advocates of the routine stop-loss order advise its placement at a standard percentage-below-cost basis. The most commonly advocated allowable losses are 10 percent, 5 percent and 15 percent. To all but the most timid market players, such losses are acceptable even though they obviously fall short of the originally intended profit result. As illustrated in Figure 23-1 (over the page), there are three objections to the use of arbitrary percentages: First, any percentage-driven order at, say, $23 would have wasted the first $1.50 below an obvious breakdown level; second, a stop at $23 would close the position just as the stock finds its next important support and probably prepares for a mild bounce-back rally.

What is tolerable in-the-noise price movement for one stock is a sign of significant change in the supply/demand balance for another because they have inherently different personalities. Because of these observable and very real differences, allowing only a single rigid percentage of breathing room on all stocks is nonsensical and basically a placebo prescription for the lazy.

A well-placed stop-loss order ought at least to take into account the natural fluctuation tendency of the stock in question rather than assume that all are alike. A staid utility is reacting to a massive change in interest rates or major risk to its dividend by falling as much as 15 percent, so here a 15 percent stop is much too loose. A wide-swinging growth stock might gyrate 20 percent around its moving average several times annually without breaking its basic upside momentum, so here a commonly advocated 10 percent or 15 percent stop-loss range will prove self-defeating from the start.

Properly, a stop-loss should be at whatever level is dictated by trend lines or support levels rather than at some percentage subtraction from a level such as entry. Take as a theoretical example a stock in an established trading channel for several months between the prices of 40 and 46. If it is clear that 39.90 is a breakdown in support, then the proper stop-loss point is 39.90, which means that if an investor buys the stock at 41, the popular 5 percent, 10 percent or 15 percent-down tolerances are too wide. And, if he buys above 44—in the upper half of the range, in the hope of a breakout—the 5 percent and 15 percent allowances are still naive in light of what the chart says. The 5 percent level would probably whipsaw the investor, getting him or her out below 42 just as the stock starts to find support in the lower end of the channel, from which it might rally again. A 15 percent allowance from 44 would be at 37.40, well after the stock will have clearly broken down.

The accompanying chart of ITT Industries (Figure 23-1) provides a real-life example of where stop-loss orders ought and ought not to be placed Notice the obvious recurring technical importance of the $24.50 to $24.75 area on the chart, first as a supply zone needing to be penetrated and, for the final five months, as a multiple bottom or support area. (This happens also to illustrate that arbitrary round numbers such as $25 are not always ideal order points.) At the time of this chart's printing,

Figure 23.1: Key Support Levels

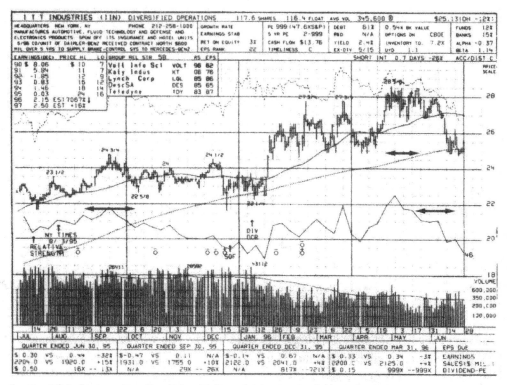

Courtesy of *Daily Graphs and Long Term Values;* P.O. Box 66919; Los Angeles, California 90066–0919.

a breakdown below $24.75 and absolutely one at $24.40 would spell significant trouble. Orders should now be placed at those levels. Previously, the stock appeared to have begun an up-trend, neatly defined by a line connecting its bottom prices in December, January and April. Each week a holder should have raised her protective stop (if any!) to just slightly below the gradually rising level of that line. By doing so, she would have been stopped out immediately as the stock broke down just below $27 in mid-June. As of two weeks later (at the very end of this chart), bargain hunters might buy at $25 but should allow no more than a half-point of downside risk, at the well-defined multiple support point. By trying to give the stock a little breathing room, say, in placing a stop at $23, one would certainly be stopped out at a doubly bad spot—too low and also approaching actual support.

The point is that stop-loss orders, if used at all, should be placed with some precision based on the market condition of the stock and not on a percentage formula. Also, it should be placed where its violation signals a significant negative move for the stock: not higher and not lower. This involves a detailed analysis of the chart and should never be related to an investor's entry point. A stop order, when used at all, is designed to protect your capital rather than to let you feel good about how tolerant you are or about how good your chances are of being proved right eventually.

Harmful Market Influences

There are times when even a technically well-placed stop-loss order can uncontrollably cause a bad execution. For example, when general market weakness takes place on rumors or in response to massive program trading, price levels in individual stocks become meaningless as usual liquidity disappears and all buyers run for cover. In this case, when the temporary but sharp overall market downdraft passes, many stop orders will have proven too tight, even if placed with good stock-specific logic beforehand. In 20/20 hindsight, it is easy to see that the investor was stopped out for market-driven rather than stock-specific reasons, and she will have cash rather than a full portfolio after the temporary panic bottom has passed and stocks (including the one now sold) have bounced back nicely.

In fast-falling markets, stop orders can be actually executed well below their stated levels; stop-limit orders can compound the problem by never being executed. Suppose you have entered a stop-loss at a properly judged level of 44. Say your stock closed yesterday at 45, comfortably above support or trend line. But there is awful overnight news—international, macro domestic or corporate. Let us say your stock opens down $1.50 at 43.50. Now, after the 43.50 opening trade, is when your order becomes a market sell order. Maybe the next trade is 43.40 or 43.10 depending on how bad the emotional climate is. And understand that opening gaps of $1.50 are by no means the limit: watch how many points a large-cap stock instantly crater when analysts are surprised by a quarterly EPS miss. So, if you use stops, you should understand their mechanics and therefore realize that your stated price very well may be above the actual execution you will realize.

Finally, it is important for an investor to fine tune the use of stops according to her broker relationship. If using a discount broker, she will need to lean more toward stops for any given situation. If using a really helpful full-service firm, she may get a warning call from the broker when a stock starts breaking down off its highs or when the news goes bad. In this way, she can sometimes get out at a higher price than by waiting for a stop to be exercised.

In essence, then, it is better to rely on broker assistance when it is being paid for than to use the mechanical stop-loss order. Some brokers occasionally accept discretion in placing an order if they cannot reach a client. If a broker agrees to operate on this basis and pays attention to stocks full time, that is yet another good reason for not using stop-losses.

Another caution is worth noting regarding placement of stops—if you use them at all. Occasionally a stock will have either one or more gaps in its chart, as illustrated in the graphs of Cooper Companies and Three-M in Figure 23-2 (opposite). These are areas where for historic reasons there simply are no orders, and such gaps tend to repeat for a while once they come to exist. Before placing any stop it would be wise always to check a chart to see whether such gaps exist. If they do, placing a stop inside the gap area will almost certainly give a bad execution; better placement would be right above the level at which the downside gap would develop if it occurred again. Right around 52 seemed to be a dangerous level in COO, and likewise about 78.50 in MMM.

Advantages of Above-Market Sell Orders

Rather than using a stop below the market, which means that the sale, if any, will occur at a price below the available price at the time the order was first entered, it is preferable to use targeted sell stops above the market. When these orders above the market are executed, they give a better price than that price prevailing when the order was entered – and even more widely favorable as compared with a stop-loss level below.

Like stop-loss orders, these orders also carry caveats and qualifiers. An above-market stop-sell order is not appropriate in all situations; sometimes a market sale is better. Any above-market stop-sell order must also be placed with precision and care.

To place an above-market, target-limit-sell accurately, first visualize what kind of overall market climate prevails and is likely to exist over the period of time your projected order will be in place. A stop-loss below market is there to provide protection against further loss, while an above-market stop-sell order should be used to exit a stock when the investor believes reasonable patience and the market's normal fluctuation working together can provide a better price. At any

Figure 23.2: Illustrations of Repeating Gaps at One Price Level

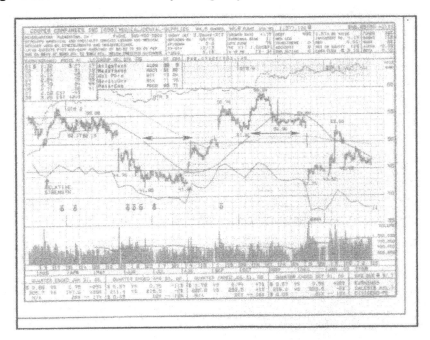

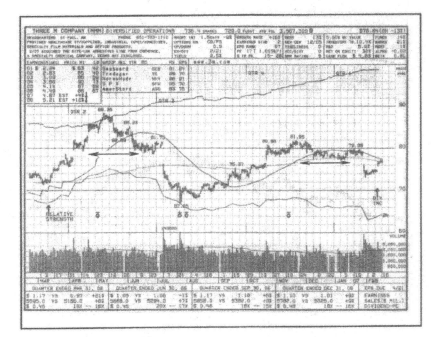

time, a reasonable expectation for upside potential is determined to some degree by the overall market trend and also by the stock's own price pattern as seen on its chart.

Going back to our imagined stock with a lengthy channel between 40 and 46, assume that a sale seems in order but is not extremely urgent. In a market moving sideways or moderately higher, an investor would be wise to set an above-market sell-stop order at perhaps around 45.70 in this situation. Reject trying to squeeze out that final dime or two.

If the overall market is quite strong but the stock remains frustratingly trapped in mid-channel, say maybe around 43, you might have more aggressive expectations for other buyable situations and so put the order at 45.40 or 550. You certainly would not put in a sell at 46.20 or higher because that would be triggered exactly and only when the stock surprises you with an upside breakout. That level would give exactly the wrong sale timing by being at a tactically wrong price. On the other hand, in a moderately weak market, the owner might be happy with anything at all in the upper half of the channel; so he might set the stop-sell at 43.50 or 44, at most.

In a violent bear move, there would be no sense in setting an above-market sell level except when a fairly sharp interim sell-off has just already been completed: if the investor is not willing to hold this stock through the coming carnage, he should assume the damage will continue and should therefore sell now at market rather than wait for a rally. Why wait for a drop through 40 to prove that the trend is clearly down?

On a short-term basis, also observe the stock's own trend and the general market in recent days: lean against it in direction and degree. If the stock and/or major averages have been up several days running (remember the discussion of extended runs in Chapter 21), any further upside attempt using a limit-sell above current levels should be quite limited. On the other hand, if the stock or market has fallen several days running on moderate volume but has not destroyed important up-trend lines or support levels, look for some rebound and place the order a bit farther away from present prices, that is, higher.

Another strategy for placing the stop-sell is to measure actual recent daily fluctuation. Calculate the actual daily price ranges for the last two to four weeks by consulting an on-line electronic data source, or from a detailed daily-basis chart service. Suppose that this discovery process reveals your stock to have an average daily range (high minus low) of $1.20. And suppose you find that on well over half of the days in the study window this issue moved by at least $0.50 above the prior day's close during the day. In this case, you might place a stop-sell about $0.30 to $0.40 above the last close, assuming that the latest close was roughly in the middle of its daily range. On average and assuming that the whole market does not collapse and that the company does not suddenly issue bad news, a few days' or a week's patience should get you out at a better price than would an unnecessarily rushed market order.

Summary of Contrasting Approaches and Results

The degree of aggressiveness in order placement compared with the actual fluctuation pattern is influenced by the direction of the stock and of the overall market. It bears repeating that if the reason for sale is bad fundamental or technical news for the company or if an exit is desired because the overall market is creating tension, an above-market sell stop is a long-odds bet against yourself.

Although having provided some degree of tutorial in stop-loss placement, this chapter actually takes the seldom-stated position that stop-loss orders should be used sparingly, if at all. Their placement should occur only after taking a close look at a stock and thus deciding-on merit and on the basis of the chart pattern-what price says to bail out and what price indicates that the market is saying something unknown is going wrong. If an investor or trader is in touch with the market on a daily basis and develops the mental discipline this book teaches, the psychological crutch of a stop will be unnecessary. He then does not need an order on the specialist's book. If he has noted the critical level in advance and is disciplined, he will prefer to sell at market when it happens. However, if an investor travels or is inaccessible or finds he always has great difficulty in pulling the selling trigger under stress, then a stop-loss order is better than costly inaction

The major message of this chapter is that well-placed above-market sell stops give a reasonable chance of better sale proceeds if there is more to be had; below-market stop-loss orders guarantee a worse price than is available right now. Do not use arbitrary percentage stops, and lean against using stop-losses as a mental crutch. Instead, it is better to face each selling decision head on, and then to do what is necessary in real time. This discipline will serve well in current dollars—as well as in greater wisdom about and feel for the market's inner workings in future situations.

CHAPTER 24

Use Special Rules for Selling Low-Priced Stocks

Keys for Successful Selling

◆ Consider Brokerage Firms' Policies

◆ Understand Margin-Loan Policies' Effects

◆ Be Aware of Maintenance Margins

◆ Watch for Non-Marginable Stocks

Three key dollar levels must be kept in mind when buying or selling low-priced stocks: $2.00, $3.00 and $5.00. Their effects are not parallel, depending on whether the low-priced stock is rising or falling through these price levels. Because the extent of their effects is more pronounced on the downside, it is important to pay close attention to selling tactics in this price-range situation. Usually anticipation will pay better than reaction.

Consider first the $2.00 price level, thought of as the badge of respectability by most brokerage houses. Investors wishing to buy a stock trading below $2.00 per share will usually be required by a full-service brokerage firm to sign what is called in the trade an unsolicited letter. This is a prewritten form letter from the client to the firm saying the stock was picked by the client, who realizes that trading in low-priced stocks is a risky business and who will not blame the firm if this stock loses money. Because of the nature of the letter, there is no requirement to sign it to sell a low-priced issue. Theoretically, the firm is supposed to have the letter signed and on file before purchase, unless the client is known and trusted. The terms of this letter requirement should serve as a mild deterrent to buying stocks under $2.00 a share.

In practice this has only a moderate effect in bull markets, when people are optimistic rather than fearful. By contrast, in bear markets the letter requirement has a chilling effect. With media headlines covering layoffs, recession, bankruptcies and similar dark omens, many investors hesitate when their broker tells them about the requirement. And that means that chances are low that the buy order will get placed, for psychological reasons.

The hesitant investor muses about the bear market, the fact that his brokerage firm seems not to want a commission, and that it appears legal defenses are being erected in advance as a condition of accepting this trade. So the effect of the unsolicited-letter rule can be a depressant on price in a bear-market climate as stocks slip below that $2.00 level. The converse, however, is not true: When a stock goes above $2.00 per share, that fact does not encourage additional buying; there is merely the removal of a constraint as brokers need not exercise the unsolicited-letter routine.

Many brokerage firms waive the rule if the stock in question is traded on a major stock exchange, so you should ask in advance. Ironically, an investor who buys shares in a profitable, dynamic company trading over-the-counter at $1.75 is required to sign an unsolicited letter. But if she buys the most shaky, debt-ridden, exchange-traded company whose sales are shrinking, whose book value is negative, and whose prospects of turning around are between slim and none, but selling at $0.30 per share higher, no letter is required. Go figure!

Another aspect of trading in lower-priced stocks is also worthy of note: the way in which brokers are compensated significantly affects their attention, which directly impacts sponsorship for a stock. Brokerage firms are becoming increasingly sensitive to legal risk, so they are taking more action to reduce exposure. One defensive brokerage weapon is the method by which firms pay their brokers. Some firms have become so risk averse and image conscious that they do not pay brokers any commission on buy orders for stocks under $2.00 per share. (An exception is made in the very rare instance when the research department is recommending the stock.)

Obviously, a broker would rather have clients investing in stocks that will generate buy-side commissions. Needless to say, if brokers are not paid for buy orders in unlisted stocks below $2.00 per share, those issues have little sponsorship in the market. If and when the price slips below that magic level, further erosion is predictable since a major source of demand—sponsorship—dries up. (See Figure 24-1, which features several charts from 1987, the most recent period of extremely widespread margin calls.) Below the $2.00 price level, it may take an unusually large amount of positive news to get the stock to move up. So keep that level in mind as a mental quitting point on stocks, especially when the overall market tone is negative and cautious. In fact, in a fear-driven market, you should plan to bail out earlier and thereby beat the crowd.

Figure 24.1: Stocks Falling through $5, $3 and $2 Levels

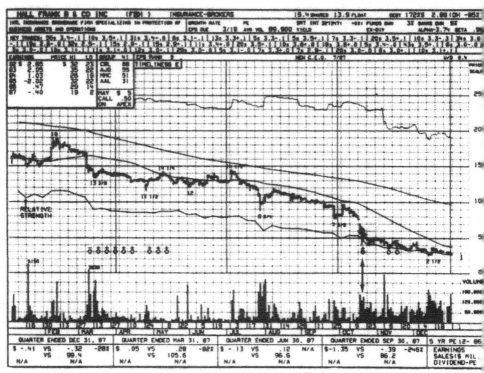

Courtesy of *Daily Graphs and Long Term Values;* P.O. Box 66919; Los Angeles, California 90066–0919.

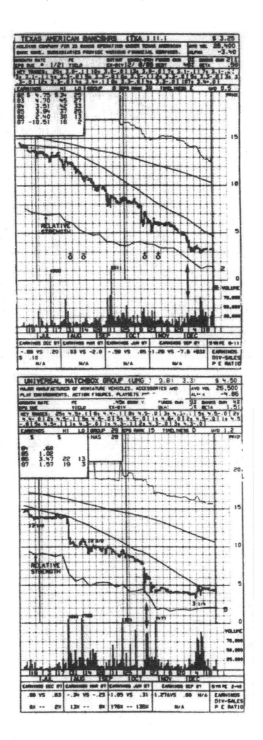

Margin-Loans Rules and Their Effects

The critical $3.00 and $5.00 levels have a somewhat different basis. These price levels have considerably more significance in terms of price effects because of the way brokerage rules work. The reason is that while the $2.00 level affects a stock's respectability, the $3.00 and $5.00 levels determine marginability. And marginability is very important to a stock, being absolute (rule driven) rather than psychological. The unsolicited-letter effect is mostly psychological, but the effect of margin requirements is very real and urgent. It definitely moves stock prices, mostly to the downside—an important point to factor into selling and holding decisions.

The power of a brokerage firm to make margin loans to purchasers of securities is governed under Regulation T of the Federal Reserve Board (and under Regulation U for commercial banks).

Basically, the Board sets as a policy the percentage of a purchase price that a brokerage firm (and, technically, a member bank) can loan to the customer. For historical reasons dating from abuses before the Great Depression, this power has sometimes been used to regulate speculation and to allocate credit within the economy. The Board can change the rules of the game at any time but in recent decades has almost never done so in general, instead focusing on specific highly volatile issues.

Consider Brokerage Firms' Policies

For many years, the going percentage has been 50 percent. An investor wishing to buy $10,000 worth of stock can do so with as little as $5,000 of his or her own equity. The brokerage firm loans its customer the remainder (and charges interest on the borrowed balance). This is a very convenient type of loan because it requires neither a credit check nor any monthly payments against principal. As long as the value of the collateral (i.e., the stock bought and held by the brokerage firm as security for the loan) is not badly impaired, the brokerage firm allows an investor to continue carrying a margin loan as long as the stock is held. When the stock is sold, the loan is automatically paid down or paid off out of the proceeds. (See Table 24-1.)

Table 24.1: Margin Loans and Maintenance Margins

	Price	Value	Less Debit	Equals	Equity
Situation #1 Just bought 1,000 at $10 borrowed $5,000	10.00	10,000	5,000	5,000	50%
Situation #2 Stock drops to $9	9.00	9,000	5,000	4,000	44%
Situation #3 Stock drops to $8.50	8.50	8,500	5,000	3,500	41%
Situation #4 Stock drops to $8.25	8.25	8,250	5,000	3,250	39%

Maintenance Margins

The level called maintenance margin is generally at 40 percent, which means the brokerage firm can let the investor's margin of equity shrink to the 40 percent level before it is forced to call for more cash (margin call).

Here is how the 40 percent maintenance margin rule works in practice. Suppose that someone buys 1,000 shares of XYZ common stock at $10 per share and puts up the minimum 50 percent required. (Here, commissions are ignored for the sake of simplicity; in actuality the commission is allowed as part of the gross amount, so the investor can borrow half of it, too – rather like financing the closing costs on a mortgage loan.) He borrows $5,000 from the brokerage firm and mails in the other $5,000. If the stock holds steady at $10 per share, obviously his equity stays at the 50 percent level (before the monthly subtraction of accrued interest charges).

But if the stock declines, the customer's percentage of equity in the position decreases. Assuming that interest charges (which increase the debit balance and thereby reduce equity), have not been taken yet (our unfortunate investor's equity will fall to the 40 percent level when his stock has declined beyond $8.34 per share.

To calculate, take the amount of the debit or loan balance, and divide by 60 percent (the complement of 40 percent) to get the minimum market value allowable. If the stock is worth $8,330 (1,000 shares times $8.33 each) and the loan is the original $5,000, the customer's remaining net equity is now just $3,330, or the new gross market value less the loan balance.

At this point, the broker must demand that by the next business day the client deposit more money to reduce the loan balance. If the investor fails to do so, the broker is required to sell sufficient stock out of the account to restore up to at least a 40 percent position.

For the sake of simplicity, the account discussed here consisted of just one stock. In actual practice, all of the stocks in the account are valued together, and the total loan balance against the stocks is calculated as a single figure. The effect of one stock dropping from $10 to below $8.34 is softened by the possibility that some other stocks in the account stayed steady or rose in value. Brokerage firms produce computerized analyses of all accounts every night; brokers get notified in the morning if any accounts need a call. The compliance department makes sure that the brokers enforce the rules by forcing their clients to meet margin calls promptly. The alternative, to stay within the rules and to protect the firm's capital, is to sell off some of the stocks. If a client does not choose which stocks to sell, the firm does it for him, and without delay. At discount brokerage firms, computers are king and the process is swift and merciless. Skip going on line one day and you could miss a margin call and find yourself sold out when you sign on during the next session!

Nonmarginable Stocks

One other critical aspect of margin rules directly affects the calculation of equity margin: the marginability of specific stocks. The Securities and Exchange Commission or the listing exchange sometimes designates certain securities as not marginable, usually because their price behavior has become highly volatile. With sharp fluctuations in prices, values in margin accounts would gyrate daily, causing margin calls and adding to market instability. To reduce this effect, some highly volatile stocks are declared nonmarginable. This act in itself tends to dampen their volatility (after a quick initial selloff) because some speculators' purchasing power is halved. Shares in Taser had this designation in 2004, for example.

Regardless of its volatility, any stock can become nonmarginable for another reason that serves (for our purposes) as an important warning: price alone can get the stock into marginability trouble. In the past, the standard rule was $5.00 per share. In recent years, during the trend toward less government regulation, determining the key price level has been left to the discretion of brokerage firms. Some have retained the traditional $5.00 rule, while others have adopted $3.00. Regardless of your firm's rule, both levels carry clear implications for the price behavior of stocks.

The $5.00 and $3.00 levels can signal significant price danger for stocks in a declining market. When a stock falls through either of those levels, its decline is likely to accelerate because of margin rules. First, the stock immediately becomes 100 percent worthless for calculating margins. That, in turn, causes the brokerage firm to send out margin calls to clients who own the stock in margin accounts and whose calculated equity has been impaired by the sudden exclusion of the stock from the margin formula.

To illustrate, suppose an investor's account consists of 2,000 shares of a stock bought at $5 per share; the minimum 50 percent or $5,000 was put up and the other $5,000 borrowed from the firm. (Any broker would be irresponsible to allow this, knowing that an urgent and major problem lurks just pennies away on the downside.) The morning after this stock declines to close at $4.99 or lower, a notice appears on the broker's desk or computer screen, highlighting the client's account. This one-stock portfolio has dropped below the marginable level.

Per the house rules, our investor now has a loan of $5,000 outstanding with zero allowable collateral behind it. He has not been wiped out because at $4.99 stock is worth $9,990; equity is $4,990 after subtracting the loan. But the rules render that stock suddenly worthless for margin calculation. He is not broke, but his credit line has been pulled.

Our unhappy investor has four choices; unfortunately, none is to call for a time-out. First, he can send or wire the broker $5,000 to pay off the loan immediately. Second, he can send in stock certificates of other companies that are marginable. But those certificates must equal $8,333 in market value of marginable stock. This strategy leaves $8,333 in countable assets to secure the $5,000 loan and a countable equity of $3,333 after the loan is subtracted; it thus restores the minimum 40 percent maintenance margin level discussed eaarlier.

A third choice is to sell without delay at least $5,000 worth of now-nonmarginable stock, or a little more than half the total position, to satisfy the compliance department and the federal regulators. A fourth option is to sell from the account at least $10,000 worth of other stocks that are still marginable, if any such are available.

Whenever maintenance calls occur, at least some traders sell part or all of the offending stock, which creates a sudden avalanche of shares coming into the market for sale at quickly declining prices. Because knowledgeable market players see the situation plainly, very few at all bid to buy the stock. If it trades over-the-counter, market-making firms lighten inventory to a minimum to control their loss exposure and bid only cautiously and in small size. In a listed stock, the floor specialist is less willing to take stock except at a price concession.

The mechanics of the market dictate that in practice this process unfolds a fraction above the key $5.00 level. Knowing how margin rules work, few informed investors or stockbrokers are willing to buy or hold a stock that has fallen from $6.00 or above toward just above $5.00; this itself adds to the weakening market.

There are three refinements in this example. First, again, most investors own more than one stock in their margin accounts. So the decline of one stock below $5.00 does not wipe out their marginable assets. Second, not all margin accounts are down to minimum equity, so a drop in one stock -- even from $5.00 to a countable zero— may not cause an immediate problem. Third, when one stock causes a problem in a margin account, no rule says this particular stock must be the one singled out for sale to satisfy the margin call, although its sale generates the most dollars to answer the call.

In practice, of course, the offending stock often is thrown overboard for psychological or financial reasons. First, when the broker says there is a margin call on XYZ stock, the investor examines his options and discovers that selling any other stock generates half its dollar value toward equity and the rest toward the loan because of the 50-percent rule and the fact that once the stock is sold, it is no longer an asset in the account against which to borrow.

But selling the offending stock, which suddenly has zero loan value, nets full, dollar-for-dollar relief. Since this is the troubled stock, the broker is quick to point out that this stock is likely to feel pressure as other people sell it to meet their margin calls. The investor is wise to sell as soon as possible to get the best price. Against these forces, an investor must be extremely stubborn or highly convinced that the intrinsic value of XYZ makes it worth holding through the storm. While there is no rule that XYZ shares must be sold, clearly they are the top candidate for dumping.

All facets of the $5.00 level apply equally at the $3.00 level for the market and for some brokerage firms. Some investors do not face a margin call generated by the $3.00 scenario until their stock slides below $3.00. But numerous other brokerage firms do still adhere to the $5.00 rule, so their clients sell stock at that level, driving the price down. These price declines at both margin-call levels have totally equal wealth-reducing effect even on investors who have no margin accounts. Foregoing a margin account certainly protects you personally from margin calls, but it does not protect against the downdraft in share prices when other investors get their calls.

In a general bear market—as opposed to a situation where just one stock is distressed due to specific news—the effect is intensified. Players are apprehensive, so fewer come up with added cash to meet their margin calls. The instinctive reaction is to sell out now. In addition, weakness in other totally unrelated stocks can cause selling in issues you own, as other investors meet their margin calls.

The bottom-line implication is that investors must draw a red zone at all times around stocks as they slip toward the $5.00 or $3.00 levels. Use perhaps a half-dollar safety zone in a normal market and a wider buffer in a bear market, particularly if it has started to become violent. Be realistic and expect the worst; anticipate trouble before it starts. Getting out at $5.50 can prevent a quick slide to $4.50 or $4.00. Regardless of the fundamental merit of a low-priced stock, it is in imminent price danger at the $5.00 and $3.00 levels because of marginability problems.

There is usually no automatic converse side to this $3.00 and $5.00 phenomenon, no automatic burst of buying. The only benefit of having a stock trade a safe distance above $3.00 or $5.00 is that it is safely marginable. Thus, at a safe distance above those levels, some buyers might buy extra shares using credit. There is no automatic surge in price when the stock edges through $5.00 on the upside. Aggressive and

Figure 24.2: Stocks Attracting Speculators When above $5

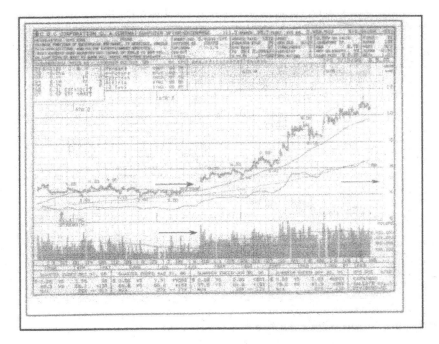

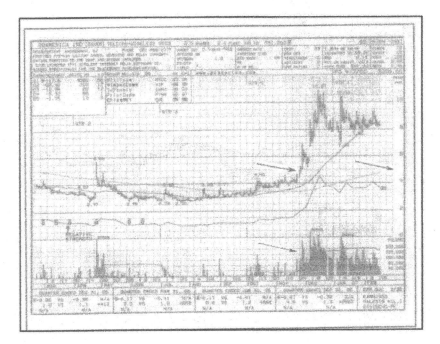

informed players know that using margin then is fraught with peril because the stock easily could slip back to $4.99.

Occasionally, however, as illustrated in the two charts comprising Figure 24-2, there may be some aggressive and probably margin-using speculators interested in a stock but unwilling to enter until it clearly passes the $5 hurdle to the upside. Look closely at the immediate and sustained higher levels of volume here as soon as these particular stocks cleared $5.00. This pattern involves a sustained rise in daily trading volume—not a crescendo but simply a whole new higher level. In such a case, if you own the stock it will probably be smart to hold off on selling until the newly aggressive speculators have finished building their positions, which will be evident once trading volume trails off. After it has escaped the tricky $5.00 zone and has picked up big volume from buyers, let the stock go where its new boosters will push it, rather than guess on an arbitrary exit level.

CHAPTER 25
Sell Smart on Good News

Keys for Successful Selling

◆ Know the Difference between Great News and Huge News

◆ Interpret News as a Temporary Crowd Creator

◆ Act Appropriately on News

Preceding chapters have dealt with technical phenomena like volume and price as clues to finding market tops. Fundamental events such as publication of positive news also accelerate intermediate or final market tops. Thus, ironic or counterintuitive as it may seem, good news can often provide a very opportune time to sell. Contrarians and students of crowd behavior find this not at all surprising, of course.

For purposes of this discussion, there are three kinds of positive news. One is such unsurprising positive news as earnings coming in on-target with estimates or the declaration of unchanged or moderately higher dividends on schedule. These events typically have no effect on stock price, although to the extent they are expected their absence would cause a drop. The past two decades have seen highly increased institutional sensitivity to the slightest shortfalls against consensus estimates, resulting in wild downside price volatility. Unsurprising events typically do not coincide with an interim price peak unless such a high proves to be reversed by a general market retreat. The two other types of positive news—or true impact news—are important to price behavior in the short term. These are events big or surprising enough to have an immediate effect on stock price. But within the impact category, the two types of news must be distinguished accurately in real time by alert market participants in order to determine proper action if any.

Great News versus Huge News

The factor that distinguishes news character is its true, long-term importance if any. Thus, what we are calling impact news includes great news and, by contrast, huge news. Great news refers to positive developments that have no major fundamental long-term significance to a company. Examples are a quarterly earnings report that comes in nicely above expectations, or the receipt of a major contract. (Occasionally a contract award might have long-term implications by signaling superior technology or a series of follow-on contracts.) On occasion directors' declaration of an unexpectedly large dividend is great news that has a short-term positive effect on a stock's price. (Remember Microsoft's famous $3 dividend in the fall of 2004? Check a long-term price chart of MSFT to see what followed.)

Any of these events is welcomed by investors and usually causes a near-term rise in stock price due to a predictable but very temporary shift in supply and demand for the shares. However, in judging positive events' significance, be coldly objective to compensate for the natural tendency toward stockholders' positive bias, and to compensate for the media buzz effect of today's big stories. Existing holders generally are in a positive mental state about owning the shares when recent price action has been rewarding. In the spirit of Chapter 8, one must be very careful not to let confusion between the stock and the company intrude. Likewise, one must not double count expected positive news.

To make an accurate and meaningful judgment about a current piece of positive news, take an imaginary look back from the future. Move forward ten years in time, and then look back at company and industry history over that period. Your key filter is the true importance—in a long-term context—of the news that looks so positive today. Is it fairly certain that today's item will be judged as one of the two or three most significant events in a decade for the company, or is it among the top dozen events in its industry? By definition, the answer in virtually every case is negative. That perspective should put above-consensus quarterly EPS reports—the day's buzz darlings of the talking heads on financial TV—into their proper light!

Thus, in very many cases today's news is great but not huge. In contrast, then, what is a huge news event? These are developments or announcements with true long-term fundamental and strategic importance to the company: usually management, technology or strategy issues rather than current financial results or growth rates, and certainly not analyst recommendations.

Changes in non-financial areas have much greater long-term significance and generally fall into the categories of blockbuster events or major unexpected changes. Examples of huge news in management are items about key individuals and shifts in types of corporate governance or management: Lee Iacocca's appointment in 1979 as head of Chrysler Corporation was a crucial turning point in the survival and interim revitalization of the number three U.S. automaker, for example. Likewise, replacement of Joseph Nacchio by Richard Notebart early in the new century was a crucial event at Qwest. A key transition in management is often necessary as a company built on entrepreneurial spirit reaches maturity. An excellent example occurred in 1983 when Apple Computer founder Steve Jobs, a technology genius, was replaced as CEO by a veteran marketing executive, John Scully, from PepsiCo.

Sometimes the retirement or death of a company officer and major stockholder proves to be huge news: Management power changes and a block of stock transfers control. Sometimes there will follow a merger or a significant change in corporate direction. Dr. Armand Hammer's death began a new era at Occidental Petroleum. The departure of a dominant founder can open up possibilities for a takeover. A possible example at this writing in mid-2007 is the passing of the restaurant chain chief at Bob Evans Farms. Critical technological advances or legal victories can also constitute huge news: One example was the issuance of an early patent on a test for AIDS to Cambridge BioSciences. As this chapter was written, Verizon and Vonage were locked in a legal battle over a key technology patent.

Finally, strategic changes in a company's direction can be huge news: abandoning a money-losing or highly competitive business, halting acquisitions in a debt-laden firm, selling off assets, working existing businesses harder and paying down debt, for example. In January 1996, Xerox Corporation announced it would withdraw from the financial services arena; investors mistakenly reacted negatively to a related write-off because the decision implied higher returns on equity and faster growth, as indicated by a 16 percent rise in dividend rate announced at the same time. The decision to cut and run was an important winner, a buy signal! Home Depot's sale of its supply business in 2007, and a related boost in its share repurchases, was a similar event. Such decisions have true longer-term strategic significance.

Strategic acquisitions or alliances that create vertical integration, a broader product mix, or strong distribution overnight are other examples. Georgia-based Colorocs— which had developed an inexpensive, high-quality color photocopier—made what appeared to be a critical positive move by acquiring control of Savin Corporation instead of risking time and capital in the creation of its own distribution infrastructure. That decision removed a major risk factor for investors and, therefore, was huge news at the time. (Unfortunately, later problems with supply from overseas undermined success.) Similarly, Research Frontiers, developer of continuously variable light-sensitive glass for use in autos and office buildings, sharply improved its prospects by licensing giant General Electric to sell its products rather than going it alone. Small drug and biotech firms commonly partner with established big-pharmaceuticals companies to get immediate distribution. Nastech is an example.

Acting on News

The critical distinction between great and huge is important because it indicates the proper tactical action for investors to take in response: whether and when to sell on strength. Great news is usually good for from one to three days of rising stock quotes, assuming a reasonably hospitable market climate at the time. Because great good news is not long-term in significance, a good short-term rally triggered by such news often provides an attractive near-term opportunity to cash in on strength by selling. This is the old buy on rumor, sell on news pattern. A stock can react with a crescendo or spike as described in Chapter 21. Urgency about selling on great news is greatest if a significant trading-volume buildup takes place following the news. Big volume means a big crowd formed and will soon be finished. Remember that a rising pace of volume is required to sustain further price increases. Given that surprising great news has already become known, how much more can be expected realistically? Where will even higher trading volume and more excitement come from? You can sell into this strength promptly and very often buy back in lower within a week or two. Don't resent the extra taxes you will owe; rejoice in the added gain you pocketed and in your rising skill at selling easily and well.

The mechanics of news dissemination and the timing of broker and investor reactions help create a typical one- to three-day pattern of rallying prices following great news. The day news is announced, assuming it comes during a market session and is carried promptly on news wires, professional traders and boardroom ticker watchers act virtually immediately. So do a few other investors whose alert brokers call to relay the developments. If the company is well known or the news has flashy camera appeal, it may get same-day financial-TV coverage.

That same news is printed the next day in daily general newspapers and in the national financial press. Now more people know, and some react. By the third day, those who got the news late or who typically are slow to act finally jump onto the bandwagon. Beyond that, there is little left in the short term. If other investors cannot justify being a buyer after seeing such a run-up, this is a perfect signal for you to sell.

The occurrence of huge news poses a more perplexing tactical challenge for the stockholder because there are likely to be two positive reactions in the stock price. In addition to judging the possible strength of the two price moves, the savvy investor confronts a psychological test: he is so pleased by the enormity of the positive development that there is a danger of losing perspective and cool judgment.

The first price reaction is a short-term burst, similar to that from great news. But there is also likely to be a second, less dramatic effect. Because of the true import of huge news, the company, in effect, rises to a new and higher level of esteem among investors—particularly among those professional money managers who look at the big picture rather than at short-term earnings momentum only. Even if the stock continues to exhibit gradual further price strength after its initial upside burst from the huge news, the tactical problem is to make a judgment about when the second effect has run its course. Clearly, this is an art rather than an exact science. Watching for when day trading volume returns to its normal pre-news range can be one help.

In general, remember that the occurrence of huge news should cause an investor to ease back on the selling trigger. And once the stock takes a rest and declines, expect it to decline less deeply than it would have on merely great news. Not only will there have been, in effect, a one-time P/E markup for the new information, but there will also be some new institutional buyers who did not jump in right away, waiting for a correction before accumulating their positions. These investors will provide the buying support for future basing and rallies in the stock. But if the stock develops a classic volume mountain and an extended string of consecutive daily rises after great or huge news, it is advisable to sell as trading volume crescendos cannot last (review Chapter 21).

No matter how fundamentally important or long-term-significant the news is, the stock cannot be expected to rise uninterrupted for an indefinite period. The formation of a flagpole advance on a volume mountain is a signal that the strength is unsustainable for at least the short term and that the stock should be sold on this rise. It can always be bought back, probably lower, later on. But because the news is huge (truly significant) you should not typically expect the entire recent price gain to be retraced, as is much more often seen in the aftermath of non-huge good news. The experience of selling and then buying back in successfully will add to your confidence about implementing this maneuver again in the future. Each time you sell well, it helps you have the courage to overcome old subconscious biases and to sell more easily thereafter.

In summary, great good news often provides a near-term selling opportunity for disciplined contrarians, who take cash from a crowd of naive players buying on good news. Huge news allows the fortunate or foresighted holder to raise her target for long-term value. But if huge news triggers a tremendous mountain of volume and an extreme short-term price advance, this too should be viewed as a gift worth accepting. Price runs do not last very long, and you can always buy back later on after the excitement and temporary price inflation have cooled off. You will buy cheaper than those who could not resist the urge to buy immediately as part of the predictable but temporary crowd. And you will have pocketed the price difference as a bonus.

CHAPTER 26

Understand How Bad the Bad News Is

Keys for Successful Selling

◆ Differentiate between Two Types of Bad News
◆ React Intelligently to Bad News

Bad news travels fast in the Internet and blog age. This truth has important price and therefore personal-wealth implications when a company's news is unexpected or highly disturbing. Too often, investors give in to emotional market swings by selling out when all seems lost, only to find later that they were part of a crowd whose selling created a panic bottom. And, especially in recent years, institutions have become extremely short-term oriented; their knee-jerk dumping on the slightest bad news drops prices sharply, adding intensity to the sense of fright that individuals must assess and learn to deal with. The impatience and often huge holdings of institutions—and especially hedge funds—have raised the severity of price reactions in recent years. This implies high importance for investors in injured-stock situations to react realistically and sometimes promptly

Before describing bad-news selling tactics, it is necessary to identify and distinguish the bad news characteristics covered in this chapter. As used here, bad news items:

◆ Relate only to company-specific news, not to market trends as measured by averages;

◆ concern sharp price declines driven by negative news, not routine price declines that are merely technical corrections;

◆ exclude acquisition situations, in which the ongoing sequence of news is highly unpredictable and where events and emotional responses are dramatic;

◆ exclude situations driven by continuous (non-discrete) outside influences, including commodity-price declines (for mining and energy companies), which have a life of their own and, therefore, are not discrete, one-day news items; and

◆ apply in the context of a sideways or higher market environment in which price reactions to bad news are worse in total but are not initially as severe as during bear markets.

Differentiating between Two Types of Bad News

In the prior chapter, two distinct types of good news were discussed, Likewise here, this chapter explores material, unexpected, and discrete bad news for a company, and contrasts it with nondiscrete)recurring) bad news. Material and unexpected are important qualifiers because other negative information does not tend to move stock prices. For example, lower quarterly EPS in line with expectations will not drive a price disaster. For purposes of this discussion, news discreteness is important conceptually because it affects the validity of certain ideas. (Discrete news developments are one-time items that do not breed suspicions of further negatives to come.) Discrete bad news usually causes two to three days of sharp declines. After some digestion the stock is able to crawl back somewhat because there is no second shoe dropping (see Figure 26-1.) Sometimes a seemingly discrete negative item is followed quickly by another unrelated and unpredictable piece of bad news. In this sort of situation, the count of reaction days begins running again. Quite often, because suspicions now have been kindled, this newly emerging apparent pattern of clustered bad news means that the stock will react as it would to a non-discrete piece of bad news. Some examples of material, unexpected, discrete bad news (or MUD for short) are as follows:

◆ For insurers, it is a storm like Hurricane Katrina in 2005 that raises loss expense beyond normal expectations.

◆ For a high-technology company, it might be the resignation or death of a key scientist or inventor.

◆ For any small company, it certainly is the death of a founder or other key person whose identity is central to the investment community's concept of the company.

◆ For a fast-growth company, it is the announcement of a competitor's major new product or technology that reduces the lead time or exclusivity enjoyed by the first company.

◆ It can be a one-quarter earnings surprise caused by nonrecurring factors such as a supplier's strike or storm damage, or by write-offs that do not form part of an established company or industry pattern.

Figure 26.1: Stocks Crawling Back after Discrete Bad News

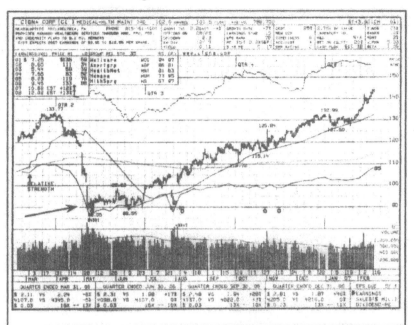

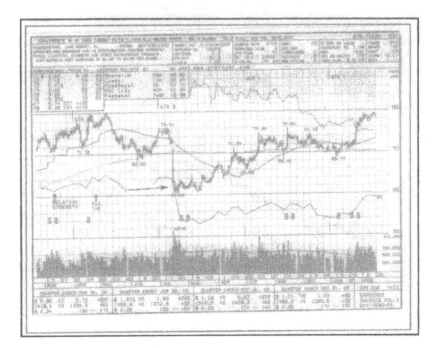

◆ A dividend reduction would be (or, in rare cases, an omission), because it usually follows other bad news.

◆ It might be damage to plant or other assets clearly caused by an outside force such as a storm or a nearby building's explosion—with fault is unlikely attributed to the company.

In contrast, these are nondiscrete negative events:

◆ For an insurance company, it might be a new law or court ruling that creates broader concepts of liability with true costs that cannot yet be calculated.

◆ It certainly would be issuance of a qualified opinion by independent auditors.

◆ It could be a major workplace or ecological accident in which the company will probably be found at fault, at least in part, and where the media hint at carelessness.

◆ For any company, it is the unexplained resignation of a very senior executive or financial officer with any hint of mystery or scandal.

◆ For a high-tech company, it is failure to secure a patent on a device or technology that had been represented to Wall Street as crucial to success.

◆ For a high-tech or fast-growth company, it could be the delayed or canceled introduction of a previously announced or expected new product. Microsoft and Apple have each occasionally fit this pattern.

◆ it might be the announcement (or the expectation) of a decline in earnings for reasons that reflect management weaknesses (poor control) or unrecognized competitive pressures in the business (lack of foresight).

◆ It is a government probe of the company for possible antitrust violations, bid rigging, contract overcharging, or false documentation (the 2006-2007 option-backdating scandal was an excellent example).

◆ It could be a SEC investigation into possible securities violations on the part of the company or one or more of its officers.

◆ It could be disclosure that one or more past financial statements were inaccurate and that time will be required for an investigation before issuing revised reports.

◆ It could be announcement that a company's board is considering or will consider reducing or omitting the dividend or declaring bankruptcy.

◆ It is a news announcement that, while appearing to be discrete, represents a contradiction of previous management representations to analysts or the press.

The key difference between these groups of examples is the apparent degree of closure versus uncertainty involving the bad news. There is an old trader's cliché that the market can handle good news and can even handle bad news, but uncertainty drives it crazy. Highly institutionally owned stocks are especially vulnerable to deep and ongoing price wounds from nondiscrete problems because portfolio managers are driven by short-term performance, do not want to list out-of-favor or tainted names on their quarterly statements, and fear firing or 20/20 hindsight misfeasance suits if they retain stocks with clearly questionable fundamentals. Widely held stocks present individual investors with a special challenge when a pattern of problems arises: while one might actually be correct in concluding that the disclosed problems will not be fatal to the company, its reputation with analysts and institutions will usually require a lengthy healing process, implying deep and long stock-price injury. Here, patience can be a negative virtue.

Reacting Intelligently to Bad News

The difference between finite, known bad news and open-ended, bad-portent news is reflected in the way investors react to it. It is all a matter of collective investor psychology. The market's reaction to open-ended news with bad implications is painfully drawn out. This is because uneasiness not only creates selling pressure at first, but it also leaves a psychological dark cloud lingering for a potentially indefinable but long time afterward. When bad news is discrete and appears to imply no further shocks, the price reaction is usually sharp but relatively brief.

MUD typically imposes a two- or three-day price drop on a stock, which is often quite sharp in percentage terms. In effect, it is a private crash. There are psycho-mechanical reasons for this pattern of typical duration, and they concern news dissemination and investors' rate of absorption and reaction to it. The sharpness of the price reaction has been compounded in recent years by the twin demons of short investment horizons and a rising concentration of institutional holdings. In very strong bull market periods, bad news sometimes triggers merciless instant selling: since investor expectations are so high and many other attractive opportunities are seen everywhere, few have patience for holding tainted issues in hope of recovery.

When news is announced, it typically has a two-day life in the media unless it is so major that prolonged follow-up coverage ensues. Major examples of the latter were Three Mile Island, the Bhopal chemical disaster, the Exxon Valdez accident, various spectacular plane crashes and major drug withdrawals on FDA orders. Early 2007 seemed to be unfolding a dangerous situation as two firms burdened with defaulting subprime mortgages declared bankruptcy. On the day of the announcement, unless the company can arrange to have the bad news released after the market closes, the item runs repeatedly on the wire services and perhaps on stock market shows (e.g., CNBC or Bloomberg TV) televised during the session.

Some investors and traders react immediately. The next day the story runs again, perhaps in greater length and detail, in national and local daily newspapers. If it makes good television, like a spectacular physical disaster or a wealthy corporate executive led away in handcuffs, it plays overnight and next morning. Then even more people react. Thus, with any meaningful negative news, generally expect a two-day price reaction at a minimum.

If the bad news occurs on a Thursday or Friday, a three-day reaction is likely because weekend researchers/investors react on reading the stock quotations in the Saturday and Sunday papers and watching the Sunday TV-magazine shows. They sell on Monday, often creating a minor third wave of price pressure. The weekend itself allows longer time for a brooding sense of panic to develop, and, in some cases, ready replacement-buy candidates are identified, adding to Monday selling orders in the tainted stock.

In cases when major bad news occurs on Friday, the three-day rule emerges if the market happens to take a serious dive (related to the company's news or otherwise) on Monday. This is followed by a Tuesday morning rout that lets further air out of the stock that has suffered bad publicity.

An important issue in the two- or three-day reaction to MUD is the extent of the price damage, specifically during the period of sharp price decline before stabilization takes place. There usually follows a period of time (perhaps two days to a week or longer) during which the stock steadies and sometimes tries to rally a bit as shorts cover and a few brave bargain hunters nibble.

Later there is most often a renewed price decline, but it is usually less dramatic than the first. (see Figure 26-2.). The second decline occurs, typically, because the stock has run out of

gas from bargain hunters attracted by the first crack; because the technical chart pattern looks weak (probably a rally on low volume or a rise into supply); because holders who refused to sell during the initial bashing waited out the storm at first but now try to sell slightly higher later on; or because of any coincidental general market weakness during which an already wounded stock cannot hold on.

With all these caveats, selling seems obvious although not easy; a pre-planned selling scenario will provide the savvy investor with necessary guidance on specific selling tactics in this environment. For an effective sale,

1. Distinguish carefully between discrete bad news and nondiscrete bad news, which have very different longer-term implications for your hold/sell decision.

2. Envision realistically in advance the decline and stabilization; this will help you keep from reacting emotionally as events play out. It is useful to know that, while the price almost certainly will not recover to its pre-news level soon, it will stop declining shortly and then provide at least two days' stability and mild bounce during which a better sale can be executed. If, due to inattention, lack of broker service, indecision, or denial, the stock has not been sold on the first day of bad news, one must understand that by the third day's arrival it is already too late; while it will be painful, at that stage briefly holding on will provide a modestly better sale opportunity sometime during the several sessions following.

Figure 26.2: Example of Extended Price Damage on Non-Discrete Bad News

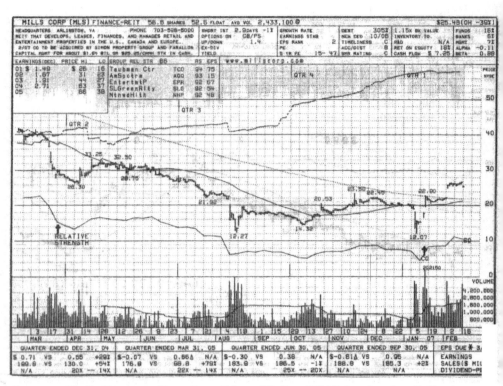

Courtesy of Daily Graphs and Long Term Values; P.O. Box 66919; Los Angeles, California 90066-0919.

What is the usual decline sequence pattern on MUD bad news? The first day's price decline is usually the worst unless the news is released late during the trading session. In that case, the second day is the worst because it absorbs the greatest barrage of selling volume. Otherwise, the second day shows a decline of from one-half to two-thirds the amount on the first (full) day, and volume starts to contract.

If there is a third day, a reversal can occur in which morning selling drives the price lower, followed around mid-session by an abatement of selling pressure and some price snap-back.

Depth of the most immediate decline can vary significantly, for any actual news severity, depending on the interaction of such factors as:

◆ Large institutional holdings (implying volume sales);

◆ bad news occurring shortly before the end of a calendar quarter (institutional window dressers do not want to show a bad holding in quarterly portfolio lists);

◆ a lengthy past period of rising EPS (implying that the shock of bad news will be harsh, as with McDonald's in early 2002, Merck in 2004 or Harley-Davidson in early 2007);

◆ stocks that traditionally trade at a high P/E (implying widespread bullish consensus of expectations and deep disappointment);

◆ stocks having recently performed very strongly rather than sideways or lower, driving a sudden scramble to lock down profits (technology/telecomm issues in late 2000);

◆ coincidence of a sharply weaker market at the same time company-specific news hits the stock itself (possible bargain hunters will stand aside);

◆ stock price fall creating a technically significant chart flaw such as a breakdown from a channel bottom or the downward resolution of a triangle (bringing in technician dumping piled on top of fundamentally disappointed sellers);

◆ bad news or any hint of possible unwinding of fortunes for companies controlled by charismatic wealthy persons (Donald Trump was a victim in the early 1990s as the tabloids dragged out his real-estate woes; ditto the Martha Stewart saga.); and

◆ bad news smacking of a currently sensitive subject such as insider trading, ecological problems, health scares, options backdating or other hot topics.

No matter what its exact timing, a price crack must be expected on major bad news, followed by calmer trading and probably a slight recovery from panic lows. A different response is called for if the bad news is open ended or if it is part of a series of bad company announcements or falls into a pattern of deterioration within an industry. Without hesitation, sell when the news indicates general corporate decay, smacks of dishonesty or falls into a pattern in a weakening industry (e.g., second and third homebuilders to report flattening backlogs in late 2005).

When seemingly discrete bad news is followed shortly by a second news item, the reaction clock starts running again for two or three days; now the situation must be considered as an erosion problem in which other investors may come to see the second announcement as no longer discrete. It begins to look like a process of going from bad to worse. A good example occurred during the early stages of the savings and loan crisis when Phoenix-based Pinnacle West Capital, the parent company of Mera Bank and Arizona Public Service, announced a dividend omission late one afternoon. The stock moved fractionally lower to the close and broke sharply the next day. The second full day of post-news trading brought a further drop on lower volume.

Normally, stabilization and a bit of a snap-back rally could have been expected. But then a major newswire interviewed a company spokesperson, who mentioned the possibility of a Chapter 11 bankruptcy filing to rid Pinnacle West of its troubled thrift unit. This second piece of bad news lengthened the period of sharp price drop for another two days. It was arrested only when an 80-point morning smash in the Dow Jones Industrials reversed itself to just a 4-point drop by the close. For any investors not already familiar with the Pinnacle West story, the second item created a new cloud of ongoing uncertainty and, in effect, a potentially life-threatening situation: The stock was no longer in the discrete bad news category, and the news continued to worsen for a long time before being turned around. A more recent example of burgeoning problems was the investigation, indictment, conviction, resignation and prison sentence in the Martha Stewart insider-trading case.

Often, as veteran observers say, the first bad news turns out not to be the last. The bottom line for investors deciding on tactics in that a two- or three-day period of near free fall is to make a realistic judgment as to whether the first bad news might be a precursor of more to come. If that is the case, while the company may well survive, its stock is destined not to prosper for an extended period as disconcerting events play out. Sometimes a useful hint as to how things may develop is gained by examining past news releases (or lack thereof) from the company. Firms that are typically closed-mouthed have a greater tendency to create huge surprises. Such a pattern is often seen in smaller companies where a founding or other controlling family owns a major block of shares and tends to treat the outside shareholders poorly by providing only minimum public information. A general pattern amounting to no comment tends to heighten suspicion when something bad happens.

CHAPTER 27
Sell on News Delays

Keys for Successful Selling

◆ Know How to Act on Pre-Scheduled Announcements
◆ Anticipate Dividend Declarations
◆ Prepare for Earnings Reports
◆ Act On Implications of Other Delays

In the investment world, no news is usually not good news. Expected but delayed news often falls into this category. There are three categories of expected news from a company: pre-scheduled announcements, dividend declarations and earnings reports. In addition, occasional unusual events will require management statements; these should be prompt and forthright.

Pre-Scheduled Announcements

The smallest and most unusual category is pre-scheduled announcements. Managements of many companies do not box themselves in by committing to an announcement on a pre-designated timetable because too much can go wrong that might require delay. Many managements will say only that they are preparing a statement and will release it as soon as possible under the circumstances.

An expected or anticipated announcement (other than periodic dividend and earnings news) usually occurs when the company is under some pressure. Something has gone awry and a response is needed. Occasionally, under such pressure, the company attempts to control the public relations damage and to ward off further telephone barrages by saying it expects to make a statement on the matter by a certain date or time. Examples included several retail chains suffering physical damage across multiple states during 2005 in the wake of Hurricane Katrina.

When the time period of news uncertainty is open ended, investors collectively are prone to suspect the worst and to invent or listen to rumors. While a delay for clarification is in effect, the stock price is likely to erode anyway. Thus, a delay in releasing follow-up news quite often means a lose/lose situation for stockholders: Continued holding simply puts money at unnecessary risk. For those who have developed the ability to sell as easily as they buy, stepping aside to evaluate from a cool distance, and perhaps to buy back lower later, is the best course.

By making a commitment to releasing news by a specified time, a company puts its reputation on the block; if that deadline passes with no further announcement, presume that the situation is more difficult or that the news and stock-price response will be more drastic or far-reaching than shareholders would wish. One situation where companies typically cannot pinpoint a future release date is when re-auditing the books is involved: Management cannot know in advance how much will be dug up or how long it will take auditors to become satisfied that they have found it all. And such investigations cot big money, often into seven digits.

While not all investors wish to, or should, take a short-term approach to the market, it is nearly always true that the first loss is the best loss. Therefore, when something goes wrong, it is most prudent to exit and re-examine the situation from a distance. By holding on in hope that the bad news will not be too bad after all, you are playing a game for minimized loss, exposing yourself to the heavier emotional baggage, greater financial loss, and more painful decision that will follow if the stock later in fact takes a big dive and increasing the odds that you eventually will capitulate and sell lower anyway as a stock's price melts in the intense heat.

Suppose a corporate treasurer suddenly resigns and the audit committee of the board suspects foul play. The company makes an announcement of the resignation. Under generally accepted standards of full and prompt disclosure, the fact that an internal investigation exists is considered material, so the company most likely feels obliged to release this information at the same time. If management announces that it expects the investigation to last for a certain number of days/week and will issue a statement at that time, expect it to make good on that representation unless the problem turns out to be particularly thorny. A delay past the appointed time without a timely and specific announcement is a danger signal.

What requires extra time? Management may have to call in independent auditors or a financial-forensics agency to uncover the full extent of a problem. Or there may be legal subtleties that require careful review because of potential litigation. Or the situation may be so significant that management wants to complete a Form 8-K filing with the SEC to cover the news before making a statement. That filing requires legal and auditor review.

Whatever the cause of delay, the outcome is much more likely to be surprisingly bad rather than happily benign or good news. Because money has a time value and because avoiding losses is very important, lean to the cautious side and anticipate bad news by selling out on the delay itself instead of waiting for some other shoe to drop. People are by nature risk- (and uncertainty-) averse. So being patient and hopeful represents paddling upstream against a strong psychological current.

Dividend Declarations

A second major category of news delays involves dividends. Not all delays are dangerous, so it helps to do some homework and have reference sources available to help distinguish between alarming and forgivable delays in time to take possible action.

Corporate boards of directors usually meet on a predictable schedule, especially for dividend declarations.(Boards usually meet more than four times a year, but shareholders seldom see any evidence of most non-dividend meetings.) As a courtesy to board members, a company usually schedules meetings on a standing basis so members can set their calendars and anticipate travel well in advance. Examples might be third Tuesdays or fourth Mondays of the month. Be aware of two wild-card factors, however: the meeting after yearend is often held later into the quarterly calendar than others, and, summer meetings are less regular because of vacations. Use the spring and fall meeting dates for best quick guidance as to likely schedule patterns.

You can readily find out when the board meets. When curious or concerned—and generally there is little cause to be worried if the latest earnings reports have been favorable and there is no pattern of trouble elsewhere in the industry—you can call the company. Its 800 number, usually going direct to the investor-relations office, is shown at the end of each press release that you will find on online chart services such as BigCharts.com or the company's own website. There are also several print and online sources of accessible history. One is Standard & Poor's individual stock reports. For dividend-paying stocks, a table shows the meeting, stock-of-record, and payable dates of the last four quarterly dividends. Also, at the company, try the corporate secretary's office rather than the PR or stockholder relations department. It is an official duty of the corporate secretary's office to schedule board meetings and notify members, so that office has the timing information readily at hand. Any refusal to release such routine information ought to raise a red flag about the company's openness.

Another widely available good source is *The Value Line Investment Survey*, although its coverage of large-capitalization companies is not all-inclusive (only about 1,800 stocks.) (Most public libraries subscribe to Value Line as do many brokerage offices.) Value Line often makes a notation in the lower left corner of its page, or some times in the lower-center footnotes, indicating the date of the next expected board meeting.

A third and highly comprehensive source is *Standard & Poor's Dividend Record*. Fewer libraries and brokerage offices subscribe, but give it a try and become familiar with it. This service tracks and reports declarations for both preferred and common stocks. Its annual, soft cover, 8 1/2 X 11-inch volumes give the same data as the S&P sheets described earlier. The monthly and weekly update supplements track the most recent declaration dates. These sheets are loose-leaf and usually filed in front.

Numerous on-line database sources are available, often at little or no cost. Unfortunately, most databases focus on past payment and XD dates but omit the declaration dates. You will be better served to look at past dates' news items on such websites as Yahoo! or BigCharts.com for recent declaration dates. Any broker with access to a Reuters or Bloomberg terminal can readily provide needed dividend-meeting information.

The reason for looking at delays in dividend meetings is cautionary. Although a delay can be innocent, it more often results from problems: if there is an earnings shortfall or a major asset write-down pending, directors may want the details before routinely declaring the regular dividend. Before calling the company, check with a broker or online news database: Scan the day's news headlines. If a news release came out too late in the afternoon yesterday, it will miss the morning papers and appear a day late. A routine dividend item will run on the ticker as soon as possible but is not as hot as other types of breaking corporate news.

Earnings Reports

By far the most perilous reason for delayed reports is bad corporate earnings. These are common during recessions, but the plethora of recent new generally accepted accounting practices (GAAP) releases also poses a burden on companies to be timely in complying even in good times. Late earnings releases most often mean trouble, but before concluding that a suspicious delay is occurring, check the facts and remember seasonal exceptions. After fiscal year-end it takes longer to release earnings (requiring auditor blessing) than it does following ends of the other three quarters. Quarterly numbers usually are unaudited. Small adjustments can be pushed from one period to the next between quarters in case something slipped by earlier. Year-end numbers are audited, however, and there is no way of taking back a year-end number without huge embarrassment and loss of credibility once it has been released. Therefore, expect yearend releases to come more slowly.

How does an investor find out when to expect earnings? A majority of brokerage firms and many online news and charting services capture and store the last 90 days' headlines from the major wires. To anticipate the release schedule rather than waiting until the news is out (always a highly useful mind-set for an investor), inquire right after a quarter's end to see on what date the prior EPS announcement was made. Add three months and mark your calendar. After more than 90 days have elapsed, the prior headline and its date typically are wiped off the quote machine or news-service memory.

An excellent hardcopy source is The Wall Street Journal Cumulative Index, which can sometimes be found in public and university libraries. It cross indexes the past year's articles in Barron's also, giving headline, date, page, and column. The release runs on the news wire one market day earlier than the print item. This source saves the amount of time it takes to look at every day's back issue in the month of the prior report. Similarly, you can narrow a daily search by looking back three months in Barron's and noting in its stock tables at which week in the previous quarter new EPS information first appeared.

Why does a company delay its announcement of earnings? If it made an acquisition or divested a business in the last one or two quarters, the accounting department is very likely still in scramble mode, putting together revised, pro-forma and continuing-operations numbers. On rare occasions, the summer vacation season might be a real excuse. Another legitimate delay is the imposition of new accounting requirements by the SEC or by the Financial Accounting Standards Board (it takes a lot less effort to change a rule than it does to comply with new ones). If many companies are noting the effects of new reporting rules, some delay is tolerable. Early in the 2000s decade, implementation of Sarbanes-Oxley became a new reason for some delay in filings, but since about 2006 that has become too old to remain credible.

Other Delays

Other delays are often harbingers of trouble. A new computer system may have been installed, which can bring a company at least temporarily to its knees. Sometimes records get lost and management loses control of operations until the loss is rectified. Such events can be true reasons but bad excuses: management arguably should have insisted that IT managers would provide for continuity by adequate systems testing before the migration was implemented. After all the Y2K preparation now long since past, computer changes are a weak explanation.

If it is not a new computer, it could be a new accounting treatment that the company has voluntarily decided to adopt or a change in fiscal yearends. Analysts usually greet such news with suspicion; sometimes the revised methods of accounting, while technically allowable, are more liberal or allow the company to cover poor performance for awhile because of lack of comparability. New accounting standards can also be more conservative, resulting in downward restatements of prior results and a drop in stock price. A delay due to new standards voluntarily adopted usually is a cause for interim concern. Remember, the market hates uncertainty.

There can also be really serious problems: A cash or inventory shortage is discovered, accounting records are falsified or operating problems have occurred and management is assessing the degree of damage and deciding how to explain what happened. Another possibility is a write-off or write-down of assets that can take extra time when independent auditors are called in to give advice and/or pre-approve the charge amounts.

Be aware of regulatory deadlines for filing SEC reports. Public companies are expected to report quarterly results no later than 45 days after that period ends; annual numbers are due in not more than 90 day. In practice, the SEC is understaffed and typically has more pressing matters to police than late reports; the exchanges and NASDAQ do monitor timeliness and will threaten delisting for noncompliance. In any event, company managements, lawyers and auditors are well aware of the rules; failure to meet a regulatory deadline is usually a sign that something meaningful is wrong (and can be a technical cause for default on corporate debt!), at least including the failure of control systems. If giants such as AT&T can get their quarterly data out in 10 days or less, surely a small company that has chosen to be publicly traded should be geared to do it in fewer than 45 days. If not, their accounting function is dangerously understaffed, and management is therefore at risk of not being in the know and in control.

One other source of concern is not an actual delay per se: a few companies routinely report results at the last possible date (the SEC deadline). Typically, such companies are extremely secretive and report only what is required and when it is due, and neither more nor sooner. They tend not to give much or any useful interim information to analysts, heightening the potential for surprises. It is often advisable to avoid investing in such companies from the beginning, unless or until they change their attitude toward public investors.

This entire area of delayed reports is one where commission phobia can get in the way. If an investor's suspicions or worst fears are proven wrong and the late news is not worse information than expected, the stock is unaffected. In such a case you will have spent a round-trip commission as insurance to be safe rather than sorry. (Possibly you will see the company more objectively from a non-holder's distance and decide not to re-enter, in which case only a single commission will have been paid.) If the news only gets worse as it emerges, you may see a gap opening of several points down (dwarfing any commission), followed by further erosion. If the news is worse than it was earlier, management credibility will have become tarnished, delaying and limiting prospects for price recovery. This admonition to be safe rather than sorry is even more forceful if the stock is widely held by institutions. In today's short-term money management culture, there is a rush to exit with huge at-market sell orders whenever any news is bad. Chapter 9 dealt with that problem in greater detail.

CHAPTER 28

Crashes: Sell versus Hold—Before, During and After

Keys for Successful Selling

◆ Review and Understand Earlier Panics

◆ Ride Out a Panic Properly

◆ Pre-Identify Stocks That Do Not Fare Well

◆ Know Panic-Resilient Stocks and Groups

Recall the chaotic pace of trading on October 19, 1987, when the Dow Jones Industrial Average lost 508 points (23 percent) and made its bottom for the move on then-record volume. Even considerably less dire but important bottoms are typically referred to as selling climaxes because they consist of prices falling in a cascade or waterfall shape (when plotted on a graph against time), accompanied by a sharp concentration of heavy trading volume as investor emotions widely take control and completely trample logic.

A more recent and somewhat different real-life market laboratory worth revisiting by reading then-current market news items is the aftermath of the September 11, 2001 terrorist attacks. The U.S. market actually closed for the rest of the week. After its re-opening on Monday, September 17, several trading sessions were required for the emotions and new thinking of the post-9/11 world to be worked out before the selling was all exhausted. Re-reading reports and looking at newspaper stock-price tables from that time will provide a vivid flavor of the fear psychology that defines a market crash. If there has not been a major crash lately when you read this, the instructive value will be all the greater.

Reviewing and Understanding Earlier Panics

On the way down, each temporary bottom during a bear trend is typically characterized by increases in fear and therefore in trading volume, with a bit of panicky dumping to mark each new interim low. The final downside climax is most violent and usually sees the greatest trading volume. Selling pressure becomes so intense that it literally cannot be exceeded; it becomes exhausted as large numbers of the previously brave finally capitulate and sell even at obvious bargain levels. As a large crowd jumps overboard simultaneously, the moment they are finished is why and when prices hit a bottom. This is the long-repeated profile of a final bottom, that is, the culmination of a selling frenzy and the end of a sharp downward movement in prices. Minyanville founder Todd Harrison, a wise commentator, says that all markets (up and down) go through three stages in sequence: disbelief, migration and panic.

The panic stage is usually followed on lower volume by timid bargain-hunting. When that process runs its course and the bulls run out of guts and/or ammunition, the initial base-building or rally falters. Such failure to hold ground leads to renewed fear, which builds in a minor crescendo to a new, sometimes lower, cascade-shaped bottom on moderately high volume. The key to note here is the less dramatic price drop and volume rise than those seen earlier; the difference proves that the prior low was one of psychological exhaustion or washout. Major market bottoms often produce a W shape on the charts over two or three months; the two bottom points need not be at exactly the same level. Examine long-term charts of SPY or DIA for July through October 2002 on your favorite charting website.

Before listing rules for selling surrounding crashes, a review of holding versus selling stocks under normal market conditions is also relevant background. Holding (which is really commission-free buying for a further holding period) should occur only if no tests for selling are failed. Company-related reasons to sell are as follows:

◆ Sell if you would not buy the stock again now at today's quoted price.

◆ Sell rather than hope against hope for a maybe price bailout.

◆ Sell if the corporate and industry news seemingly cannot get any better.

◆ Sell when your original scenario has been fulfilled.

◆ Sell if things did not go as planned.

◆ Sell when analysts' advice goes from buy to hold or equivalent euphemisms.

◆ Sell if company fundamentals are getting sick.

◆ Sell on the rebound in the aftermath of material, unexpected, discrete bad news.

◆ Sell in certain cases when expected news is delayed.

General market-climate or behavioral indicators for selling are as follows:

◆ An extended market advance has far exceeded realistic growth rates.

◆ Prevalence of general euphoria but then this unusually illogical positive climate, seemingly overnight, turns surprisingly nasty and stocks suffer sudden sharp losses.

◆ Widespread public participation (a strong final-stage indicator). Remember 1999-2000? It was classic.

◆ The is heavy and increased market coverage in TV news, general-interest news magazines and local newspapers.

◆ Sell when your portfolio shows all or virtually all gains (a fairly rare condition).

◆ Sell after gloating or counting the chips.

◆ Sell and step aside when experiencing a personal losing streak.

Price-specific conditions for selling are as follows:

◆ Sell when a stock reaches your original price target.

◆ Sell on an unsustainable upward price spike or crescendo on very heavy volume.

◆ Sell if the stock is lazy money and likely to stay that way.

◆ Sell when price is unusually far above its moving average (the MACD indicator, Chapter 20).

◆ Sell using above-market limit orders, letting the market come to your price and free you from a decision while giddy, greed and celebrating.

◆ Sell stocks promptly that break down on a chart basis.

◆ If you use stop-loss orders, never remove or lower them.

If you sell stocks in a disciplined manner using the preceding guides, you are likely to end up with a good deal of cash before the market moves into an obvious bear cycle. Relatively few of one's holdings will fail to hit one of the 23 triggers noted in those lists. Stocks that do survive will tend to be high-quality issues that have continued to perform fundamentally and have not run up to unreasonable price levels. Some experts refer to these as core holdings or businessman's risk foundation stocks. They are stocks that have given consistent indications that they can be held through good and bad in the market. All other stocks will have become sales well before you face a market-wide panic bottom because:

1. They worked as planned, achieving your price targets.
2. They acted too well for a brief period of time.
3. They gradually became unreasonably priced.
4. They were wasting your capital's time value by going nowhere.
5. They developed significant fundamental problems.
6. General market blow-off symptoms, described above, became evident.

Very few stocks can escape all such screens for long late in a bull market. Thus, as an investor cashes in as prescribed and follows a buying discipline that rejects new positions when valuations get too pricey, she ends up still holding very few stocks as the market gets toppy. These combined technical-analysis and value disciplines, of course, work very nicely by protecting capital. Moving to increased cash will make her feel a bit lonely in a bull market's late stages, as certain speculative stocks skyrocket and prompt regrets of being left behind. However, she can be assured that her selling discipline will be rewarded when the prevailing psychology, eventually, first loses its bravado and then later turns ugly and savage. That experience deepens her understanding of the way the market works. Probably most of all, having won at a difficult game, she develops the wisdom and courage to succeed in similar market stages in the future. And that provides the opportunity to make big profits in the handful of similarly dramatic cycles that will occur in future years. She will know beyond any shadow of a doubt, from personal experience, that contrarian investing philosophy works and that deliberately doing what is emotionally taxing will produce handsome financial gains once the market crisis passes.

To strengthen your big-picture perspective, review the descriptions presented in our very early chapters of the mechanical supply/demand processes and factors such as sponsorship that make stock prices rise. Recall that if such processes and factors supporting further price advance are absent, an investor should not hold because the stock will not go up.

Looking now at stock-price trends not from a mechanical viewpoint but from a big-picture perspective, there are two major price-driving forces: fundamentals (which control the long term) and psychology (which rules the short and medium term). Review Chapters 8 and 13. Fundamental and psychological factors affect stocks in both directions. As an overlay, understand that they can affect a stock either directly (because of the company behind the stock itself) or indirectly (because the industry group's or the over all market's trend is so forceful—up or down—that virtually no stocks can buck it). Of course the effects are hugely stronger on the downside than on the upside: fear is a much more powerful driver than greed.

Weathering a Panic

When you are caught in a market panic, the bottom-line reality question is whether capitalism in the United States and other major Western nations will continue to function after the panic ends. If the answer is yes, then there is no reason to sell at foolish levels. In fact, the only rational thing to do is take courage and make buys. Being gutsy enough to act on our contrarian test—refusing to sell good stocks cheap because Wall Street and Main Street have lost faith for a few days—ensures that your earlier selling at better levels, or not at all, will prove appropriate. It will be emotionally difficult to buy in a panic. Those who can do so are demonstrably rational and therefore also calm enough to sell with discipline as the prior highs approached.

A central concept of this chapter is the occasional need to play when it is painful. But this concept specifically and only applies to stocks being affected solely by the overwhelming negative psychological forces that occasionally cause selling routs or panics in the whole market. To put this very important limiting caveat another way, when a crash or panic is in process, stocks should be held only if they are going down solely because of market factors and not at all because of company factors. This should relate to only a few issues for you, however, because investors following the suggestions in this book should have already weeded out their bad performers and taken profits in their stellar performers well before a bear market arrives, let alone reaches its final climax proportions.

Thus, when appropriate selling has left an investor with only a few, high-quality stocks, he can and should hold onto those gems and play through the difficult experience of a panic or crash. He will be holding only a relatively small portfolio (having followed the other cashing-in suggestions well before the bottom nears), so his level of pain will be no worse than moderate. His cash holdings will give emotional comfort and provide the resources for acquiring stocks advantageously when prices get really low and buying feels scary. A comforting perspective for those less than 50 percent committed to stocks is that each decline means their cash is gaining stock-buying power faster than their remaining holdings are losing cash value! Think about that.

There is one more qualifier on whether to hold or sell after a panic has passed. Once the panic subsides, there is a lift in the market. But its effect is significantly different across various kinds of stocks. For some issues, there is a sharp snap-back rally; for others, very little improvement. Just as it is not advisable to sell directly into the panic, it is prudent to reassess positions after the selling frenzy has subsided and an initial bounce in prices has begun.

The object, as always, is to decide in real time what to sell and what to hold. Selling should not be urgent because pre-bear-phase tactics will have raised a lot of cash, so there is no need to sell to raise cash for margin calls or for new buying. But because the goal is always to maximize return on capital and to take advantage of the time value of money, look closely at what to hold and what to sell now that the panic's dust has cleared. One must look forward at future prospects rather than backward at now-irrelevant old (higher) prices.

Some readers may see a contradiction in this advice to hold the remaining few gems through the worst psychological heat, because earlier they were counseled that avoiding losses is the first priority and the best reason for selling. But taking a limited short-term dose of paper losses in a crash—by holding a few items of real quality— is a lesser risk than selling out during the fury and hoping to have the courage and good timing to get back in at lower prices shortly afterward.

Stocks That do not Fare Well

If an investor is down to just a few core holdings anyway, he is better advised to tough it out. The very experience of playing in pain through a temporary crash is of enormous instructional value and thus actually worth the modest monetary cost involved. The process of crisis thinking and the need to make wrenching decisions that prove valid in short order will serve a person well for the rest of his or her investment career. Once an investor has successfully navigated the worst of the choppy investment seas, she will have learned survival lessons and will have internalized feelings and a vivid experience that will be of permanent psychological and instructive value.

Stocks that tend to be sub-par performers in a post-crash environment are the following:

◆ low-priced stocks

◆ lower-NASDAQ issues

◆ small total-capitalization issues

◆ thinly traded, analyst under-covered or non-covered stocks

◆ fundamental in-industry laggards

◆ stocks in recession-sensitive industries

◆ brokerage firms' own stocks (the public will be slow to return to active investing)

◆ discredited groups

◆ stocks in panic-trigger related groups

Because of fear, nervousness and absence speculative appetite after a crash or panic, the first six groups (some of which will overlap for individual stocks) lack sponsorship. In addition, because market panics generate immediate scare headlines in the media, predictably there will be talk of recession (or depression) and parallels drawn with 1929. Recall the October 1987 and October 1989 bashings and the smaller one-day drubbings during the early and middle 1990s; depression talk was rampant in post-9/11 months until mid-2002. The final two categories should be off your hold list for similar reasons. Sometimes there is an industry or category of stocks related to the news that triggers the panic. Even immediately after any panic itself has passed, investors and traders will have keen memories of what started the debacle, and will avoid such stocks for an extended time. If the mid-2007 trouble with sub-prime mortgage losses drives a major drop, banks will be on the defensive thereafter, even if they look cheap.

It is highly important to make hold/sell calls with an eye on prevailing drivers of market selling. In 1962 (deep history), it was steel stocks sensitive to pricing confrontation with the Kennedy administration. Then, any industry that needed price freedom became one to avoid. Brokerage stocks would have been poor choices to hold after the 1987 crash because of all the controversy surrounding program trading. The

1989 echo-crash was triggered by the collapse of a proposed buyout of United Air lines, so airlines and other possible leveraged-buyout candidates were identifiable as the trigger-related groups at that time. Large international banks were laggards in the fallout after the LTCM hedge-fund debacle in 1998 because of their lending exposure. Anything with a Latin American tinge became taboo for a while after the Mexican peso devaluation in late 1994. Technology remained in the doghouse for seemingly a dog's age after the 2000 bubble burst. The common thread is that while certain stock groups may indeed be cheap they will be not yet ready to rebound soon after a related crisis. Forgetting pain takes time.

Discredited groups, which will vary from one market period to another, will depend on what was in the headlines in recent months. Basic industry stocks were taboo in the early 1980s, known as the rust-belt period. Airline stocks suffered prolonged underperformance (six years as of 2007) after 9/11 and then a string of related bankruptcies, and then rising fuel costs, occurred.

Make sure that your expectations are not in direct conflict with prevailing consensus and not based alone on your personal judgment of what may or should happen. If the (correct) bet is no recession, the reward will be smaller and slower if a second (correct) bet is market expectation of a recession (whether it comes or not). The investor must submerge his or her ego to the realities of the emotional climate (this may be one reason that women have become known as better investors). It is better to be richer today than to be vindicated slowly (economist and market player John Maynard Keynes is reputed to have remarked that the market can stay irrational longer than you can remain solvent). In the next major post-decline phase that occurs after you read this chapter, carefully note the events on which that decline was blamed, and avoid for some time stocks/industries associated with those concepts; they will have a difficult time regaining sponsorship quickly. Therefore, recession-sensitive groups of stocks do not bounce back much for a period of time, even if later hindsight shows that no recession occurred or that the economic downturn is statistically well past.

Panic-Resilient Stocks

There are, by contrast, several groups that tend to act well in a post-panic environment, especially if the crash itself drives prices to incredible levels. Of course, the more unusual the values created, the briefer the opportunity window and the sharper will be the initial snap-back rally. Some of the groups most likely to snap back are as follows:

◆ recession-resistant industries (foods, grocers, drugs, utilities)
◆ non-cyclical blue chips driven well down (oils)
◆ big names with corporate staying power (e.g., IBM, ExxonMobil, General Electric, P&G, McDonald's)

- ◆ Fortune 100 and similar companies with good yields
- ◆ trade-down concepts such as low-cost restaurants and discount retailers (recession beneficiaries)
- ◆ companies with low P/Es or low price/cash flow ratios not already otherwise in the above list
- ◆ companies selling at or below book value and with positive earnings-trend estimates
- ◆ companies with low debt/equity ratios (perceived as low in risk)
- ◆ unleveraged closed-end non-junk bond funds (see ETFconnect.com)
- ◆ panic-trigger beneficiaries (e.g., oil-service and insulation stocks after OPEC raised oil prices in 1973; solar-power plays in the mid-2000s after oil spiked to $80/barrel; temporary employment services and outsourcing manufacturers after a downsizing-driven recession such as that of 1991)

All of these groups are recession resistant or perceived as among the most likely to survive hard times. They retain market sponsorship and are soonest to regain steady sponsors and buyers. Related positively to the trigger event, they have high visibility because investors remember the concept vividly and relate to it readily.

Humorists are fond of saying that the stock market has forecast ten of the past three recessions. There may, in fact, turn out to be no recession at all following a market's dramatic down-move (as in 1998 and again 2002), but perception and expectation drive stock prices in the near term more than facts do. Thus, cyclicals such as autos, steels, chemicals, papers and capital-goods producers are not prime early choices for participating in the bounce. Similarly, vacation-related (airline, hotel and casino) and luxury stocks fare poorly early on.

Again, remember that longer-term perspectives may prove that the fear about leading companies in discredited groups was unfounded. More important from a tactical investment perspective in the healing phase after a crash is the reality that few investors/analysts/money managers will quickly have renewed courage to sponsor tarnished-image-group stocks with either money or written advice. Such issues will nearly always prove early-recovery laggards.

CHAPTER 29

Use This Hold/Sell Decision Checklist

Keys for Successful Selling

◆ Use These 20 Questions to Focus the Hold Versus Sell Decision
◆ Evaluate Your Answers Later, to Fine-Tune Your Skills

This chapter contains a list of questions that summarize key points developed earlier to help investors create a selling strategy. The questions were originally adapted from a session developed for brokers in an award-winning regional retail brokerage firm's training program. They have proved notably useful for two reasons: they deal with a relatively unfamiliar facet of the investment process (i.e., selling stocks), and they help focus thinking in ways that encourage rational decisions and sometimes free up lazy funds for better re-use.

Readers are encouraged to photocopy these pages and to keep copies in three places: in your workplace, from where broker conversations or online trading may take place; at home, near your PC where market studying and decision making tends to take place; and in your broker's office if you still use a full-commission rep, so that he or she also might spend time thinking about these issues and be able to help a wayward reader/investor back onto the path should there be any straying from coolly logical thinking.

Each stock should have its own separate checklist page; keeping these in a three-ring notebook, including beyond when sales have been completed, will create over time a highly useful record that can reveal recurring patterns of strength and weakness.

20 Questions to Focus the Hold-Versus-Sell Decision

At the Time of Purchase:

1. What is the date the stock was bought?

2. Price paid did you pay? (For reference, also DJIA level on that date), Bought @ market, or on limit?

3. What was your price target? (Implied P/E ratio?) Sell order entered?

4. What is the target sale date? (Calculate projected annualized return from #s 1,2, and 3)

5. What events or changes should make this stock go up (specific expectations)?

Reviewing the Position at a Later Date:

6. Are you currently more, less, or equally excited and sure about the company versus when stock was first bought?

7. Has the story expected in answer #5 played out yet? If no, is there still a concrete chance the story will work? If yes, did the stock go up at all on any related or partial news? If yes, did the stock reach your objective in question 3?

8. What is the stock's price now? (Compare with answers # 2 and 3; note answer #6 also.)

9. What do you now expect to happen fundamentally? (Compare with question 5.) If discussed originally with friends, relatives, or colleagues, would the stock be discussed as enthusiastically now and be purchased today?

10. Due to answer #9, what price is expected now? (Compare with question 3.)

11. When is the price in answer 10 projected? (Compare with question 4.) What is the revised estimated annualized percent return derived from questions 8, 10 and 11?

12. What is the downside price risk from current prices if nothing happens; that is, if the story or concept in question 5 or question 9 proves false or faulty?

13. Is the reward/risk balance favorable from current prices? (Compare answers 10 and 12 with current price.) Many strategists require a 3:1 or better expected ratio!

14. Where is the DJIA now? (Compare with DJIA level in answer #2.) Is the stock's relative performance surprising? Acceptable?

15. Have there been negative surprises from the company or its industry since your purchase? How if at all did these affect your thinking? Why/why not?

16. Since purchase, did you almost decide to sell, only to hold on for a little more? Was a mental or actual stop-loss point set but later reduced or removed as the stock weakened?

Analyzing Whether to Hold or Sell Now:

17. Considering answers to #9 through #12, specifically why should this stock still he held?

18. With your updated knowledge, would you buy this stock right now, at today's price?

19. Have you identified significantly better opportunities for purchases right now?

20. Does the answer to question #17 square with those to #3, #18 and #19?

Evaluating Your Answers

Written responses to these questions are recommended for two reasons: the discipline of thinking through the exercises in detail and the creation of an archival record that can be used for later reference, comparison and learning. Number a piece of paper from 1 to 20, put a blank line for the stock's name on the top, and photocopy this answer grid in some quantity for future use.

Start filling out the sheet at the time of purchase by answering questions 1 through 5 immediately when the buy order is placed. There will then be no need to search back for data for 1 and 2 and, most significantly, there will be no fudging of responses to questions 3 through 5.

Later, answer questions 9 through 11 with your responses 3 through 5 covered up: merely copying will render the exercise useless. The quality of your investment and trading decisions will be enhanced by the honesty and rigor with which you carry out this process.

Note that these questions have a built-in bias toward making one feel a bit defensive about holding a stock. This creates a presumption in favor of selling when things have not gone as planned. If a holding is not working, that position needs to be fixed.

If time has gone beyond the period indicated by answer 4 or if the stock actually has traded at or above your target in answer 3, something has gone wrong with your plan or execution. If there are differences between the answers to questions 3 through 5 as compared with those for 9 through 11, study them again for an implied corrective action.

An affirmative answer to question 15 or to either part of question 16 indicates lack of decisiveness or consistency in dealing with this situation. Either greed arose when things went well or denial arose as events turned sour. It is only human to shift ground (rationalize) in an effort to be tolerant of the stock's performance (one's own judgment) or of one's less-than-perfect strategy and execution. Learn from past strategy executions, and make a special effort to avoid falling into this pattern again. Continuing to do what is most comfortable will not improve results and is likely to hamper them.

The heart of things is 18. If it cannot be answered in the affirmative with total honesty and enthusiastic conviction (use the subpart of question 9 as an acid test), then stop this deteriorating process by selling. If you would not buy today, why should you envision others doing so? If other investors cannot reasonably be expected to be buyers, such failure of sponsorship and support implies and forecasts lower prices. So why will you hold?

How soon or how often this exercise should be conducted for each stock held is a reasonable question. It is advisable to create a tickler file in which you place each sheet for review 90 days from the buy date (or at the date noted in question 4, if that is sooner). If the review results in a hold decision, file the page for re-review at the date in question 11.

Use of this questionnaire is not a guaranteed cure-all. Nor will it automatically make every position profitable. But it will usefully help to impose closure on situations that are not working out as expected. Use it to generate urgency by examining and overlaying the time value of money; and to serve as a reminder that a decision to hold should be an active and reasoned act of the mind instead of a lazy default. A decision to hold should be every bit as active as a decision to buy or to sell, missing only the need to telephone your broker or sign on to your online account.

To be successful, an investment must be not only bought well but also sold right. Until a sale occurs, the outcome is only a temporary paper result. A handsome profit can still melt away at any moment (due to sudden bad news or a crash) until it is actually closed out. This questionnaire should be used as a reminder, guide, and prompting tool to sharpen decision-making skills and thereby improve sale executions. It will almost surely make you uncomfortable at first. But as some famous multi-step programs note, becoming unhappy with our present state is the required first step for achieving constructive change.

CHAPTER 30
Summing Up: The Winner's Test

Keys for Successful Selling

◆ Define the Ultimate Test
◆ Consider the Mother Test
◆ Apply the Time-Value Test
◆ Apply the Ultimate Test: How Often?

You now recognize and understand the many externally-imposed and internally-created roadblocks to successfully selling your investments. To counteract those forces, you have begun to develop a newly activist mind-set about closing out your investment positions. A significant element of that revised way of looking at selling involves having adopted a contrarian's outlook toward the markets in both short- and long-term contexts. Prior chapters in this final section have equipped you with several specific tactics for executing your position-liquidating decisions effectively and profitably, and under a variety of particular market circumstances. This final chapter names a single critical test that should be applied frequently to each of your holdings; its answer will sharply focus and define your choice between holding and selling.

You own a stock; you have been watching its progress (or lack thereof) both in absolute terms and against the market background. When first buying, you had in mind a scenario or rationale that involved a view about future company developments, a time frame in which such events should materialize, and also a price target you envisioned as credible, driven by your story. No investor's crystal ball is perfect; unforeseen positive and/or negative events in the world or specifically pertaining to your stock will have arisen since your original purchase action. Those now-known factors cannot be ignored, but neither should you be so totally focused on them that you mourn over (or continue to celebrate) them. What is of most practical importance in defining the remaining outcome of this investment position is the future. The future is all you can do anything about. This perspective defines, and highlights the importance of, the ultimate hold-versus-sell test.

The Ultimate Test

Here is the overriding primary test, followed by observations on why it is so critically important: Knowing all that you now know and expect about the company and its stock (not what you originally believed or hoped at time of purchase), and assuming that you had available capital, and assuming that it would not cause a portfolio imbalance to do so, would you buy this stock today, at today's price? No equivocation. Yes or no? Answers such as maybe or probably are not acceptable since they are ways of dodging the issue. No investor probably buys a stock; they either place an order or do not. Here is the implication of your answer to that critical test: if you did not answer with a clear affirmative, you should sell; only if you said a strong yes, are you justified to hold.

Some would object that this test is quite harsh. Indeed, it is sharply framed. But it is neither unfair nor less than 100 percent logical.

If you would not buy now, saying that you are nevertheless willing to hold amounts to playing a greater-fool game: holding in hope of higher prices implies your expectation that other investors will be more naive or less discerning than you since you have said that at present levels and with what you know, you would not be a buyer. Instead, as (illogical) justification for your continuing to hold you would be counting on other investors to do what you would not do: buy the stock today and in the future at present and at higher levels. Stock prices do not rise by magic or merely because people hope they will; rising prices require buying pressure that exceeds selling pressure. Buying pressure comes from buy orders generated by positive, proactive decisions. If you would not be a part of the source of new buying orders, you are counting on others to make a decision you cannot justify. Such a decision to hold, therefore, is based on fanciful and unreasoning hope rather than on logic. Stating the point plainly: What you would not buy, you should not hold.

In case you harbor any doubts about whether holding is logically the same as buying, consider this: holding is redeploying capital for another time period, whether that be a moment, a day, a month, or longer. Purchasing an investment is deploying your capital by changing your wealth's form from cash (or a money market fund or margin buying power) into a certain number of shares of a given stock. When you have cash, becoming a stockholder requires deciding to exchange your cash for a chosen security. When you are already an owner of a stock, holding also implies a decision, namely, the choice to retain the security position rather than exchange it back for cash at its current dollar value. Thought of in another (albeit unusual) way, holding represents invisibly exchanging an owned stock for its cash value and then deciding to immediately trade that cash back for the same shares to hold for another moment, day or longer. Holding is commission free and requires no contact with your brokerage firm, electronic or traditional. But, in all other ways, it is a recommitment of capital to the same stock for a further future time period. Since holding is every bit as much a choice as was the purchase itself, holding should be an active choice rather than a default due to inertia or inattention.

What you would not buy, you should not hold. Therefore, you should sell it. There is no other available choice. Avoidance by a non-holder is driven by the same perceptions and expectations as sale by a current holder: Cash or something else is preferable to this stock. What you would not buy (i.e., would avoid if not already involved with) is nothing other than a sale awaiting your action. Stripping away questions of tax effects (dealt with earlier), for an owner to hold rather than to sell what he would otherwise avoid (reject buying) is completely irrational.

Consider the Mother Test

When considering the hold-versus-sell question, you might also usefully frame the issue in terms of your author's mother/mother-in-law tests. (Again: Remember that holding is the equivalent of buying!) Suppose your mother requested that you select a stock for her to purchase today and, for the sake of argument, assume that you share identical investment objectives and risk tolerances. Ask yourself whether you would recommend this stock (that you already own) to Mom for purchase (yes or no, not maybe). You love her and you wish her success rather than grief and loss. You dread the possibility that you might at some future date need to justify or explain away a possible mistake in your selection. You realize you are human and therefore fallible and can only exercise your best overall judgment in Mom's behalf. But you would really prefer to be right rather than wrong. Your mother might forgive you an error, but you will still feel bad for having made it. This is a difficult screen for your stock to pass, is it not? Well, treat yourself as well as you would hope to treat Mom! What you would not suggest she buy, nor should you buy—and holding is a commission-free buy as shown earlier. How can you justify holding what you would not advise a loved one buy?

A variant of that test involving Mom is the mother-in-law version. Here, since the relationship between you may have a somewhat different driving dynamic, your attention is probably focused more strongly on first avoiding damage than on trying to create success. In the real world of spouses and in-laws, of course, you would most likely demur at an opportunity to render any investment advice. But as a mental measure of your true confidence in this stock, an imaginary mother-in-law test will serve well. Here, suppose that you want her to think well of you and to benefit rather than hurt from your advice. And also assume you will not have another visit for awhile. During that time while you will be out of touch, the stock in question will be moving either up or down; your feedback will undoubtedly come at your next family gathering. Would you name this stock today as your buy choice for your mother-in-law? Again, only an unqualified yes or no is acceptable. If your expected risk of loss is not clearly overshadowed by your perceived likelihood of gain, you would not suggest buying. If you like the stock generally but would rather be a new buyer down five points from current levels, again you have defined a clear answer: you should sell now and place a limit buy at that lower price level of greater comfort. Why willingly tolerate a suspected price retrenchment? Once again, treat yourself no less well than you would your mother-in-law. Avoid that anticipated remorse and that difficult review from 20/20 hindsight. What you would not tell her to buy, you should not hold either! What is not a buy is not a hold, so selling is the only alternative.

Without question, investing is an art rather than a science. You should not expect to achieve near-perfect results; you must be able to forgive your own human imperfection. Your judgments regarding buying, holding and selling must always be made under uncertainty and without sure knowledge of the future. Diligent best effort at making reasonably sound decisions each time is all you can require of yourself. Desperately seeking all possible added information takes so long that the situation will have changed in the intervening time, requiring unending further reconsideration, and so on. (If you cannot function short of certainty, you are not well suited for investing—especially in individual stocks.) For these reasons, the preceding discussion of whether to sell or hold must be interpreted in a fair and realistic context: Given what you know, and exercising best available judgment while admitting that errors are an obvious possibility, what would you find seems best to do? In that spirit, more-detailed scenarios under which to define answers to your sell/hold question are offered next.

Your Stock Is Down

Clearly, something has gone awry since you made that purchase. Has the overall economic or interest-rate climate worsened in a way that will require considerable added time for recovery? Did your original assumptions (price driven by story in an assumed time frame) prove inaccurate? Has the company jolted your thinking (and, clearly, the overall market of investor opinion) by producing one or more important negative surprises? Perhaps new competitors emerged or existing ones jumped ahead, leaving your choice in the shadows. Whatever has driven the downside price action, you need to reassess realistically. The basic and most fundamental test remains whether you would buy it today, knowing what you now do. If your added knowledge points to a more modest target price or, realistically, a longer period of time to justify your original goal, that implies a lower rate of return from today forward compared with whatever return you originally projected and also considered adequate for risking your capital on this purchase.

Given your inability to change past events, your only relevant consideration is a revised future whose shape you now find less attractive than you first envisioned. Is the implied return, starting from today, one that would cause you to buy this stock here and now? What you would not buy, you should not hold. Thousands of other investment possibilities exist, so do not remain stuck with a past choice merely to prove that you can come out without a loss or without having made a demonstrable mistake. Time is money. Holding this thus far underachiever should require a stiff mental hurdle. Do you have a compelling reason to expect (not merely hope) that events will now start unfolding promptly so that a high rate of return is therefore predictable? It needs to be a rate high enough to make up for time already lost and thus get your stock back to the target/time you first set out. If you cannot make such a case, looking elsewhere is likely to be a better choice than holding and hoping. Getting even is not a relevant issue; a good return on your capital from today forward is the test.

Apply the Time-Value Test

Always respect the time value of money. Due consideration of that factor can be very useful in your work on the sell/hold issue for each stock. Occasionally reviewing Chapter 10 on this critical perspective may be of great value.

If Your Stock's Price Has Gone Nowhere

Considering your hold/sell choice with time value in mind should prove helpful regardless of where your stock's price has gone since purchase. Many investors are most careful to reconsider their positions when paper losses have occurred, and that discipline definitely earns due credit (anything that causes an investor to conduct an active hold/sell re-examination is healthy). But equally, a mental sell versus hold exercise should be undertaken if your stock has gone sideways.

Assuming that price inertia cannot be blamed on the overall market, it would now appear that this stock may take more time to work out than you first thought. If that is because some expected news has failed to appear or because earnings growth has not materialized, you have some serious and honest re-assessing to do. Your stock has not treated you as badly as a decliner would have. But in fact it has failed to meet your original studied expectations, and it has wasted some of your capital's valuable time. Putting it briefly, something (even if you don't know exactly what) has gone wrong—even if that something is not so severe as to have caused an actual price decline. Assuming that an overall negative market environment has not caused your problem, the most likely reason your dollars have been asleep is that your original scenario was either overly optimistic or already obvious to much of the world by the time you jumped aboard at what general opinion now knows was a full or inflated price. (Another possibility is that some investors are beginning to sense some fundamental challenges for the company but consensus sentiment has not yet turned clearly negative.)

Bottom line, as with that other stock that actually declined: You need to have convincing reasons to expect that this one will start making up lost time. Given that something has been amiss to date, such a scenario might well be on the optimistic side of real. Remember, in order for you to achieve your initial expectations by still riding this vehicle, something good enough must start happening to justify an annualized return on investment greater than what you originally projected. Stocks sometimes do emerge from dormancy to act very well, but wishing alone will not make it so. What will be needed for these shares to rise is better fundamental performance in a large enough dose to attract sponsorship and, therefore, active buying pressure. As elsewhere, would you actually buy it again today? Your answer tells whether to hold or sell.

If Your Stock Is Up Ahead of Schedule

This is, of course, the most pleasant scenario: your purchase judgment has not only been vindicated but your pick has actually been working out more rapidly than you had originally hoped. Surprisingly, such a favorable experience contains very subtle but powerful aspects that can undermine your success. When your stock has done unexpectedly well, it is probably because of well-publicized good news, rotation of its industry into market leadership, or even just because it is a volatile stock doing well in a generally strong market. Psychologically, your tendency in such times is to be in love with both this stock/company and your own brilliance. The natural tendency is to project recent facts, with which we are now comfortable, into the future. What has done quite well we subconsciously condition ourselves to expect to continue prospering. Just when a maximum number of analysts and investors (and traders) adopt this same belief, by definition current buying pressure will reach a zenith, and price must soon thereafter begin to decline. Identifying the exact moment of maximum adulation for a stock is seldom possible, but an objective examination (such as a contrarian non-owner might make) can usually spot a period of bubbly enthusiasm unlikely to be long sustained.

Once again, the operative and defining question is whether you would buy it today. If the stock now sits well above that imaginary line of progression from your buy to your sell target (Figure 12-1), only a highly significant, previously unimagined development should prompt you to raise your target and thereby justify continued holding. Expected good news or presumed solid earnings progress does not count; those were reasons you bought and were already factored into your price/time target. If your stock has thus far done very well, those plus factors are surely now already in the price. Without some very significant new factor, when your stock is well above trend it is most likely a timely current sell candidate from either of two perspectives. First, on a shorter-term basis, the thrust of its recent rise is very probably unsustainable. In the vernacular, this (good) can't go on like this forever. From a longer-term perspective, again without some new fundamentally up-shifting development, the remaining path from today's advanced price to your original price/

time target has a slope much flatter than your required rate of return. Therefore, while this stock might still go up in the long run, it will be a relative laggard from here to your original target time and price.

Your comfort level about the company and how well you feel you understand its stock will tempt you to stay with a familiar vehicle you know rather than to move elsewhere. Cold logic would say this stock is overheated and cannot be expected to provide an adequate return from here to your old target. The bottom line is that if you would not dare buy more atop this recent pleasant rise, you ought not to hold it from here. Selling will reduce your risk of loss and disappointment and at the same time will take money off the table. You can use that cash either to buy another stock or to wait and repurchase this known winner a bit more reasonably after it corrects. The better a stock has treated you, the more strongly it will beguile you into holding at just those times when it is due for a price correction. Remember, elevated price is elevated risk.

Applying the Ultimate Test: How Often?

In the purest of theory, our would you buy? test could be applied at every moment the market is open. In fact, active day traders and other aggressive short-term market participants tend to do just that. But most people are occupied with job pursuits throughout the market day (or, if retired, 'have a life' outside the markets). Those time demands render constant testing impractical –all the more so when not just one stock but a whole list of holdings bears watching! Many readers do in fact look at their favorite newspaper's quotations pages, or log onto their brokerage account or favorite charting website, daily. If your attention is actually that frequent, you should ask yourself what your purpose is in doing such intense watching. Checking stock prices daily should have a very different basis than watching the daily sports box scores to follow your favorite players or teams. In the sports example, you are powerless to take action and are clearly a permanently passive spectator. With your stocks, daily tracking really should only be practiced if you are prepared any day to take action based on latest developments.

Daily tracking can be dangerous in at least two senses: (1) Unless you have a firmly disciplined contrarian's mind-set, close daily watching (especially via financial TV) can lure you into following current trends: You will fall prey to selling in panic or to buying what has recently become too hot. (2) Daily tracking with absolutely no intention of taking counter-trend actions (selling up or buying on big dips) actually acts to numb your senses and to dampen the likelihood you will take action, particularly to sell. The more days you practice a habit of passively watching the market just to see what comes next, the less likely it is that you will be in an alert, activist frame of mind and actually take action when a decision does become warranted. Over-observing from a resting position makes you too forgiving and also fills your mind with myriad data elements that overload your circuits and contribute to confusion. A hundred days, half up and half down, will give you numerous paralyzingly equal reasons to hold and to sell, which will breed inaction from an overwhelming sense that there is no single clear answer since there are so many countervailing factors in the picture.

Much better than daily watching with no real intent of acting is the practice of regular weekend reviewing. Saturday and Sunday are safe times since you cannot make an immediate transaction. This trading hiatus allows reflection, a trip to the library, or a purposeful scan of your favorite investment-information databases. Also, net price moves for a week are larger than daily moves; bigger numbers are more likely to jar you into considering seriously whether a recent rise might be getting overdone, due for a correction. Finally, once-weekly portfolio work simply takes less time out of your life. Weekend market tracking presents a suitable balance (for other than active traders) between loss of perspective and overburdened time on the daily side, and being out of touch and too relaxed on the longer end of the spectrum. One may intend to be a long-term investor, but reality in an age of fast-moving markets dominated by huge institutions argues for vigilance more constant than one might actually prefer. A weekly review strikes a healthy balance.

Your review should include writing down the latest price for each stock held and probably also its high and low. Such a record becomes a ready reference, allowing you to recycle old newspapers promptly. Earnings and dividend developments can be noted, most easily in Barron's if not through an on-line website. Company announcements can be noted and studied. (BigCharts.com, in its upper indicators feature, shows dates of stock splits, EPS news and ex-dividend events.) Such news should be evaluated against your written plan (Chapter 29) for each stock. Are things going as anticipated, or is something perhaps beginning to smell a bit strange here? Has the stock reached your price target? Has it run well ahead of that imaginary progress line, implying that it is overheated and likely due for cooling down? Where is your stock on its chart? Has it reached a supply area or a channel top (sell on the good fortune), or is it ominously breaking down technically (the world now knows something that you did not foresee)? The checklist offered in the previous chapter should serve as a reminder and guide about why you bought and what you expected to happen. Comparing latest information against your blueprint for each stock will go far in guiding you to a hold/sell decision for the coming week. That point raises a possible caution: just because you make a decision on the weekend does not mean it necessarily must be executed at Monday's opening. Think tactically about how you might get a good execution, rather than dumping in a sell order before the opening just to be done.

Finally, after sorting through the latest relevant facts you will probably be well served to calibrate prices of your stocks against others in their industries or sectors. This can be done easily by choosing a comparative chart format, perhaps at EquityTrader. com or BigCharts.com. Look at your stock against a suitable ETF first and then move on to comparisons with other individual issues. Having done this, you now come again to the bottom-line question: knowing all you do now, would you buy this stock again here at today's price? Your answer says whether to hold or sell.

As you learn to do your selling more easily, your increased practice will produce more and richer feedback, enabling you to succeed at a task that other people find elusive for a whole investment lifetime: selling when the time is right. Perfection is impossible, but a good batting average in this underemphasized skill is highly sufficient.

Final Words

This book has been aimed at tuning you in, more sharply and insightfully, to how Wall Street really works and at helping you become intellectually and emotionally better prepared to pull that all-important selling trigger. Stocks are made to be sold as well as bought. Only a complete combination of those two actions, each reasonably well executed, results in a profit. Much help on the subject of buying (to be sure, of enormously varying true value) is available elsewhere. Your author's intent has been to enrich you and your investment experience, both mentally and in dollar terms, by adding a measurable contribution to the sadly limited resources to which you can turn for making informed decisions about selling. So now... go forth and do better!

Useful Reading and Other Resources

The following is a highly selective reading and resources list on the subject of stock market investment. The items, grouped by subject, are useful to both a specialist and non-specialist audience.

Organizations

American Association of Individual Investors, a not-for-profit educational association with chapters across the United States, offering investor-improvement tools and local speakers. 625 N. Michigan Ave., Suite 1900, Chicago, IL 60611; (800) 428-2244. www.AAII.com

Market Technicians Association, a membership group for both individuals and professionals, offering the CMT designation; local chapters offering speaker programs. 61 Broadway, Suite 514, New York, NY 10006, 646-652-3300. www. MTA.org

Better Investing (formerly National Association of Investors Corporation), the organizing force behind local investment clubs and a source of excellent stock-valuation worksheets ("Stock Selection Guide"). 711 W. 13 Mile Road, Madison Heights, MI 48071; (877) 275-6242. www.Better-Investing.org

Charts

Free online charts: www.
BigCharts.com, www.StockCharts.com, www.EquityTrader.com

Daily Graphs, William O'Neil & Co., Inc. (one-year, daily NYSE, ASE, and OTC charts with price and volume). Published on trial and subscription basis: William O'Neil & Co., Inc., P.O. Box 66919, Los Angeles, CA 90066. For current rate quotes, phone (213) 472-7479.

Long-Term Values. William O'Neil & Co., Inc. (15-year, monthly graphs of 4,000 companies, showing EPS, dividends, and prices); great for perspective. Published on trial and subscription basis: Source contact information as above.

Books on Selling

Fraser, James L. *The Art of Selling Stocks*. Burlington VT: Fraser Publishing Co., 1983 reprint. A valuable pamphlet offering wisdom from the single best source of contrarian investment publications. (800) 253-0090. www .FraserPublishing.com

Mamis, Justin, and Robert Mamis. When *to Sell: Inside Strategies for Stock Market Profits*. New York: Simon & Schuster, 1977. One of the few works entirely on selling stocks (the last prior to this volume).

Rogers, Donald I. *How Not to Buy a Common Stock*. New Rochelle, NY: Arlington House, 1972. How and when not to buy is exactly when to sell.

Contrarianism

Neill, Humphrey B. *The Art of Contrary Thinking*. Caldwell, ID: The Caxton Printers, Ltd., 1967. The classic; absolutely basic to the subject.

Dreman, David. *The New Contrarian Investment Strategy*. New York: Random House, 1982. Deals with both contrarian theory and self understanding.

Ellis, Charles D. *Investment Policy: How to Win a Loser's Game*. Homewood, IL: Dow-Jones Irwin (now McGraw-Hill), 1985. Setting reasonable rules to help overcome emotion and illogic.

Browne, Harry. *Why the Best Laid Investment Plans Usually Go Wrong*. New York: William Morrow and Co., Inc. 1987. A lot of contrarianism here; easily his most useful volume.

History and Perspective

Galbraith, John Kenneth. *The Great Crash of 1929*. Boston: Houghton Mifflin Company, 1954. History now sadly becomes dim. Lest we forget!

Galbraith, John Kenneth. *A Short History of Financial Euphoria*, Nashville, TN: Whittle Direct Books, 1990. Documents conceptually the several common threads signaling climactic stages of market blow-offs followed by crashes.

Sobel, Robert. *Panic on Wall Street new York*: The Macmillan Company, 1968. A very useful history of panics in the USA, 1792 to 1962.

Katsenelson, Vitaliy N. *Active Value Investing: Making Money in Range-Bound Markets*. New York: Wiley Finance, 2007. Incisive analysis of history and a very strong case against mindless buy-and-hold.

Technical Analysis

Achelis, Steven B. *Technical Analysis from A to Z*. New York: McGraw-Hill, 2000. Highly readable quick reference to numerous systems, so one can investigate further those making intuitive sense.

Edwards, Robert D., and John Magee. *Technical Analysis of Stock Trends*. Boston: John Magee Inc., 1979. The bible for the technical approach. Expensive but worth it.

Arms, Richard W. *Profits in Volume*. Larchmont NY: Investors Intelligence, Inc., 1971. Describes Equivolume charting, a useful way of measuring resistance that defines a top.

Cassidy, Donald L. *Trading on Volume*. New York: McGraw-Hill, 2001. Covers crescendos, spikes, and other volume phenomena in more detail than this volume's Chapter 21.

Psychology of Investing and Trading

Mamis, Justin. *The Nature of Risk, Stock Market Survival and the Meaning of Life*. Reading, MA: Addison-Wesley Publishing Co., 1991. Insightfully probes our innermost drives, motives and fears, showing that the greatest risks for investors lie inside ourselves.

Plummer, Tony. *The Psychology of Technical Analysis*. Burr Ridge, IL: Irwin Professional Publishing (now McGraw-Hill), 1992. Explains why technical analysis cannot be ignored; especially good on crowd dynamics.

Anthony, Joseph. *The Stock Market Saga*. Los Angeles: The Nowadays Press, 1972. Humorous brief rhymes with wisdom about wrong-way market psychology.

Commission Discounts

AAII Journal, January issue. (Annual: detailed tabular listings of updated rate structures, phone numbers, website URLs.) From American Association of Individual Investors (contacts provided above under Organizations). Check also the websites of major discount brokerages by name for possible rate changes.

Author's Website

See. www.R-I-I.org, website of the Retirement Investing Institute, a 501(c)(3) educational foundation dedicated to educating investors without exposing them to sales pitches. Contains a more lengthy book list.

INDEX